What readers have said about
Where Is God When It Hurts?

I know firsthand that pain and paralysis sometimes seem to push away the presence of God. To ask *Where Is God When It Hurts?* is honest, reasonable even. And thank the Lord, Philip puts our questions into perspective, helping us find out exactly where God really is when we hurt.

—Joni Eareckson Tada

I started to read it thinking I was going to read a pleasant little easy-to-read book on the subject of pain; I finished feeling as if I had read a classic. It probes aspects of pain that C. S. Lewis never touches and draws upon the lives of suffering saints from John Donne to Joni Eareckson Tada. But I was most impressed with Philip's honesty and willingness to admit the inadequacy of words to unravel problems that go back to the patriarch Job.

—William J. Petersen

I've read everything I can get my hands on about the problems of pain and evil, and this book is the clearest, most practical thing I've read.

—Keith Miller

If I expected to find inside a shallow theoretical treatise unworthy of such a profound question, that's not what I found . . . by the time you get to the end of these chapters your heart is crying out, "Thank you, God, for pain!"

—Paul Harvey

Also by Philip Yancey,
available in Large Print
from Walker and Company

The Jesus I Never Knew

WHERE IS GOD WHEN IT HURTS?

Philip Yancey

Walker and Company
New York

Large Print edition published by arrangement with Zondervan Publishing House, 1988.

Published simultaneously in Canada by Thomas Allen & Son Canada, Limited, Markham, Ontario.

Library of Congress Cataloging-in-Publication Data
Yancey, Philip.
    Where is God when it hurts?/Philip Yancey.
        p. cm.
    1st Large print ed.
    Previously published: New York: Phoenix Press, 1990.
    ISBN 0-8027-2709-3 (pbk.)
    1. Suffering—Religious aspects—Christianity. 2. Large print
    books. I. Title
  [BT732.7.Y36]
  248.8'6—dc20   96-22273
        CIP

Material from "A Luckless City Buries Its Dead," © 1976, reprinted by permission of Time, Inc.

Material from Chapter 3 of *Philosophy of Religion*, © 1963, reprinted by permission of Prentice-Hall, Inc.

Material from *Children of Crisis, Vol. 2: Migrants, Mountaineers, and Sharecroppers*, © 1971, reprinted by permission of Little, Brown, and Co., in association with Atlantic Monthly Press.

Revised Large Print Edition, 1996
Walker and Company
435 Hudson Street
New York, New York 10014

Printed in the United States of America

10 9 8 7 6 5 4 3 2

To Dr. Paul Brand,
who unselfishly shared with me a lifetime of
medical and spiritual wisdom

If you are only able to read large print, you may qualify for Wolfner Library services which include free access by mail to:

- Over 350,000 titles in audio and other formats
- Use of audio playback devices
- DVDs with descriptive narration
- Over 70 audio magazines

Wolfner Talking Book and Braille Library

Email: Wolfner@sos.mo.gov
Toll free: 800-392-2614 (in Missouri)
Phone: 573-751-8720

Contents

Part 5: How Does Faith Help?

Preface

There's a cardinal rule in book publishing that applies equally to brain surgery and auto mechanics: "If it ain't broke, don't fix it." Since people are still buying the original *Where Is God When It Hurts?* I may be breaking that rule by attempting a major revision.

I wrote *Where Is God When It Hurts?* back in the mid-1970s, when I was in my mid-twenties. In the years that have passed since then, I have never ceased thinking about the subject. Like a dog on a fresh spoor I keep circling around the problem of pain, searching for clues. In that time I have also heard from hundreds of readers, many of whom wrote wrenching letters describing their own odysseys with pain. For these reasons I felt it necessary to go back to a work I had completed long ago and bring it up to date.

Many biblical scholars date the book of Job as the oldest in the Bible, and it amazes me that the questions Job voiced so eloquently have not faded away. They have grown even louder and shriller over the centuries. A recent novel, *The Only Problem*, gets its title from a phrase in a conversation about how a good God can allow suffering. "It's the only problem, in fact, worth discussing," concludes the main character.

Another thing amazes me. Books on the problem of pain divide neatly into two groupings. The older ones, by people like Aquinas, Bunyan, Donne, Luther, Calvin, and Augustine, ungrudgingly accept pain and suffering as God's useful agents. These authors do not question God's actions. They merely try to "justify the ways of God to man." The authors wrote with confidence, as if the sheer force of their reasoning could calm emotional responses to suffering.

Modern books on pain make a sharp contrast. Their authors assume that the amount of evil and suffering in the world cannot be matched with the traditional view of a good and loving God. God is thus bumped from a "friend of the court" position to the box reserved for the defendant. "How can you possibly justify yourself, God?" these angry moderns seem to say. Many of them adjust their notion of God, either by redefining his love or by questioning his power to control evil.

When you read the two categories of books side by side, the change in tone is quite striking. It's as if we in modern times think we have a corner on the suffering market. Do we forget that Luther and Calvin lived in a world without ether and penicillin, when life expectancy averaged thirty years, and that Bunyan and Donne wrote their greatest works, respectively, in a jail and a plague quarantine room? Ironically, the modern authors—who live in princely comfort, toil in climate-controlled offices, and hoard elixirs in their medicine cabinets—are the ones smoldering with rage.

After reading several shelffuls of such books I asked myself, "Does the world really need another book on the problem of pain?" As I spent time among suffering people, however, I had to conclude yes. I learned that many books on pain seem oddly irrelevant to suffering people. For them the problem of pain is not a theoretical problem, a theology game of lining up all the appropriate syllogisms. It is a problem of relationship. Many suffering people want to love God, but cannot see past their tears. They feel hurt and betrayed. Sadly, the church often responds with more confusion than comfort.

Fifteen years ago, at an age when I had no right to tackle the daunting problem of pain, I wrote *Where Is God When It Hurts?* for those people. Partly because I have heard from so many of them, I have now revised and expanded that book. In a sense, this new edition represents a dialogue with my readers, the next step in my own pilgrimage.

I have especially expanded the section "How Can We Cope with Pain?" because I believe God has given the church a mandate of representing his love to a suffering world. We usually think of the problem of pain as a question we ask of God, but it is also a question he asks of us. How do we respond to hurting people?

In this revision, I have drawn from several of my articles published in *Christianity Today* as well as the booklet *Helping the Hurting*, published by Multnomah Press. I am grateful to them for permission to incorporate that material.

Think too
of all who suffer
as if you
shared their pain.

Hebrews 13:3 (J. B. PHILLIPS)

PART I

———◇◇◇◇———

Why Is There Such a Thing
as Pain?

1

————◦◦◦————

A Problem That Won't Go Away

Meanwhile, where is God? This is one of the most disquieting symptoms. When you are happy, so happy that you have no sense of needing Him, if you turn to Him then with praise, you will be welcomed with open arms. But go to Him when your need is desperate, when all other help is vain and what do you find? A door slammed in your face, and a sound of bolting and double bolting on the inside. After that, silence. You may as well turn away.

C. S. Lewis
A Grief Observed

I feel helpless around people in great pain. Helpless, and also guilty. I stand beside them, watching facial features contort and listening to the sighs and moans, deeply aware of the huge gulf between us. I cannot penetrate their suffering, I can only watch. Whatever I attempt to say seems weak and stiff, as if I'd memorized the lines for a school play.

One day I received a frantic plea for help from my close friends John and Claudia Claxton. Newlyweds in their early twenties, they were just beginning life together in the Midwest. I had watched in amazement as the experience of romantic love utterly transformed John Claxton. Two years of engagement to Claudia had melted his cynicism and softened his hard edges. He became an optimist, and now his letters to me were usually bubbly with enthusiasm about his young marriage.

But one letter from John alarmed me as soon as I opened it. Errors and scratches marred his usually neat handwriting. He explained, "Excuse my writing . . . I guess it shows how I'm fumbling for words. I don't know what to say." The Claxtons' young marriage had run into a roadblock far bigger than both of them. Claudia had been diagnosed with Hodgkin's disease, cancer of the lymph glands, and was given only a fifty percent chance to live.

Within a week surgeons had cut her from armpit to belly, removing every visible trace of the disease. She was left stunned and weak, lying in a hospital bed.

At the time, ironically, John was working as a chaplain's assistant in a local hospital. His compassion for other patients dipped dangerously. "In some ways," he told me, "I could understand better what other patients were undergoing. But I didn't care any more. I only cared about Claudia. I wanted to yell at them, "Stop that sniveling, you idiots! You think you've got problems—my wife may be dying right now!"

Though both John and Claudia were strong Christians, an unexpected anger against God surged up—anger against a beloved partner who had betrayed them. "God, why us?" they cried. "Have you teasingly doled out one happy year of marriage to set us up for this?"

Cobalt treatments took their toll on Claudia's body. Beauty fled her almost overnight. She felt and looked weary, her skin darkened, her hair fell out. Her throat was raw, and she regurgitated nearly everything she ate. Doctors had to suspend treatment for a time when her swollen throat could no longer make swallowing motions.

When the radiation treatments resumed, she was periodically laid out flat on a table, naked. She could do nothing but lie still and listen to the whir and click of the machinery as it bombarded her with invisible particles, each dose aging her body by months. As she lay in that chill steel room, Claudia would think about God and about her suffering.

Claudia's Visitors

Claudia had hoped that Christian visitors would comfort her by bringing some perspective on what she was going through. But their voices proved confusing, not consoling.

A deacon from her church solemnly advised her to reflect on what God was trying to teach her. "Surely something in your life must displease God," he said. "Somewhere, you must have stepped out of his will. These things don't just *happen*. God uses circumstances to warn us, and to punish us. What is he telling you?"

A few days later Claudia was surprised to see a

woman from church whom she barely knew. Evidently, this plump, scatterbrained widow had adopted the role of professional cheerleader to the sick. She brought flowers, sang hymns, and stayed long enough to read some happy psalms about brooks running and mountains clapping their hands. Whenever Claudia tried to talk about her illness or prognosis, the woman quickly changed the subject, trying to combat the suffering with cheer and goodwill. But she only visited once, and after a while the flowers faded, the hymns seemed dissonant, and Claudia was left to face a new day of pain.

Another woman dropped by, a faithful follower of television faith healers. Exuding confidence, she assured Claudia that healing was her only escape. When Claudia told her about the deacon's advice, this woman nearly exploded. "Sickness is never God's will!" she exclaimed. "Haven't you read the Bible? The Devil stalks us like a roaring lion, but God will deliver you if you can muster up enough faith to believe you'll be healed. Remember, Claudia, faith can move mountains, and that includes Hodgkin's disease. Simply name your promise, in faith, and then claim the victory."

The next few mornings, as Claudia lay in the sterile cobalt treatment room, she tried to "muster up" faith. She wondered if she even understood the procedure. She did not question God's supernatural power, but how to go about convincing God of her sincerity? Faith wasn't like a muscle that could be enlarged through rehabilitation exercises. It was slippery, intangible, impossible to grasp. The whole notion of mustering up faith seemed awfully exhausting, and she could never decide what it really meant.

Perhaps the most "spiritual" woman in Claudia's church brought along some books about praising God for everything that happens. "Claudia, you need to come to the place where you can say, 'God, I *love* you for making me suffer like this. It is your will, and you know what's best for me. And I praise you for loving me enough to allow me to experience this. In all things, including this, I give thanks.'"

As Claudia pondered the words, her mind filled with rather grotesque images of God. She envisioned a figure in the shape of a troll, big as the universe, who took delight in squeezing helpless humans between his fingernails, pulverizing them with his fists, dashing them against sharp stones. The figure would torture these humans until they cried out, "God, I love you for doing this to me!" The idea repulsed Claudia, and she decided she could not worship or love such a God.

Yet another visitor, Claudia's pastor, made her feel she was on a select mission. He said, "Claudia, you have been appointed to suffer for Christ, and he will reward you. God chose you because of your great strength and integrity, just as he chose Job, and he is using you as an example to others. Their faith may increase because of your response. You should feel privileged, not bitter. What we see as adversity, God sees as opportunity." He told her to think of herself as a track star, and to view adversity as the series of hurdles she would need to leap over on the way to the victory circle.

Sometimes the notion of being a privileged martyr appealed to Claudia, in a self-pitying sort of way. Other times, when the pain crescendoed, when she vomited up food, when her facial features aged, Claudia would call out, "God, why me? There are millions of Christians stronger and more honorable than I—couldn't you choose one of them instead?" She didn't feel like a track star at all, and she wondered why God would deliberately place hurdles in the path of someone he loved.

I, too, visited Claudia, and found her desperately confused by all these contradictory words. She repeated for me the advice given her by well-meaning Christians, and I listened to her bewildered response. Which of these lessons was she supposed to be learning? How could she have more faith? Who should she listen to? In the midst of much confusion, Claudia had one certainty: her happy world with John was disintegrating. Above all, she didn't want that to end.

I had little advice for Claudia that day. In fact, I came away with even more questions. Why was she lying in a hospital bed while I stood beside her, healthy? Something inside me recoiled as I heard her repeat the clichéd comments from her visitors. Is Christianity supposed to make a sufferer feel even worse?

At the time I visited Claudia, I was working for *Campus Life* magazine while also moonlighting as a free-lance journalist. In a short span I wrote six "Drama in Real Life" stories for *Reader's Digest*.

I interviewed a young Canadian couple who had been mauled by a grizzly bear. Although both survived, the young man lost one eye, and no amount of plastic surgery could hide the scars across his face. In another city, two young adults told me the story of a childhood camping trip taken with their father up Mount Rainier. Caught in a blizzard, they frantically dug a snow cave. Their father, lying protectively across the face of the cave, froze to death overnight.

All these people repeated their own versions of the cacophony of voices from Christian "comforters." One amputee told me, "My religious friends were the most depressing, irritating part of the entire experience." That pattern disturbed me greatly. Something was wrong. A faith founded on the Great Physician should bring peace, not confusion, at a time of crisis.

Why do people have to suffer so? What does the Bible really say? Because of the questions that arose from my contacts with Claudia* and others like her, I began a quest that culminated in this book. I have looked for a message we Christians can give to people who are suffering. At the same time, I've hunted for a message that can strengthen my own faith when I suffer. Where is God when it hurts? Is he trying to tell us something through our pain?

---

*Claudia's dilemma was eventually resolved when the cobalt treatments effectively destroyed the cancer cells. She's had no recurrence of the disease.

A Personal Approach

After an extensive tour of the United States, the well-known German pastor and theologian Helmut Thielicke was asked what he had observed as the greatest deficiency among American Christians. He replied, "They have an inadequate view of suffering." I have come to agree with him.

That deficiency stands out as a huge blemish to the non-Christian world. I've asked college students what they have against Christianity, and most of them echo variations on the theme of suffering: "I can't believe in a God who would allow Auschwitz and Cambodia"; "My teenage sister died of leukemia despite all the Christians' prayers"; "One-third of the world went to bed hungry last night—how can you reconcile that with Christian love?"

No other human experience provokes such an urgent response. No one sits in smoky coffeehouses late into the night debating the cosmic implications of the sense of smell or taste. Smell! Why this strange sensation? What did God intend? Why was scent apportioned so capriciously, lavished on roses but not on oxygen? And why must humankind get by with one-eighth the sensory ability of the dog? Oddly, I hear no one debating "the problem of pleasure"; why do we take for granted sensations of pleasure but react so violently against pain?

As I did library research on the problem of pain, I discovered that many great philosophers, otherwise sympathetic to Christian principles and ethics, have stumbled over this problem of pain and suffering, ultimately rejecting Christianity because of it.

C.E.M. Joad wrote, "What, then, are the arguments which for me have told so strongly against the religious view of the universe? . . . First, there was the difficulty presented by the facts of pain and evil."[1] Other philosophers, such as Bertrand Russell and Voltaire, share Joad's complaint.

The messy problem of pain and suffering keeps popping up despite erudite attempts to explain it away. The great British writer C. S. Lewis offered perhaps the most articulate treatment of the subject in this century with *The Problem of Pain*, written at the height of his intellectual powers. But years later, after his own wife died of bone cancer, Lewis wrote another book, *A Grief Observed*, which he published under a pseudonym. It covers the same topic, but in a very different way. As the quote at the beginning of this chapter reveals, Lewis's confidence had been shattered, his emotions stretched to the breaking point—stretched beyond the breaking point. "You never know how much you really believe anything until its truth or falsehood becomes a matter of life and death to you," he said.

As in Hercules's battle against the Hydra, all our attempts to chop through agnostic arguments are met with writhing new examples of suffering. Novelist Peter De Vries has called the problem of pain "the question mark turned like a fishhook in the human heart." And too often the Christian defense sounds like a red-faced, foot-shuffling, lowered-head apology.

"The problem of pain" represents a profound riddle, and the philosophers' approach to the subject sometimes takes the form of abstract reasoning, such as you might find in a textbook on pure mathematics. I will not attempt to address philosophers with this book; others with far more training have done that. Rather, I have tried to keep before me the scene of my friend Claudia Claxton lying on a hospital bed. Most of our problems with pain are not exercises in mental gymnastics. They are problems like Claudia's: the loss of youth, an ulcerous throat, the prospect of a new marriage gouged by death, the paralyzing fear of the unknown. Claudia heard much conflicting advice about these problems from fellow Christians. What can we believe with confidence?

To prepare for this book, I talked to Christians who suffer at a level far worse than most of us will ever experience. For some of them, pain nearly defines life. It is the first sensation to greet them in the morning and the last they feel before drifting off to sleep, if they are lucky enough to fall asleep despite it. Ironically, I also spent time among people with leprosy, who feel no pain physiologically but desperately wish they could. With such people as my guides, I have entered the world of the sufferer to find out what difference it makes to be a Christian there.

First, I will examine pain biologically—through the microscope, you might say—to see what role it plays in life. Then, stepping back, I will look at our planet as a whole, asking what God is up to. Is suffering God's one great goof? And, finally, I will ask what response we can give when suffering strikes, and how we can also reach out to others.

Perhaps the next time I'm sick, when the flu hits and I toss in bed, fighting off waves of nausea, perhaps then my conclusions about pain will offer no solace. But as a Christian trying to fathom what God is up to in this world, I have learned a great deal. And as I've come to better understand the suffering of this world, my attitude toward God has changed dramatically.

2

The Gift Nobody Wants

The symptoms and the illness are not the same thing. The illness exists long before the symptoms. Rather than being the illness, the symptoms are the beginning of its cures. The fact that they are unwanted makes them all the more a phenomenon of grace—a gift of God, a message from the unconscious, if you will, to initiate self-examination and repair.

M. Scott Peck
The Road Less Traveled

I am sitting in Chicago's ornate Orchestra Hall. I have exulted in the works by Beethoven and Mozart, but the long, complex concerto by Prokofiev is another matter. As energy-giving blood is shunted away from my brain down toward my stomach to help digest the Sunday brunch, I find it increasingly difficult to stay awake.

The concert hall is warm and stuffy. Gradually the sounds from various instruments begin to meld together into one muted tone. My eyelids sag. Catching myself, I glance around and see scores of

well-dressed concertgoers who have already succumbed. And so I rest my chin on my right hand
and prop my elbow on the wooden armrest. The
music fades. . . .

THUNK!! My limbs are splayed out in all directions. People in surrounding seats are glaring at me,
their necks craned in my direction. My overcoat is
on the floor. Startled and embarrassed, I retrieve the
overcoat, straighten in my seat, and try again to attend to the music. Blood is now pounding in my
head.

What happened? Even as I was drifting into
dreamland, my body was loyally working to protect
me. Though my conscious brain had already shut
down, my reflex system had not. When my head
nodded forward, two small sacs in my inner ear,
filled with fluid and lined with ultrasensitive hairs,
detected an alarming shift in my equilibrium. Just
at the last moment, as my head was about to crash
downward to the armrest, the inner ear sounded an
all-points-alert. Suddenly my arms jerked out, my
head shot upward, and my whole torso twitched in
a spasm. The dramatic act, an embarrassment to me,
was merely my body's emergency effort to prevent
injury. And all these complex maneuvers took place
while I was drifting off to sleep.

The mechanism of pain in the human body operates much like the warning system I experienced
in Orchestra Hall. Pain sensors loudly alert my body
to danger—It hurts! —and force me to concentrate
on the problem area.

Sometimes the reaction occurs at an involuntary

level. For example, when I go to the doctor for a checkup and he taps my knee with a rubber hammer, my leg straightens violently. Why? The doctor's tap gives the knee the impression that it is bending: his hammer hits the same nerves that would be affected if my knee suddenly buckled while walking. My body rushes to compensate, lest I stumble and experience a greater pain. The reaction is too spontaneous and lightning-quick to allow the brain time to reason that I'm seated on a table, not standing, and no actual danger of falling exists.

Marks of a Designer

Yet despite the obvious protective value of these millions of warning sensors, the pain network is easily the most unappreciated bodily system. It attracts mostly abuse and bad feelings. I have never read a poem extolling the virtues of pain, nor seen a statue erected in its honor, nor heard a hymn dedicated to it. Pain is usually defined as "unpleasantness."

Christians, who believe in a loving Creator, don't really know how to interpret pain. If pinned against the wall at a dark, secret moment, many Christians would confess that pain was God's one mistake. Really, he should have worked a little harder to devise a better way for us to cope with danger. I used to feel that way exactly.

Now, however, I am convinced that pain gets a bad press. Perhaps we should see poems, statues, and hymns to pain. Why has my attitude changed? Because up close, under a microscope, the pain network is seen in an entirely different light. My discussion of pain, then, must begin with a look at the human body. Why do I need pain? When I hurt, what is my body telling me?

I begin here, with the closeup view, because that perspective is the one most often overlooked by people fumbling with the question "Where is God when it hurts?" I have read scores of philosophical and theological books on "the problem of pain," but at best these give token acknowledgment to the fact that pain may serve some useful biological purpose. The pain network deserves far more than token acknowledgment. It bears the mark of creative genius.

Consider a single organ from the human body: the skin, a flexible-yet-tough organ that stretches over the body's frame as an advance guard against the dangers of the outside world. Millions of pain sensors dot the surface of the skin, scattered not randomly, but in precise accord with the body's specific needs. Actually, the body does not seem to have any dedicated "pain cells," for the sensation of pain ties in with an elaborate network of sensors that also report information about pressure, touch, heat, and cold.

Scientists blindfold their research subjects (usually hapless medical students) and measure their skin sensitivity. For example, how much pressure must be applied before a blindfolded person becomes aware of an object touching his skin? The scale, called the absolute threshold of touch, is measured in grams (per square millimeter of skin surface), and this is what researchers have discovered:

Absolute Threshold of Touch

Pressure applied to:	Sensitive to:
Tip of tongue	2 grams of pressure
Fingers	3 grams of pressure
Back of hand	12 grams of pressure
Back of forearm	33 grams of pressure
Sole of foot	250 grams of pressure

Thus the skin, a single organ, displays a very wide range of sensitivity to pressure. We use our tongues for such intricate acts as forming words and picking food particles from between our teeth. We use our fingers for playing the guitar, writing with a felt-tip pen, and the caresses of love. These areas of the skin require a fine-tuned sensitivity.[1]

But less critical areas hardly need such sensitivity: we would tire very quickly indeed if our brains had to listen to such dainty pressure reports from the foot, which faces a daily rigor of stomping, squeezing, and supporting weight. Thus, while fingers and tongue can detect a feather touch, other parts of the body need a good sound slap before they report unusual activity to the brain.

These measurements of threshold barely scratch the surface of the marvels of the pain network. For example, sensitivity to pressure varies depending on context. I can distinguish a letter that weighs 1 1/4 ounces from one that weighs 1 1/2 ounces just by holding it in my hand. But if I'm holding a ten-pound package, I could not discern that difference; I would need a change of at least three ounces before noticing.

Another test assesses the absolute threshold of pain. In this test, the scientist measures how much pressure must be applied to a very sharp needle before the subject begins to experience pain.

Absolute Threshold of Pain

Pressure applied to:	Amount of pressure to produce painful sensation:
Cornea	0.2 grams
Forearm	20 grams
Back of hand	100 grams
Sole of foot	200 grams
Fingertip	300 grams

Note how these figures contrast with the thresholds of pressure.[2] The fingertip, for example, shows an astounding difference: it can detect a mere 3 grams of pressure, but not until that pressure exceeds 300 grams will I feel pain there! Why? Think about the fingers' activities. The concert violinist must sense an amazing range of pressures to produce perfect sound and volume. A skilled baker, swishing his hands through batches of dough, can notice as little as a two percent variance in the "stickiness" or consistency. Cloth feelers in textile industries compare the qualities of cloth by touch. The fingertips must be incredibly sensitive to the slightest differences in touch.

But sensitivity to touch is not enough. The fingertips must also be tough in order to withstand rigorous activity. Feel the calloused, scaly hand of a carpenter or a professional tennis player. Life would be miserable indeed if the fingertip fired a message of pain to the brain each time a person squeezed a tennis racket or pounded a hammer. So the design of the body includes a fingertip extraordinarily sensitive to pressure, but relatively insensitive to pain. Hands and fingertips serve us well as the most used parts of our bodies.*

The cornea of the eye, however, lives a different existence. Due to its transparency—essential, to admit light rays—it has a limited blood supply and is thus very fragile. A small wound could cause blindness, and any intrusion in the eye, a wood splinter or

---

*We have exactly as many pain sensors as we need. Scientists measure another phenomenon of the nervous system called the two-point threshold. They press two stiff bristles against the skin of a blindfolded person to determine how close together they must be brought before that person feels one pinprick rather than two. In other words, it demonstrates how close together the individual pain sensors are. On the leg, I can no longer distinguish two pinpricks when the pins are brought in to a distance of 68 mm. But I can distinguish two pinpricks on the back of the hand at a distance of 32 mm, and on the fingertip at only 2 mm. The tip of the tongue, however, has sensors every 1 mm. This explains the common phenomenon I feel when food is caught between my teeth. With my tongue I can search it out and quickly determine in what crevice the food is caught. But with the fingertip, the food is harder to locate. Spaces between the teeth "feel smaller" with the finger than with the tongue.[3]

a speck of dirt, represents a serious threat. Therefore the cornea's pain sensors have an electronic hot line to the brain.

I have seen a World Series baseball game delayed for the simple reason that the pitcher got a stray eyelash in his eye. The infielders and umpires gathered around while he looked in a mirror and fished it out. He could not possibly continue pitching until he removed the source of the pain. Such an eyelash lying on his nose, arm, or any other part of the body would go unnoticed.

Colic, Kidney Stones, and Ice Cream Headaches

Inside, the body presents even more evidence of the pain network's intelligent design. Pinpricks and heat burns, the scientists' favored techniques for measuring pain on the skin surface, prove useless on internal organs, which simply don't respond to those stimuli. Why should they? Since the body has designated the skin to sort through alarms from cuts and burns and pressures, internal organs can get along without such elaborate warning systems.

Slip past the skin's defenses with the aid of a local anesthetic, and you could burn the stomach with a match, insert a needle through the lung, cut the brain with a knife, crush the kidney in a vise, or bore through bone, all without causing the patient any discomfort. Such internal pain signals would be redundant—the skin and skeleton already protect internal organs from such dangers.

Instead, the body's sheltered organs possess

unique sets of pain receptors specific to the dangers they face. If a doctor inserts a balloon inside my stomach and fills it with air to distend my stomach slightly, urgent messages of pain would shoot to my brain—the pain of colic, or gas. The stomach's pain network is custom-designed to protect it from specific dangers. Likewise, the kidney sends out excruciating signals of pain when a BB-sized kidney stone is present. Linings of the joints, which are insensitive to a needle or knife, are very sensitive to certain chemicals.[4]

On rare occasions, an internal organ must inform the brain of an emergency that its pain sensors are not equipped to handle. How can it alert the brain to the damage it senses? In this event, the organ uses the remarkable phenomenon of **referred pain**, recruiting nearby pain sensors to sound the alarm. For example, heart attack victims may notice a burning or constricting feeling in the neck, chest, jaw, or left arm. Skin cells there, though perfectly healthy, obligingly send off alarm messages to the brain as if *they* were damaged, when in fact the problem lies with their neighbor the heart. In this way the skin "loans" its pain sensors to the heart as a relay warning station.

Anyone who has eaten homemade ice cream too fast on a hot summer day may experience a related phenomenon. Suddenly a headache strikes, just behind the eyes. Quite obviously, ice cream is not entering the forehead. Rather, the stomach's vagus nerve is sending out strong signals of cold to the brain; at the junction with the trigeminal nerve from the face, forehead, and jaw, pain jumps across from one nerve to the other and the chill in the stomach is felt as pain in the head.

The mystery of referred pain can make for some challenging medical diagnoses. Spleen injuries are sometimes felt in the tip of the left shoulder. A damaged appendix may borrow pain sensors in a variety of places, on either side of the abdomen. A neck injury may cause pain in the arm. Each of these demonstrates how the body's backup systems cooperate to warn of possible injury.

Medical libraries contain massive volumes filled with amazing facts about the operation of the body's pain network, and I have mentioned a mere sampling. Such facts as these—the exact distribution of needed pain cells, the customized pressure/pain thresholds, and the backup system of referred pain—convince me that, whatever it is, the pain network is not an accident.

Pain is not an afterthought, or God's great goof. Rather, it reveals a marvelous design that serves our bodies well. Pain is as essential to a normal life, it could be argued, as eyesight or even good circulation. Without pain, as we shall see, our lives would be fraught with danger, and devoid of many basic pleasures.

But Must It Hurt?

My appreciation for the engineering aspects of the pain network traces back to the beginning of my friendship with Dr. Paul Brand. I came across his name in 1975, when I was first researching the topic of pain. Already I had read many books on the subject. But one day my wife, who was rummaging through a closet at a medical supply house, came across a pamphlet with the unusual title, "The Gift of Pain." Its author was Dr. Brand. A short time later, we met together on the grounds of the leprosarium in Carville, Louisiana, and since then we have collaborated on two books (*Fearfully and Wonderfully Made* and *In His Image*).

Dr. Brand has received widespread recognition for his medical work, including awards from the Albert Lasker Foundation, the U.S. Public Health Service, and also from Queen Elizabeth II, who made him Commander of the British Empire. Yet, oddly, he got most of his recognition as a crusader on behalf of pain. Without hesitation Dr. Brand declares, "Thank God for inventing pain! I don't think he could have done a better job. It's beautiful." As one of the world's foremost experts on leprosy, a disease of the nervous system, he is well-qualified to make such a judgment.

Once, in fact, Dr. Brand received a several-million-dollar grant for the express purpose of designing an artificial pain system. He knew that people with diseases like leprosy and diabetes were in grave danger of losing fingers, toes, and even entire limbs simply because their warning system of pain had been silenced. They were literally destroying themselves unawares. Perhaps he could design a simple substitute that would alert them to the worst dangers.

In this project Dr. Brand had to think like the Creator, anticipating the needs of the body. For assistance, he signed on three professors of electronic engineering, a bioengineer, and several research biochemists. The team decided to concentrate on fingertips, the part of the body most often used and therefore most vulnerable to abuse. They developed a kind of artificial nerve, a pressure-sensitive transducer that could be worn on the finger like a glove. When subjected to pressure, the electronic nerve triggered an electric current which in turn set off a warning signal.

Dr. Brand and his assistants confronted daunting technical problems. The more they studied nerves, the more complex their task appeared. At what level of pressure should the sensor sound a warning? How could a mechanical sensor distinguish between the acceptable pressure of, say, gripping a railing and the unacceptable pressure of gripping a thornbush? How could it be adjusted to allow for rigorous activities like playing tennis?

Brand also recognized that nerve cells change their perception of pain to meet the body's needs. Due to the pressure of inflammation, an infected finger may become ten times more sensitive to pain. That's why a finger swollen from a hangnail feels awkward and in the way: your body is telling you to give it time to heal. Nerve cells "turn up the volume," amplifying bumps and scrapes that would normally go unreported. In no way could these well-funded scientists duplicate that feat with current technology.

The artificial sensors cost about $450 each, and it took many of them to protect a single hand or foot, but each new design would deteriorate from metal fatigue or corrosion after a few hundred uses. Each month Dr. Brand and his colleagues gained more appreciation for the remarkable engineering of the body's pain network, which includes several hundred million sensors that function maintenance-free throughout a healthy person's life.

At first Dr. Brand sought a way to make his artificial pain system work without actually hurting the patient. He had read the complaints of various philosophers against the created world. Why hadn't God designed a nervous system that protects us, but without the unpleasant aspects of pain? Here was his chance to improve on the original design with a protective system that did not hurt.

First his team tried sending an audible signal through a hearing aid, a signal that would hum when tissues were receiving normal pressures and buzz loudly when they were actually in danger. But the signal proved too easy to ignore. If a patient with a damaged hand was turning a screwdriver too hard, and the loud warning signal went off, he would simply override it and turn the screwdriver anyway. This happened not once, but many times. People who did not feel pain could not be persuaded to trust the artificial sensors.

Brand's team next tried blinking lights, but soon eliminated them for the same reason. Finally they had to resort to electric shock, taping electrodes to a still-sensitive portion of the body, such as the armpit. People had to be forced to respond; being alerted to the danger was not enough. The stimulus had to be unpleasant, just as pain is unpleasant.

"We also found out that the signal had to be out of the patient's reach," Brand says. "For even intelligent people, if they wished to do something which they were afraid would activate the shock, would switch off the signal, do what they had in mind to do, and then switch it on again when there was no danger of receiving an unpleasant signal. I remember thinking how wise God had been in putting pain out of reach."

After five years of work, thousands of man-hours, and several million dollars, Brand and his associates abandoned the entire project. A warning system suitable for just one hand was exorbitantly expensive, subject to frequent mechanical breakdown, and hopelessly inadequate to interpret the profusion of sensations. A system sometimes called "God's great mistake" was far too complex for even the most sophisticated technology to mimic.

That is why Paul Brand says with utter sincerity, "Thank God for pain!" By definition, pain is unpleasant, enough so to force us to withdraw our fingers from a stove. Yet that very quality saves us from destruction. Unless the warning signal demands response, we might not heed it.

Listen to Your Pain

The typical American response to pain is to take an aspirin at the slightest ache and silence the pain. That approach only deals with the symptom of the problem. We dare not shut off the warning system without first listening to the warning.

A tragic example of someone not heeding the

warning occurred in an NBA basketball game in which a star player, Bob Gross, wanted to play despite a badly injured ankle. Knowing that Gross was needed for the important game, the team doctor injected Marcaine, a strong painkiller, into three different places of his foot. Gross did start the game, but after a few minutes, as he was battling for a rebound, a loud snap! could be heard throughout the arena. Gross, oblivious, ran up and down the court two times, then crumpled to the floor. Although he felt no pain, a bone had broken in his ankle. By overriding pain's warning system with the anesthetic, the doctor caused permanent damage to Gross's foot and ended his basketball career.

Pain is not God's great goof. The sensation of pain is a gift—the gift that nobody wants. More than anything, pain should be viewed as a communication network. Just as the warning system of my equilibrium saved me in the embarrassing episode at Orchestra Hall, a remarkable network of pain sensors stands guard duty with the singular purpose of keeping me from injury.

I do not say that all pain is good. Sometimes it flares up and makes life miserable. For someone with crippling arthritis or terminal cancer, pain dominates so much that any relief, especially a painless world, would seem like heaven itself. But for the majority of us, the pain network performs daily protective service. It is effectively designed for surviving life on this sometimes hostile planet.

In Dr. Brand's words, "The one legitimate complaint you can make against pain is that it cannot be switched off. It can rage out of control, as with a terminal cancer patient, even though its warning has been heard and there is no more that can be done to treat the cause of pain. But as a physician I'm sure that less than one percent of pain is in this category that we might call out of control. Ninety-nine per cent of all the pains that people suffer are short-term pains: correctable situations that call for medication, rest, or a change in a person's lifestyle."

Admittedly, the surprising idea of the "gift of pain" does not answer many of the problems connected with suffering. But it is a beginning point of a realistic perspective on pain and suffering. Too often the emotional trauma of intense pain blinds us to its inherent value.

When I break an arm and swallow bottles of aspirin to dull the ache, gratitude for pain is not the first thought that comes to mind. Yet at that very moment, pain is alerting my body to the danger, mobilizing anti-infection defenses around the wound, and forcing me to refrain from activities that might further compound the injury. Pain demands the attention that is crucial to my recovery.

3

———◆◆◆◆◆———

Painless Hell

He jests at scars who never felt a wound.
> William Shakespeare
> *Romeo and Juliet*

Almost by definition, if we have pain we don't want it. Why would Dr. Brand and his associates spend so much time and energy trying to create pain even as most other medical professionals were working diligently to silence it?

I had learned many facts about the design of the pain network. I had even come to see it as a "gift." But knowledge alone was not enough to overcome my instinctive resistance to pain. I had strong doubts until I spent a week in Louisiana with Dr. Brand, the crusader for pain.

Dr. Brand came to appreciate pain by living among people with leprosy. It was he who discovered that leprosy patients suffer for the simple reason that they have a defective pain system.

The word leprosy conjures up exaggerated images: stubby fingers, ulcerous wounds, missing legs, distorted facial features. Literature and movies such as *Ben Hur* and *Papillon* (frequently inaccurate) have conditioned us to view leprosy as an unbearably cruel affliction. It is the oldest recorded disease, and one of the most feared. For centuries leprosy victims had to call out "Unclean! Unclean!" whenever someone approached.

Leprosy is indeed cruel, but not in the manner of most diseases. Primarily, it works like an anesthetic, attacking the pain cells of hands, feet, nose, ears, and eyes to produce numbness. Not so bad, really, one might think. Most diseases are feared because of their pain; what makes a painless disease so horrible?

Yet leprosy's numbing quality is precisely the reason for the fabled destruction of tissue. For thousands of years people thought the disease itself caused the ulcers on hands and feet and face that so often led to infection and ultimately loss of limbs. Dr. Brand's pioneering research in India established that in virtually all cases leprosy only numbs the extremities. Tissue damage results solely because the warning system of pain has fallen silent.

How does the damage occur? Dr. Brand asked himself that question thousands of times as he treated the infected hands of Indian villagers. It seemed a losing battle. He would heal wounds and bind them up, only to have the patients come back several months later with far worse damage. Like other leprosy workers, he assumed the disease worked like a fungus, destroying tissue indiscriminately.

But Brand soon learned to question his patients

carefully about any activities that might have contributed to the injury. He once watched horrified as a person with leprosy reached directly into a charcoal fire to retrieve a potato someone had dropped. Brand knew he would soon be treating sores on that patient's hand—sores caused by burns from the fire, not by leprosy. The villager, insensitive to pain, had unwittingly exposed his hand to terrible abuse.

Brand started following around the patients at the leprosarium in India. How else might they be damaging themselves? He saw one man hard at work in the garden, oblivious to blood running down his hand; Brand examined the shovel and found a nail protruding just at the spot his hand had been gripping. Other leprosy patients would reach over and extinguish a burning wick with their bare hands, or walk barefoot across broken glass. Watching them, Brand began formulating his radical theory that leprosy was chiefly anesthetic, and only indirectly a destroyer. He would need much more evidence, however, to overturn centuries of medical tradition.

One day, in the midst of this time of field research, Dr. Brand went to fetch some supplies from a little storeroom behind the hospital. He tried to open the door, but a rusty padlock would not yield. Just at that moment, one of his youngest patients strolled by—an undersized, malnourished ten-year-old. Brand liked the boy for his pleasant, cooperative spirit.

"Oh, sahib doctor, let me try," the boy said, and reached for the key. With a quick jerk of his hand he turned the key in the lock. Brand was dumbfounded. How could this weak youngster, half his size, exert such force?

His eyes caught a telltale clue. Was that a drop of blood on the floor? Upon examining the boy's index finger, Brand discovered the act of turning the key had gashed it open to the bone; skin, fat, and joint were all exposed. Yet the boy was completely unaware of it! To him, the sensation of cutting his finger to the bone was no different from that of picking up a stone or turning a coin in his pocket.

After that incident, Brand redoubled his efforts to test his theory about leprosy being a secondary, not primary cause of injury. He began measuring the fingers of his patients each day, and tried to account for every blister, ulcer, and cut. He learned that his patients were living in great danger because of their painlessness.

Foot injuries were easy to explain. If an ankle turned, tearing tendon and muscle, the leprosy patient would simply adjust and walk with a crooked gait. No warning system of pain announced the need to rest the ankle or seek treatment, and the injury would then lead to permanent damage. The most puzzling injuries, though, occurred at night. How could pieces of fingers and toes disappear while the patients were sleeping? Brand found the unsettling answer: rats were coming into the open-air wards and nibbling on unsuspecting patients. Feeling no pain, the patients would sleep on, and not until the next morning would they notice the injury and report it to Dr. Brand. That discovery led to a firm rule: every patient released from the hospital had to take along a cat, for nocturnal protection.

Listening to Dr. Brand tell these horror stories, I could easily understand why he could say with absolute conviction, "Thank God for pain!" For him, pain represents God's great gift, one Brand desperately desires to share with fifteen million victims of leprosy.

After twenty years in India, Dr. Brand moved to the Hansen's disease* research center and hospital in Carville, Louisiana. There, under the auspices of the U.S. Public Health Service, he could continue his research and potentially help many more patients worldwide.

I first met Dr. Brand at the Carville hospital, a visit that changed forever the way I think about pain. Because of the stigma of leprosy, the hospital is remote and difficult to reach. It was built in the 1890s on the swampy site of a plantation by the banks of the Mississippi. (Land was purchased under the pretense of starting an ostrich farm so that neighbors would not suspect the buyers' true intent.)

The leprosy center stretches out over 337 acres and includes a nine-hole golf course and a stocked lake in addition to modern medical facilities. Barbed wire around Carville has come down, and visitors are now welcome. Tours are conducted three times daily.

A pleasant environment, buildings designed for wheelchair patients, the best medical care, free treatment with the latest drugs—on the surface life

---

*The medical name for leprosy.

in this shaded plantation setting seems almost enviable. The disease is under control now, and most cases can be arrested in early stages. But, as I quickly learned, one horrible aspect of leprosy remains: the loss of pain sensation.

Visit to Carville

I am visiting a patient clinic at Carville. Two physical therapists, a nurse, and Dr. Brand are seated in chairs arranged in a semicircle around a TV monitor. Together they will examine three patients with health problems.

The first enters, a middle-aged Hawaiian man named Lou (not his real name). I notice that Lou has more visible deformities than most patients here. He came to Carville with an advanced case of leprosy. His eyebrows and eyelashes are gone, which gives his face a naked, unbalanced appearance. Because his eyelids are paralyzed, tears tend to overflow and he seems to be perpetually crying.

Dr. Brand has already told me that Lou is virtually blind. Blind from lack of pain: tiny pain cells on the surface of his eye stopped signaling the irritation and discomfort that call for blinking, and as his dulled eyelids blinked less frequently Lou's eyes gradually dried up. Preventing blindness is a real challenge at Carville. A few patients destroyed their eyes by the simple act of washing their faces, their hands not sensitive enough to warn of scalding water.

In addition to blindness, Lou suffers from many other side-effects of leprosy. His feet are smooth stumps, without toes—all ten toes were lost due to inadvertent injury and infection. His hands are lined with deep cracks and thickened scars. But Lou's main problem, the reason he has come to the clinic, is more psychological than physical.

Lou feels a door has been shut between him and the rest of the world. He can't see people. Having lost so much sensation, he cannot feel a handshake or any other form of human touch. His last remaining unaffected sense is hearing, and that is the source of his fear. A new experimental drug is causing some loss of hearing.

His voice trembling, Lou tells the group how much he loves the Autoharp. He can strum the Hawaiian melodies of his childhood and dream of younger days. A devout Christian, he sings as a form of praise to God, and sometimes volunteers to play hymns for his church. In order to play, Lou must tape the pick onto the one patch of his thumb that still has some sensation. With that sensitive spot, he can detect enough variation in pressure to know how to strum the chords correctly.

But Lou's thumb is not sensitive enough to recognize dangerous pressures. Hours of practicing the Autoharp have left calluses on the thumb, and now an ulcer has broken out. He has been afraid to come to the clinic until now. "Can you find some way for me to continue playing without damaging my hand?" he asks in a thick accent, almost pleading.

The committee of doctors and physical therapists view Lou's hand on the TV monitor. They are using thermography, a process by which a machine detects differing temperature bands and projects them visually as bright colors. Weather satellites use the same technology.

On the thermogram Lou's hand appears as a psychedelic pattern of chartreuse, yellow, scarlet, and all shades in between. The coolest portions show up green or blue. Bright red is a danger sign that indicates an infection: blood has rushed to the site, raising the temperature. Yellow shows extreme danger. It's easy to see the single most useful spot on Lou's thumb, for constant use has inflamed the area, and it now stands out as a yellow pinpoint of heat.

Thermography has revolutionized treatment at Carville because for the first time it offers a warning system for painless persons. Unfortunately, unlike the pain network, this technology detects danger after the period of stress, not during it. A person with a healthy pain system would have sought treatment long before. His or her thumb would throb all day long, loudly demanding attention and rest. But Lou has no such advantage. He never knows when he is further damaging the tiny spot of infection in his thumb.

The committee designs a glove to fit Lou's hand, one that will relieve some of the pressure of the Autoharp pick. Dr. Brand delivers a stern lecture about the need for Lou to give his thumb a rest, to wear the glove at all times, and to report in every few days. But after Lou leaves, the physical therapist expresses pessimism. "Lou hates gloves. They call attention to his hands, and undoubtedly he'll lose some control over the pick. Probably he'll try it for a day, then throw it away."

Already Lou is withdrawing from people, cutting off contact as his senses of sight, hearing, and touch gradually fade. Now his last great love, his self-expression through music, is also threatened. He may return to the clinic in a few weeks with a further infection that has caused permanent damage to his thumb. He may even lose the thumb. But at Carville treatment is voluntary. Without his own pain network to force him to act, Lou has the risky option of ignoring the thermogram's warning.

A Mop and a Shoe

Another patient, Hector, enters the room. Although his face shows none of the deformities of Lou's, still I must catch myself from gasping when I see it. By now I have grown accustomed to seeing colors projected on a thermogram monitor, but not on a man's face. Hector has blue skin! Dr. Brand, noticing my reaction, whispers to me that Hector has shown resistance to the sulfone drugs most commonly used for treatment, and the team has been experimenting with a new drug that happens to be a blue dye. Hector has gladly forfeited normal flesh tones in hopes of halting the spread of leprosy in his body.

Hector, a most cooperative patient, answers all the committee's questions thoughtfully, speaking in a deep Texas drawl. No, he's had no problems since the last checkup. Hector's thermogram, however, disagrees, revealing a vivid red danger spot in the webbing between his right thumb and forefinger. A callus has hidden any external signs of infection, but underneath an infection is festering.

Quizzing him like a police investigation team, Dr. Brand and the others ask Hector to trace his day's activities. How does he shave? Put on his shoes? Does he have a job? Does he play golf? Shoot pool? At some point in his day, Hector has been grasping something too firmly between his thumb and forefinger. Unless they can find the faulty activity and get him to stop, his hand will deteriorate further.

At last, in the course of the grilling, Hector identifies the problem. After each day's mild work as a canteen cashier, he helps with the cleanup, mopping the floor to erase any spilled soft drinks or candy. That back-and-forth motion, coupled with Hector's inability to sense how firmly he is squeezing the mop handle, has damaged tissue inside his thumb. The mystery is solved.

Hector thanks the group profusely. A physical therapist makes a note to ask the canteen supervisor to substitute some other activity for Hector.

One more patient comes in—Jose. In contrast to most people at Carville, Jose is wearing the latest in fashion. His pants have a sharp crease, and his all-cotton shirt is neatly tapered to fit. His shoes are nothing like the dull, black orthopedic shoes I have seen on most patients. They have a contemporary, narrow-toe design and are polished to a high brown gloss.

Jose's shoes are, in fact, the problem. He dresses meticulously because of his full-time job as a furniture salesman back in California. Carville therapists have tried to persuade Jose to wear less stylish, and safer, shoes, but he has always refused. His job and image are more important to him than the condition of his feet.

When Jose removes his shoes and socks, his feet show the worst injury I have seen. I cannot find the slightest nub where his toes should be. After years of infection, his body has absorbed the bone tissue, and Jose now walks on rounded stumps, like an amputee. With no toes to cushion the impact when his heel lifts upward, he is systematically wearing down even the stumps. Thermography graphically illustrates the ongoing problem. Dr. Brand calls Jose's attention to bright yellow patches marking the extent of infection.

Normally, a person would automatically limp, or change walking styles, to break in a new pair of shoes, and if the feet hurt too badly, out would come a more comfortable pair. But Jose can't feel the danger signs. Members of the committee take turns trying to impress on Jose the gravity of the problem, but he is politely unyielding. He will not wear Carville-made shoes. To him, they look like training shoes for cripples, and they'd tip off his customers that something is wrong. His facial features and hands are almost normal; he won't let his feet betray him.

Finally, Dr. Brand calls in the shoemaker and asks him to make some minor adjustments on Jose's shoes that may partially relieve the pressure.

At the end of the clinic, after the last patient has left, Dr. Brand turns to me and says, "Pain—it's often seen as the great inhibitor, keeping us from happiness. But I see it as a giver of freedom. Look at these men. Lou: we're desperately searching for a way to allow him the simple freedom of playing an Autoharp. Hector: he can't even mop a floor without harming himself. Jose: he can't dress nicely and walk normally. For that, he would need the gift of pain."

A Deadly Indifference

Leprosy is not the only affliction that muffles the protective warnings of pain. The research at Carville has also been applied to other medical conditions of insensitivity. In advanced cases, diabetics lose pain sensations and face exactly the same dangers. Many have lost fingers, toes, and entire limbs as a result of preventable injuries. Alcoholics and drug addicts can likewise deaden their sensitivity: each winter alcoholics die of exposure, their bodies numb to the biting cold.

A few people, however, are born with a defective pain network, and some of these too have sought treatment at Carville. Victims of the rare condition known informally as "congenital indifference to pain" have a warning system of sorts, but, like Dr. Brand's flashing lights and audible signals, theirs does not hurt. To them, running fingers over a hot stove gives the same sensation as running fingers over an asphalt driveway. They feel both as neutral sensations.

Congenital indifference to pain poses unique problems of child-rearing. One family told of a horrifying incident that occurred when their infant daughter grew four teeth. The mother, hearing the baby daughter laughing and cooing in the next room, went in expecting to find some new game the child had discovered. She screamed. Her daughter had bitten off the tip of her finger and was playing in the blood, making patterns with the drips.

How do you explain the danger of matches, knives, and razor blades to such children? How do you punish them? The little girl, seeing the effect of her "game" on her mother, started using it mischievously. Whenever her mother forbade her to do something, the girl would put her finger in her mouth and begin to bite it. By the time she reached sixteen, she had chewed off all her fingers.

About a hundred cases of this strange affliction have been reported on in medical literature. One seven-year-old picked at her nose until her nostrils became ulcerated. An eight-year-old English girl, in a fit of anger, pulled out all but nine of her teeth and poked both eyes out of their sockets. Afflicted children can impress their friends with bizarre feats like pushing a straight pin through their fingers.

But insensitivity to pain dooms such people to lives of constant peril. They can sprain a wrist or ankle without knowing it, or bite through their tongues while chewing gum. Joints deteriorate because they fail to shift weight while sleeping or standing. One afflicted woman lost her life because she could not feel a simple headache, the warning symptom of a serious illness.[1]

These people can undergo surgery without anesthesia, but how do they know when surgery is required? Whereas a healthy person would feel symptoms in advance of a heart attack or appendicitis, they feel nothing. Where most people would respond immediately, spurred on by pain, the congenitally insensitive must consciously attend to the faintest clues and ponder the appropriate response. A tickling sensation in the abdomen . . . does that mean my appendix has burst?

Medical textbooks had done much to convince me of pain's value before I visited Carville. Already I was beginning to see that, even in Claudia Claxton's case, pain was not the root problem—the disease was. Pain was merely her body's loyal way of informing her that cancer cells and cobalt rays were harming her. Apart from these warnings she might have died, unaware of the disease's presence.

The week at Carville left me with indelible memories. Whenever I am tempted to curse God for pain, I remember Lou: his eyes running, his face scarred, oblivious to human touch, longing for a way to retain his music, his last love in life. Pain allows us, the fortunate ones at least, to lead free and active lives. If you ever doubt that, visit a leprosarium and observe for yourself a world without pain.

Pain is not an unpleasantness to be avoided at all costs. In a thousand ways large and small, pain serves us each day, making possible normal life on this planet. If we are healthy, pain cells alert us when to go to the bathroom, when to change shoes, when to loosen the grip on a mop handle or rake, when to blink. Without pain, we would lead lives of paranoia, defenseless against unfelt dangers. The only safe environment for a painless person is to stay in bed all day . . . but even that produces bedsores.

4

—◦◦◦—

Agony and Ecstasy

How singular is the thing called pleasure and how curiously related to pain, which might be thought to be the opposite of it . . . yet he who pursues either is generally compelled to take the other; their bodies are two but they are joined by the same head.

Socrates

When confronted with the facts, most of us will admit that pain—some pain, at least—serves a good and useful purpose. Apart from the warning system it provides, hidden dangers would shadow our everyday existence. Even more neglected, however, is the intimate connection that links pain and pleasure. The two sensations work together so closely they sometimes become almost indistinguishable.

Pain is an essential component of our most satisfying experiences. Does that sound odd? It may, for modern culture barrages us with opposite messages. We are told that pain is the antithesis of pleasure. If you feel a slight headache, dull it immediately with the newest extra-strength pain reliever. If your nose drips more than a drop, by all means reach for the latest sinus decongestant spray. At the slightest cramp of constipation, visit a drugstore and select from the dazzling display of candies, liquids, pills, and enemas.

I think back to Thielicke's criticism of Americans' "inadequate view of suffering." Little wonder. We moderns have cut ourselves off from the stream of human history, which has always accepted pain as an integral part of life. Until very recently, any balanced view of life had to account for pain as a normal, routine occurrence. Now it looms as the great intruder.

Let me quickly add that I buy shrink-wrapped, bloodless hunks of meat in grocery stores, work in an air-conditioned office, and wear shoes to protect my feet from Chicago sidewalks. But in doing so I realize that abundant luxuries and conveniences such as these give me a perspective on the world and on pain that was not shared by any other century and is still unrealized by two-thirds of the world. I, along with most Americans, tend to see pain as a sensation that can and should be mastered by technology. That distorted viewpoint helps foster the notion that pain and pleasure are diametrically opposed: our lifestyles murmur it to us every day.

Nobel Prize winner George Wald reflected on this fact: "Just realize, I am 69 and have never seen a person die. I have never even been in the same house while a person died. How about birth? An obstetrician invited me to see my first birth only last year. Just think, these are the greatest events of life and they have been taken out of our experience. We somehow hope to live full emotional lives when we have carefully expunged the sources of the deepest human emotions. When you have no experience of pain, it is rather hard to experience joy."

Buzzed Brains

In some ways the human brain resembles an electronic amplifier, coordinating input from a bewildering array of sources. Instead of phono turntables, VCR machines, compact disc players, and tape decks, we have such input sources as touch, vision, hearing, taste, and smell. In a healthy body, pain is just one of many input sources assigned to report on the state of the extremities.

When a sense organ begins to degenerate, the brain automatically turns up the volume control. Sometimes a person with leprosy will not notice a loss of touch sensation until it fades completely; his brain has compensated by increasing the volume of the slight impulses until the sensors die and give off no more impulses.

Modern culture saddens me because, while it seeks to turn down the volume on pain, it constantly turns up the volume from all other sources. We have ears: they are bombarded with decibels until the subtle tones are lost forever. Listen to music from any other century, twelfth, sixteenth, even nineteenth, and compare it to what most people listen to today. We have eyes: the world assaults them with neon lights and phosphorescent colors until a sunset or butterfly pales in comparison. Imagine what a glimpse of a tiger swallowtail butterfly did for the senses in a village of medieval Europe—compared to the same butterfly in downtown Las Vegas today. We have noses: chemical droplets come printed like ink on magazine pages so that we need only scratch and sniff. Take away the spray cans from our closets indoors and the pollution particles from the air outdoors, and most of us would have no idea how the natural world is supposed to smell.

We use the word "stoned" for people so blitzed with sensations, often chemically induced, that they are dulled almost senseless. I prefer the word "buzzed," following the brain/amplifier analogy. In such a high-tech environment, it is easy for the young, especially, to mistake vicarious pleasure for true fulfillment—life as video game. They don't see pleasure as something to reach out for and actively attain after struggle. Pleasure is something done to you; merely strap yourself in the amusement-park ride.

The drug problems in the U.S. demonstrate this pattern: by heightening powers of perception, chemical stimulants open up a new world to a generation that has never learned to appreciate fully the world we have. It is not enough to walk alongside a swamp and listen to the frogs and crickets, to watch the turtles plop like bloated submarines into the water, to seek out the faint scent of wildflowers. It is not enough, even, to visit the outer reaches of wilderness, where nature is far from subtle. Instead, too often we experience all these things vicariously, slumped in front of a flickering television with its beams of Trinitron color and low-frequency radiation, receiving sensory stimulation through our eyes alone. We have been to Everest and back, we think, when in fact some of us have never climbed the Appalachians.

Substituting vicarious and artificial sensations for natural ones takes a toll on the human body. Like muscles, our senses can atrophy. French scientists have proved this in experiments with darkened isolation chambers in which volunteers float in tepid water. In the absence of outside stimuli, the senses have nothing to report, and begin to fail. Soon the subjects become restless and disoriented, and before long begin to hallucinate. High altitude jet pilots and military sentinels in isolated outposts have experienced similar hallucinations. When deprived of sensory reports from the body, the brain appears to manufacture its own.

On the other hand, through regular use our sensory faculties can develop even more responsiveness. Nerve endings actually "improve" with use. Some scientists theorize that fingertips develop their incredible sensitivity due to our constant reliance on them from infancy onwards. Similarly, you can increase skin sensitivity by brushing your own arm daily with a nylon brush. Eventually the skin surface there will detect a much wider range of pleasure and pain sensations.

Going barefoot also helps to vary skin sensation, especially if you walk on the sand of a beach or on grass. The subtle variations in a lawn's shape and texture feed the brain with needed sensory input, which is vital for the brain's healthy development.

For this reason Dr. Brand, half in jest but half seriously, suggests that babies should be raised on coarse coconut matting rather than on down comforters and blankets. Surrounding babies with softness and neutral sensations stifles their nerve-growth and limits their range of interpreting the world. Brand also confesses his wife discouraged him from stringing barbed wire around his children's playpens. Cruel? It would merely train a child to accept a world where certain things (like sharp objects and hot stoves) are off-limits and painful. The more you coddle children, he says, the more you condition them to an insulated, sensation-starved life.

Dr. Brand tries to follow this principle throughout his life, even as he approaches the last decades of his life. "At one time, I thought of pain as the opposite of happiness. I would have illustrated life by drawing a graph with a peak at each end and a trough in the middle. The peak at the left would represent the experience of pain or acute unhappiness. The peak at the right would represent pure happiness or ecstasy. In between is quiet, normal living. My goal, I thought, was to face firmly toward happiness and away from pain. But now I see things differently. If I drew such a graph today, it would have a single, central peak with a surrounding plain. The peak would be Life with a capital *L*, the point at which pain and pleasure meet. The surrounding plain would be sleep or apathy or death."

Pain and Pleasure

Nature, ever economical, uses the same nerve sensors and pathways that convey messages of pain to carry also messages of pleasure. At the cellular level, the sensation of a mosquito-bite itch (unpleasant) and that of a tickle (pleasant) are virtually identical, the difference being that tickling involves the motion of something acting upon you—a feather pulled across skin, a finger wiggled on a sensitive area. The same nerve sensors are involved, firing off identical responses to the brain, but we interpret one action as pleasant and one as unpleasant.

The body contains no dedicated "pleasure" sensors. Sensors in your fingers that report to your brain information about heat, or the extent of a mild electric shock, or the degree of coarseness of a rough surface, are the same sensors that convey to you the feel of velvet or satin. Indeed, even the sensors that produce feelings of sexual pleasure are the same ones that carry messages of alarm. Dissection of the erogenous zones yields an abundance of touch and pressure cells (which explains why those areas are so sensitive to pain), but no cells devoted to pleasure. Nature is never so lavish.

Some pains—the sharp prick of a fingernail to stop the itching of a mosquito bite, or the twang of a sore muscle being stretched after a hard day's work—are perceived as more pleasant than unpleasant. After skiing all day in the mountains, I want the hottest Jacuzzi available. I wait a few minutes, then gingerly lower a hand or leg into the water. Ouch! A stinging shot of pain. I withdraw, then try again.

Up to my ankles now, and the pain is far less. I gradually lower my body into the water. The same water that a moment before caused me pain now feels wonderful. My sore muscles feel better than they have felt all day. (Liniments like Ben Gay work on the same principle: they slightly irritate the skin, which causes something akin to a "burning" sensation. Blood rushes to the site, bringing relief to overtaxed muscles.)

This close association between pain and pleasure holds true not just on the cellular level, but in many experiences that involve the whole body working together. Often the most intense pleasure comes after prolonged struggle.

I once went on a stress camping trip, designed after the Outward Bound program, in the north woods of Wisconsin. Such programs offer an instant cure for anyone who feels isolated from the natural world, or from pain. Getting awakened at 4:00 A.M., scrambling up a bare rock wall with no gloves, running a marathon race after ten days in the woods, invading the world headquarters of black flies and "no-see-ums"—such delights await the soft city slicker. I have never felt more tired at the end of a day as I forced weary muscles into a sleeping bag still damp from last night's dew. Even so, I have never gotten less sleep, thanks mainly to the nocturnal "no-see-ums," smaller than any mosquito net opening and fiercer than any killer bee.

Yet what I now remember most about that week is how it affected my senses. They seemed to come alive. When I breathed in, I could "taste" the air—

and in an entirely different way than I taste the air around my Chicago home. I noticed things with my eyes and ears that I would normally overlook.

Once, after an afternoon of hiking in the dust and heat, while loaded down with seventy-pound packs, we paused for a brief rest stop. One of the group followed a honeybee to a small patch of wild strawberries growing nearby. No self-respecting grocery store would ever have accepted these strawberries. They were small and scrawny, and coated with dust. We didn't care; they were food, and perhaps contained some moisture. I picked a handful, popped them into my mouth, and was immediately overwhelmed by the incredible flavor of sweet, luscious strawberry juice. These desiccated little berries were the best I had ever eaten! I spent my rest time picking more and stuffing them into plastic bags for an afternoon snack.

At first I thought we had stumbled upon a new species, the discovery of which would revolutionize the fruit-growing industry. Gradually I figured out that the taste had to do with *my* physical condition, not the strawberries'. The process of using my body and connecting with all my senses had freed up a whole new level of pleasure awareness. The extraordinary, delicious taste of those strawberries would never have been mine if I had not first felt the heat and toil of hiking all day, as well as the pangs of hunger that sharpened my senses.

Athletes know well this strange brotherhood. Watch an Olympic weight lifter. He approaches the steel bar with its bulging wheels of weight. He takes deep breaths, grimaces, flexes his muscles. Reaching down, he gives a few preparatory tugs to limber up. Then he squats, sucks in air, tenses his body in one mighty reflex, and begins to hoist. Oh, the pain in a weight lifter's face. Each millisecond it takes him to jerk the weight to his shoulders and raise it over his head etches lines of agony on his face. His muscles scream for relief.

If he succeeds, he drops the bar with a tremendous thud on the floor and jumps in the air, his hands clasped above his head. In a millisecond, absolute ecstasy replaces absolute agony. One would not have existed without the other. Ask the weight lifter what he thought of the pain—and he will stare at you, bewildered. He has already forgotten, for it has been swallowed up in pleasure.

Lin Yutang describes an ancient Chinese philosophy in his book *My Country and My People*: "To be dry and thirsty in a hot and dusty land—and to feel great drops of rain on my bare skin—ah, is this not happiness! To have an itch in the private part of my body—and finally to escape from my friends and to a hiding place where I can scratch— ah, is this not happiness!" In Yutang's long list of happiness experiences, virtually every one combines pain with pleasure.

Augustine's *Confessions* contains a remarkably similar passage. "What is it, therefore," he begins, "that goes on within the soul, since it takes greater delight if things that it loves are found or restored to it than if it had always possessed them?" Augustine proceeds to mention a victorious general who experiences the greatest satisfaction when the danger is greatest, a seafarer who exults in calm seas after a violent storm, and a sick man who upon recovery walks with a joy he had never known before his illness.

"Everywhere a greater joy is preceded by a greater suffering," Augustine concludes.[1] Like other church fathers, he understood that depriving some senses, such as through fasting, heightened others. Spiritual experience is nourished best in the wilderness.

When I am old, I hope I do not spend my days between sterile sheets, hooked up to a respirator in a germ-free environment, protected from the hazards of the world outside. I hope I'm on a tennis court, straining my heart with a septuagenarian overhead smash. Or perhaps on a final hike, huffing and puffing along a trail to Lower Yosemite Falls for one more feel of the spray against my wrinkled cheek. In short, I hope I do not so insulate myself from pain that I no longer feel pleasure.

Befriending Enemies

Athletes and artists alike learn that a long period of struggle and effort precedes nearly all worthwhile human accomplishments. It required years of toil and misery for Michelangelo to create the Sistine Chapel frescoes that have since given pleasure to so many others. And anyone who has built cabinets in a kitchen or tended a vegetable garden knows the same truth in a more mundane way: the pleasure, coming after the pain, absorbs it. Jesus used childbirth as an analogy: nine months of waiting and preparation, intense labor, then the ecstasy of birth (John 16:21).

I once interviewed Robin Graham, the youngest person ever to sail around the world alone. (His story was told in the book and movie *Dove*.) Robin set sail as an immature sixteen-year-old, not so much seeking his future as delaying it. In the course of the long voyage, he was smashed broadside by a violent ocean storm, had his mast snapped in two by a rogue wave, and barely missed annihilation by a waterspout. He went through such despair in the Doldrums, a windless, currentless portion of the ocean near the Equator, that he emptied a can of kerosene in his boat, struck a match, and jumped overboard. (A sudden gust of wind soon caused him to change his mind and he jumped back in to extinguish the blaze and continue the voyage.)

After five years, Robin sailed into the Los Angeles harbor to be greeted by boats, banners, crowds, reporters, honking cars, and blasts from steam whistles. The joy of that moment was on a different level from any other experience he had known. He could never have felt those emotions returning from a pleasure outing off the coast of California. The agony of his round-the-world trip had made possible the exultation of his triumphant return. He left a sixteen-year-old kid and returned a twenty-one-year-old man.

Impressed by the sense of health that self-accomplishment could bring, Robin immediately bought a farm plot in Kalispell, Montana, and built a cabin from hand-cut logs. Publishers and movie agents tried to entice him with round-the-country publicity trips, talk show engagements, and fat expense accounts, but Robin declined them all.

We moderns, in our comfort-controlled environments, have a tendency to blame our unhappiness on pain, which we identify as the great enemy. If we could somehow excise pain from life, ah, then we would be happy. But, as experiences like Robin's show, life does not yield to such easy partitioning. Pain is a part of the seamless fabric of sensations, and often a necessary prelude to pleasure and fulfillment. The key to happiness lies not so much in avoiding pain at all costs as in understanding its role as a protective warning system and harnessing it to work on your behalf, not against you.

I have learned that this same principle applies not only to pain, but to other "enemies" as well. When I encounter an apparent enemy, I ask myself, Can I find even in this a reason for gratitude? To my surprise, the answer is almost always yes.

What about fear, for example—Why be grateful for fear? I know the physiology behind fear, the way in which the body uses minute quantities of adrenaline to speed heart rate, increase skin friction, heighten reaction time and supply added strength—all this in a millisecond of fear. I try to imagine a sport like downhill skiing without the protective response of fear that keeps me from being even more foolhardy. Fear, like pain, serves as a warning system, only with the added benefit of functioning in advance of harm.

Someone asked the Swiss physician and author Paul Tournier how he helped his patients get rid of their fears. He replied, "I don't. Everything that's worthwhile in life is scary. Choosing a school, choosing a career, getting married, having kids—all those things are scary. If it is not fearful, it is not worthwhile."

Consider another apparent enemy: guilt, a universal human response that many people want to purge from their lives. But try to envision a world without guilt, a society with no curbs on behavior. The U.S. court system defines sanity as the ability to discern between good and evil, and a world with no guilt would tilt toward insanity.

Guilt is a pain message to the conscience, informing it that something is wrong and should be dealt with. Two steps are necessary. First, the person must locate the cause of the guilt, just as a person must locate the cause of his or her pain. Much of modern counseling deals with this process of weeding out reasons for false guilt. But a further step must follow, a pathway out of the guilt.

The perceived function of guilt, like pain, is an impulse to get rid of the unpleasant sensation. Underlying that, however, is the more significant purpose of dealing with the root cause. In the long run, it won't help you to try to purge authentic guilt feelings unless you first let them guide you toward forgiveness and reconciliation. Guilt by itself doesn't lead you anywhere, just as pain does not: both are directional, symptoms of a condition that requires your urgent attention.

Or, I think of a world without another pain, the pain of loneliness. Would friendship and even love exist apart from our inbuilt sense of need, the prod that keeps us all from being hermits? Do we not need the power of loneliness to pry us away from isolation and push us toward others?

I do not mean to gloss over or discount the very real suffering in this world. Nevertheless, when something bad happens and we feel we have no control over the tragedy itself, we still have some control over our own responses. We can lash out in bitterness and anger against the unfairness of life that has deprived us of pleasure and joy. Or, we can look for good in unexpected sources, even our apparent enemies.

I heard recently about a poll of senior citizens in London. To the question, "What was the happiest period of your life?" sixty percent answered, "The Blitz." Every night squadrons of fat Luftwaffe bombers would dump tons of explosives on the city, pounding a proud civilization to rubble—and now the victims recall that time with nostalgia! In those dark, fearful days, they learned to huddle together and strive toward a common goal. They learned such qualities as courage, and sharing, and hope.

When something bad happens—a disagreement with my wife, a painful misunderstanding with a friend, an ache of guilt over some responsibility I have let slide—I try to view that occurrence as I would view a physical pain. I accept it as a signal alerting me to attend to a matter that needs change. I strive to be grateful, not for the pain itself, but for the opportunity to respond, to form good out of what looks bad.

Surprised by Happiness

Jesus captured succinctly the paradoxical nature of life in his one statement most repeated in the Gospels: "Whoever finds his life will lose it, and whoever loses his life for my sake will find it." Such a statement goes against the search for "self-fulfillment" in advanced psychology—which turns out to be not advanced enough. Christianity offers the further insight that true fulfillment comes, not through ego satisfaction, but through service to others. And that brings me to the last illustration of the pain/pleasure principle: the Christian concept of service.

In my career as a journalist, I have interviewed diverse people. Looking back, I can roughly divide them into two types: stars and servants. The stars include NFL football greats, movie actors, music performers, famous authors, TV personalities, and the like. These are the people who dominate our magazines and our television programs. We fawn over them, poring over the minutiae of their lives: the clothes they wear, the food they eat, the aerobic routines they follow, the people they love, the toothpaste they use.

Yet I must tell you that, in my limited experience, these "idols" are as miserable a group of people as I have ever met. Most have troubled or broken marriages. Nearly all are hopelessly dependent on psychotherapy. In a heavy irony, these larger-than-life heroes seem tormented by incurable self-doubt.

I have also spent time with servants. People like Dr. Paul Brand, who worked for twenty years among the poorest of the poor, leprosy patients in rural India. Or health workers who left high-paying jobs to serve with Mendenhall Ministries in a backwater town of Mississippi. Or relief workers in Somalia, Sudan, Ethiopia, Bangladesh, or other such repositories of world-class human suffering. Or the Ph.D.'s scattered throughout jungles of South America translating the Bible into obscure languages.

I was prepared to honor and admire these servants, to hold them up as inspiring examples. I was not, however, prepared to envy them. But as I now reflect on the two groups side by side, stars and servants, the servants clearly emerge as the favored ones, the graced ones. They work for low pay, long hours, and no applause, "wasting" their talents and skills among the poor and uneducated. But somehow in the process of losing their lives they have found them. They have received the "peace that is not of this world."

When I think of the great churches I have visited, what comes to mind is not an image of a cathedral in Europe. These are mere museums now. Instead, I think of the chapel at Carville, of an inner-city church in Newark with crumbling plaster and a leaky roof, of a mission church in Santiago, Chile, made of concrete block and corrugated iron. In these places, set amidst human misery, I have seen Christian love abound.

The leprosarium in Carville, Louisiana, offers a wonderful example of this principle in action. A government agency bought the property and promised to develop it, but could find no one to clear the roads, repair the plantation's slave cabins, or drain the swamps. The stigma of leprosy kept everyone away.

Finally an order of nuns, the Sisters of Charity, moved to Carville to nurse the leprosy patients. Getting up two hours before daybreak, wearing starched white uniforms in bayou heat, these nuns lived under a more disciplined rule than any Marine boot camp. But they alone proved willing to do the work. They dug ditches, laid foundations for buildings, and made Carville livable, all the while glorifying God and bringing joy to the patients. They learned perhaps the deepest level of pain/pleasure association in life, that of sacrificial service.

If I spend my life searching for happiness through drugs, comfort, and luxury, it will elude me. "Happiness recedes from those who pursue her." Happiness will come upon me unexpectedly as a by-product, a surprising bonus for something I have invested myself in. And, most likely, that investment will include pain. It is hard to imagine pleasure without it.

PART 2

Is Pain a Message from God?

5

—◦◦◦—

The Groaning Planet

Imagine a set of people all living in the same building. Half of them think it is a hotel, the other half think it is a prison. Those who think it a hotel might regard it as quite intolerable, and those who thought it was a prison might decide that it was really surprisingly comfortable. So that what seems the ugly doctrine is one that comforts and strengthens you in the end. The people who try to hold an optimistic view of this world would become pessimists: the people who hold a pretty stern view of it become optimistic.

C. S. Lewis
God in the Dock

Consider earth, our home. Let your eyes savor the brilliant hues and delicate shadings of a summer sunset. Tunnel your toes into wet sand, stand still, and feel the dependable foam and spray of an ocean tide. Visit a butterfly garden and study the abstract designs: 10,000 variations, more imaginative than those of any abstract painter, all compressed into tiny swatches of flying fabric. Belief in a loving Creator is easy among these good things.

Yet the sun that lavishes dusk with color can also bake African soil into a dry, cracked glaze, dooming millions. The rhythmic, pounding surf can, if fomented by a storm, crash in as a twenty-foot wall of death, obliterating coastal villages. And the harmless swatches of color fluttering among wild-flowers survive on average two weeks before succumbing to the grim ferocity of nature's food chain. Nature is our fallen sister, not our mother. And earth, though God's showplace, is a good creation that has been bent.

Witness the human species. The fatherland of Bach, Beethoven, Luther, and Goethe also gave us Hitler, Eichmann, and Goering. A nation weaned on the Bill of Rights also brought us slavery and the Civil War. As a species and as individuals, in every one of us wisdom, creativity, and compassion vie with deceit, pride, and selfishness.

And so it is with pain. Up close, pain may seem a trusted, worthy friend. From the myopic perspective of, say, a bioengineer, the pain network surely appears as one of creation's finest works. The nervous system, bearing the stamp of genius, merits admiration and awe, like an exquisite Rembrandt painting.

Yet most often pain comes to our attention not through a microscope eyepiece, but through unwelcome tokens of personal misery. If you relate each warning signal to a specific cause, the pain network may seem rational and well-designed. But if you step back and view all humanity—a writhing, starving, bleeding, cancerous progression of billions of people marching toward death—there, a problem arises.

The "problem of pain" encompasses far more than the loyal responses of nerve cells. What about the side effects of pain as it grinds down the soul toward despair and hopelessness? Why the caprice of some lives dominated by arthritis, cancer, or birth defects, while others escape unafflicted for seven decades? The poet William Blake summed up human existence this way:

My mother groaned, my father wept,
into the dangerous world I leapt . . .

Philosophers love sweeping discussions of the sum total of human suffering, as if all human pain could be extruded into one great cauldron and presented to God: "Here is the pain and suffering of Planet Earth. How do you account for all this misery?" But as Ivan Karamazov pointed out in Dostoyevksi's great novel, pain comes to one person at a time, and the undeserved suffering of a single human being—a child beating its breast with its fist—raises the problem just as acutely.

Pain may have been intended as an efficiently protective warning system, but something about this planet has gone haywire and pain now rages out of control. We need another word for the problem: perhaps "pain" to signify the body's protective network and "suffering" to signify the human misery. After all, a leprosy patient feels no pain, but much suffering.

Though some people stay mercifully free of

acute physical pain, everyone has a form of suffering that will not go away: a personality flaw, a broken relationship, an unhealed childhood memory, a suffocating guilt. To understand suffering we must step away from the microscope, with its array of nerve cells obediently responding to stimuli, and look full in the face of agonized human beings. The question "Where is God when it hurts?" becomes "Where is God when it won't stop hurting?" How can God allow such intense, unfair pain?

Best Possible World?

For centuries philosophers have debated the question "Is earth the best of all possible worlds?" The debate follows from the presumption that an all-knowing, all-powerful, all-loving God naturally would have created a wonderful domain for his creatures. But look around at some of the features of our planet—the AIDS virus and Down's syndrome, spina bifida and poliomyelitis, scorpions and tsetse flies, earthquakes and typhoons. Couldn't God have done a better job? As Voltaire put it sarcastically in *Candide*, "If this is the best of all possible worlds, then what are the others like?"

In former times, Christian theologians such as Augustine and Thomas Aquinas argued that God had indeed created the best of all possible worlds. Nowadays, after the twentieth century's display of natural and man-made horrors, only the bravest of thinkers would make such an assertion.

I certainly would not attempt to build a case that earth represents the best of all possible worlds. But one reason I have spent so much time on the biology of pain is that I believe modern philosophers may fail to appreciate the difficulties involved in the act of creation. They presume all God has to do is wave a magic wand to eliminate most hazards of life on earth.

In order to make their point convincingly, critics of this planet need to describe a superior universe, with a complete system of natural laws that would result in significantly less human suffering. Imagine a few possibilities. Why not simply do away with bacteria? That would be a disaster: 24,000 different species of bacteria have been identified, only a few score of which cause illness. Eliminate bacteria and we would never be able to digest food. Typhoons? Bangladesh and India have learned painfully that the earth's climatic system depends upon such major disturbances; in years that typhoons stay away, rains stay away as well.

Creation involves a selection from alternatives. If I break my leg skiing I might wish for stronger bones. Perhaps bone could have been made stronger (though scientists have not been able to find a stronger, suitable substance for implanting), but then my legs would be thicker and heavier, probably making me too bulky and inert to ski at all. If my fingers were thicker and more durable, many human activities—such as playing the piano—would be impossible. A creator had to make those difficult choices between strength and mobility and weight and volume.

Dr. Paul Brand had a taste of such difficult

choices when he was trying to design a simple pain sensor to protect the hands of his leprosy patients. This is what he learned:

The more I delve into natural laws—the atom, the universe, the solid elements, molecules, the sun, and even more, the interplay of all the mechanisms required to sustain life—I am astounded. The whole creation could collapse like a deck of cards if just one of those factors were removed. Some people really believe that all the design and precision in nature came about by chance, that if millions of molecules bombard each other long enough a nerve cell and sensory ending at exactly the right threshold will be bound to turn up. To those people I merely suggest that they try to make one, as I did, and see what chance is up against.

I have spent most of my life in the field of hand surgery. I could fill a good-size room with books that explain various techniques for repairing damaged hands. But I have never seen one procedure—not one—that suggests a way to improve a healthy hand. The design is incredible, and pain is, of course, a part of that design. Ninety-nine out of 100 hands are perfectly normal. But the statistics are exactly reversed for those people insensitive to pain: 99 percent of them have some sort of malformation or dysfunction, simply because their pain network has not been working properly.

Much of the suffering on our planet has come about because of two principles that God built into creation: a physical world that runs according to consistent natural laws, and human freedom.

By committing himself to those two principles, both good principles in themselves, God allowed for the possibility of their abuse. For example, water proves useful to us and all creation because of its "softness," its liquid state, and its specific gravity. Yet those very properties open up its rather disagreeable capacity to drown us—or the even more alarming possibility that we might drown someone else.

Take another example, from wood. It bears the fruit of trees, supports leaves to provide shade, and shelters birds and squirrels. Even when taken from the tree, wood is valuable. We use it as fuel to warm ourselves, and as construction material to build houses and furniture. The essential properties of wood—hardness, unpliability, flammability—make possible these useful functions.

But as soon as you plant a tree with those properties in a world peopled by free human beings, you introduce the possibility of abuse. A free man may pick up a chunk of wood and take advantage of its firmness by bashing the head of another man. God could, I suppose, reach down each time and transform the properties of wood into those of sponge, so that the club would bounce off lightly. But that is not what he is about in the world. He has set into motion fixed laws that can be perverted to evil by our misguided freedom.

(God may have had something like this argument in mind in his address at the end of Job. After listening to Job's complaints, thirty-five chapters' worth, he finally makes a personal appearance,
blasting Job off his feet with magnificent descrip-
tions of the created world. God points with pride to
a few of the most remarkable features of creation,
then gives Job a chance to suggest improvements.
Would he care to propose how to run the world differently? You might say that God and Job compare
résumés—guess who wins?)

Is God somehow responsible for the suffering of
this world? In this indirect way, yes. But giving a
child a pair of ice skates, knowing that he may fall,
is a very different matter from knocking him down
on the ice.

In a world that runs according to fixed laws and
is populated by free human beings, the protective
pain network, a wonderful gift, is likewise subject
to abuse. Could God have done it another way?
Could he have maintained some of the benefits of
the pain network without the disadvantages? There
is some question as to whether any warning system
that excludes the element of suffering would work
effectively. As Dr. Brand's experiments and the experience of painless people show, it is not enough
for us to be alerted when pain is present. It must
hurt, so as to demand action.

One can argue forever about whether God could
have designed our world differently. A cut-off
switch for pain? Tropical storms but not hurricanes?
One less virus, or three less bacteria? None of us

knows the answer to those questions, or even to the prior question of how a specific virus entered the world. (Was it a direct creative activity of God? A consequence of the Fall? An act of Satan? A genetic mutation?) But such speculation is mooted by God's own straightforward answer to the question, "Does earth represent the best of all possible worlds?" And that answer is an unqualified *NO!*

The Wild Animal

The Bible traces the entrance of suffering and evil into the world to the grand but terrible quality of human freedom. What makes us different from porpoises, muskrats, and grizzly bears? Alone, *homo sapiens* have been released from the unbreakable pattern of instinctual behavior. We have true, self-determining choice.

As a result of our freedom, human beings introduced something new to the planet—a rebellion against the original design. We have only slight hints of the way earth was meant to be, but we do know that humanity has broken out of the mold. "We talk of wild animals," says G. K. Chesterton, "but man is the only wild animal. It is man that has broken out. All other animals are tame animals; following the rugged respectability of the tribe or type."[1]

Man is wild because he alone, on this speck of molten rock called earth, stands up, shakes his fist, and says to God, "I do what I want to do because I want to do it." As a result, a huge gulf separates us, and this planet, from God. Most remarkably, God allows us the freedom to do what we want, defying all the rules of the universe (at least for a time). Chesterton again: "In making the world, He set it free. God had written, not so much a poem but rather a play; a play He had planned as perfect, but which had necessarily been left to human actors and stage-managers, who have since made a great mess of it."[2]

Theologians use the term "the Fall" to summarize the massive disruption of creation caused by the initial rebellion when evil first entered the world. The shorthand account in Genesis 3 gives a bare sketch of the consequences of that rebellion, but enough to indicate that all of creation, not just the human species, was disrupted. As Milton said in *Paradise Lost*, "Earth felt the wound, and Nature from her seat / Sighing through all her works gave signs of woe, / That all was lost."

The apostle Paul expressed it this way: "The creation waits in eager expectation for the sons of God to be revealed. For the creation was subjected to frustration, not by its own choice, but by the will of the one who subjected it. . . . We know that the whole creation has been groaning as in the pains of childbirth right up to the present time" (Romans 8:19–20, 22).

Somehow, pain and suffering multiplied on earth as a consequence of the abuse of human freedom. When man and woman chose against God, their free world was forever spoiled. As Paul sees it, since the Fall the planet and all its inhabitants have been emitting a constant stream of low-frequency distress signals. We now live on a "groaning" planet.

Thus, any discussion of the unfairness of suffering must begin with the fact that God is not pleased with the condition of the planet either. The story of the Bible, from Genesis to Revelation, is the story of God's plan to restore his creation to its original state of perfection. The Bible begins and ends with the same scene: Paradise, a river, the luminous glory of God, and the Tree of Life. All of human history takes place somewhere between the first part of Genesis and the last part of Revelation, and everything in between comprises the struggle to regain what was lost.

To judge God solely by the present world would be a tragic mistake. At one time, it may have been "the best of all possible worlds," but surely it is not now. The Bible communicates no message with more certainty than God's displeasure with the state of creation and the state of humanity.

Imagine this scenario: vandals break into a museum displaying works from Picasso's Blue Period. Motivated by sheer destructiveness, they splash red paint all over the paintings and slash them with knives. It would be the height of unfairness to display these works—a mere sampling of Picasso's creative genius, and spoiled at that—as representative of the artist. The same applies to God's creation. God has already hung a "Condemned" sign above the earth, and has promised judgment and restoration. That this world spoiled by evil and suffering still exists at all is an example of God's mercy, not his cruelty.

The Megaphone

What can God use to get our attention? What will convince human beings, we who started the rebellion, that creation is not running the way God intended?

C. S. Lewis introduced the phrase "pain, the megaphone of God." "God whispers to us in our pleasures, speaks in our conscience, but shouts in our pains," he said; "it is His megaphone to rouse a deaf world."[3] The word "megaphone" is apropos, because by its nature pain shouts. When I stub my toe or twist an ankle, pain loudly announces to my brain that something is wrong. Similarly, the existence of suffering on this earth is, I believe, a scream to all of us that something is wrong. It halts us in our tracks and forces us to consider other values.

The animal fable *Watership Down* tells of a colony of wild rabbits uprooted from their homes by a construction project. As they wander, they come across a new breed of rabbits huge and beautiful, with sleek, shiny hair and perfect claws and teeth. How do you live so well? the wild rabbits ask. Don't you forage for food? The tame rabbits explain that food is provided for them, in the form of carrots and apples and corn and kale. Life is grand and wonderful.

After a few days, however, the wild rabbits notice that one of the fattest and sleekest of the tame rabbits has disappeared. Oh, that happens occasionally, the tame rabbits explain. But we don't let it interfere with our lives. There's too much good to enjoy. Eventually, the wild rabbits find that the land is studded with traps, and death "hangs like a mist" over their heads. The tame rabbits, in exchange for their plush, comfortable lives, had willingly closed their eyes to one fact: the imminent danger of death.

Watership Down is a fable with a moral point. Like the fat, sleek rabbits, we could—some people do—believe that the sole purpose of life is to be comfortable. Gorge yourself, build a nice home, enjoy good food, have sex, live the good life. That's all there is. But the presence of suffering vastly complicates that lifestyle—unless we choose to wear blinders, like the tame rabbits.

It's hard to believe the world is here just so I can party, when a third of its people go to bed starving each night. It's hard to believe the purpose of life is to feel good, when I see teenagers smashed on the freeway. If I try to escape toward hedonism, suffering and death lurk nearby, haunting me, reminding me of how hollow life would be if this world were all I'd ever know.

Sometimes murmuring, sometimes shouting, suffering is a "rumor of transcendence" that the entire human condition is out of whack. Something is wrong with a life of war and violence and human tragedy. He who wants to be satisfied with this world, who wants to believe the only purpose of life is enjoyment, must go around with cotton in his ears, for the megaphone of pain is a loud one.

Three centuries ago the French mathematician Blaise Pascal worried about some of his friends who seemed to him to be avoiding the most important issues of life. Here is how he characterized them, almost in a parody:

> I know not who put me into the world, nor what the world is, nor what I myself am. I am in terrible ignorance of everything. . . . All I know is that I must soon die, but what I know least is this very death which I cannot escape.
>
> As I know not whence I come, so I know not whither I go. I know only that, in leaving this world, I fall forever either into annihilation or into the hands of an angry God, without knowing to which of these two states I shall be for ever assigned. Such is my state, full of weakness and uncertainty. And from all this I conclude that I ought to spend all the days of my life without caring to inquire into what must happen to me. Perhaps I might find some solution to my doubts, but I will not take the trouble, nor take a step to seek it.

Pascal shook his head in perplexity over people who concern themselves with trifles or even with important matters, all the while ignoring the most important matter of all. "It is an incomprehensible enchantment, and a supernatural slumber," he said.[4]

Some other religions try to deny all pain, or to rise above it. Christianity starts, rather, with the assertion that suffering exists, and exists as proof of our fallen state. One may dismiss the Christian explanation for the origin of suffering—that it was introduced into the world as a consequence of man's aborted freedom—as being unsatisfactory. But at least the concept of a great-but-fallen world matches what we know of reality. It fits the dual nature of this world, and of us.

We are like the survivors of a wreck, like Crusoe cast ashore with relics from another land. It is this aspect of Christianity that made Chesterton say, "The modern philosopher had told me again and again that I was in the right place, and I had still felt depressed even in acquiescence. But I had heard that I was in the wrong place, and my soul sang for joy, like a bird in spring." Optimists had told him the world was the best of all possible worlds, but he could never accept it. Christianity made more sense to him because it freely admitted that he was marooned on a mutinous planet.

"The important matter was this," Chesterton concluded, "that it entirely reversed the reason for optimism. And the instant the reversal was made it felt like the abrupt ease when a bone is put back in the socket. I had often called myself an optimist, to avoid the too evident blasphemy of pessimism. But all the optimism of the age had been false and disheartening for this reason, that it had always been trying to prove that we fit in to the world. The Christian optimism is based on the fact that we do *not* fit in to the world."[5]

The megaphone of pain sometimes, of course, produces the opposite effect: I can turn against God for allowing such misery. On the other hand, pain can, as it did with Chesterton, drive me to God. I can believe God when he says this world is not all there is, and take the chance that he is making a perfect place for those who follow him on pain-racked earth.

It is hard to be a creature. We think we are big enough to run our own world without such messy matters as pain and suffering to remind us of our dependence. We think we are wise enough to make our own decisions about morality, to live rightly without the megaphone of pain blaring in our ears. We are wrong, as the Garden of Eden story proves. Man and woman, in a world without suffering, chose against God.

And so we who have come after Adam and Eve have a choice. We can trust God. Or we can blame him, not ourselves, for the world.

Hearing the Echoes

If you doubt the megaphone value of suffering, I recommend that you visit the intensive care ward of a hospital. There you'll find all sorts of people pacing the lobby: a mixture of rich, poor, beautiful, plain, black, white, smart, dull, spiritual, atheistic, white collar, blue collar. But the intensive-care ward is the one place in the world where none of those divisions make a speck of difference.

In an intensive care ward, all visitors are united by a single, awful thread: concern over a dying relative or friend. Economic differences, even religious differences, fade away. You'll see no sparks of racial tension there. Sometimes strangers will console one another or cry together quietly and unashamedly. All are facing life at its most essential. Many call for a pastor or priest for the first time ever. Only the megaphone of suffering is strong enough to bring these people to their knees to ponder ultimate questions of life and death and meaning. As Helmut Thielicke has wryly observed, there is a hospital chaplaincy but no cocktail-party chaplaincy.

That, I believe, is the megaphone value of suffering. This planet emits a constant "groaning," a cry for redemption and restoration, but very often we ignore the message until suffering or death forces us to attend. I do not say that God permits suffering because of its megaphone value. (Nor do I believe it carries a specific message—"You're suffering as a consequence of this action"—as the next chapter will make clear.) But the megaphone of pain does announce a general message of distress to all humanity.

John Donne, a seventeenth-century poet, found himself listening to the megaphone of pain. An angry father-in-law got him fired from his job and black-balled from a career in law. Donne turned in desperation to the church, taking orders as an Anglican priest. But the year after he took his first parish job, his wife Anne died, leaving him seven children. And a few years later, in 1623, spots appeared on Donne's own body. He was diagnosed with the bubonic plague.

The illness dragged on, sapping his strength almost to the point of death. (Donne's illness turned out to be a form of typhus, not the plague.) In the midst of this illness, Donne wrote a series of devotions on suffering which rank among the most poignant meditations ever written on the subject. He composed the book in bed, without benefit of notes, convinced he was dying.

In *Devotions*, John Donne calls God to task. As he looks back on life, it doesn't make sense. After spending a lifetime in confused wandering, he has finally reached a place where he can be of some service to God, and now, at that precise moment, he is struck by a deadly illness. Nothing appears on the horizon but fever, pain, and death. What to make of it?

What is the meaning of disease? John Donne's book suggests the possibility of an answer. The first stirrings came to him through the open window of his bedroom, in the form of church bells tolling out a doleful declaration of death. For an instant Donne wondered if his friends, knowing his condition to be more grave than they had disclosed, had ordered the bell to be rung for his own death. But he quickly realized that the bells were marking a neighbor's death from the plague.

Donne wrote Meditation XVII on the meaning of the church bells, one of the most celebrated passages in English literature ("No man is an island. . . . Never send to know for whom the bell tolls; it tolls for thee"). He realized that although the bells had been sounded in honor of another's death, they served as a stark reminder of what every human being spends a lifetime trying to forget: We will all die.

> When one man dies, one chapter is not torn out of the book, but translated into a better language; and every chapter must be so translated; God employs several translators; some pieces are translated by age, some by sickness, some by war,

some by justice; but God's hand is in every trans-
lation, and his hand shall bind up all our scattered leaves again for that library where every
book shall lie open to one another. . . . So this bell
calls us all; but how much more me, who am
brought so near the door by this sickness.[6]

Three centuries before C. S. Lewis, Donne used
a different phrase than "pain, the megaphone of God"
to express the same concept: the singular ability of
pain to break through normal defenses and everyday
routines. "I need thy thunder, O my God; thy music
will not serve thee," he said.[7] The tolling of the bell
became, for him, an advance echo of his own death.
For the dead man, it was a period, the end of a life;
for Donne, clinging to life, it was a penetrating question mark. Was he ready to meet God?

The tolling of that bell worked a curious twist in
Donne's progression of thought. The megaphone, or
thunder, of pain caused Donne to reexamine his life,
and what he saw was like a revelation. "I am the man
that has seen affliction," he had once told his congregation, in a self-pitying mood. But it now seemed
clear that the periods of sharpest suffering had been
the very occasions of spiritual growth. Trials had
purged sin and developed character; poverty had
taught him dependence on God and cleansed him of
greed; failure and public disgrace had helped cure
worldly ambition. A clear pattern emerged: pain
could be transformed, even redeemed.

Donne's mental review next led him to reflect on
present circumstances. Could even *this* pain be re-

deemed? Illness prevented him from many good works, of course, but his physical weakness surely did not curb all spiritual growth. He had much time for prayer: the bell had reminded him of his less fortunate neighbor, and the many others suffering in London. He could learn humility, and trust, and gratitude, and faith. Donne made a kind of game of it: he envisioned his soul growing strong, rising from the bed, and walking about the room even as his body lay flat.

In short, Donne realized that his life, even in his bedridden state, was not meaningless. He directed his energy toward spiritual disciplines: prayer, confession of sins, keeping a journal (which became *Devotions*). He got his mind off himself and onto others.

Devotions records a seismic shift in Donne's attitude toward pain. He began with prayers that the pain be removed; he ends with prayers that the pain be redeemed, that he be "catechized by affliction." Such redemption might take the form of miraculous cure—he still hoped so—but even if it did not, God could take a molten ingot and through the refiner's fire of suffering make of it pure gold.

6

⌐○○○⌐

What Is God Trying to Tell Us?

I can read my affliction as a correction, or as a mercy, and I confess I know not how to read it. How should I understand this illness? I cannot conclude, though death conclude me. If it is a correction indeed, let me translate it and read it as a mercy; for though it may appear to be a correction, I can have no greater proof of your mercy than to die in thee and by that death to be united to him who died for me.

John Donne
Devotions

A *Time* magazine report from Yuba City, California:

Flanked by weeping relatives, a Spanish-American couple sat in the shimmering heat of Sutter Cemetery, holding hands and staring dully at the bronze coffin that held the remains of their 17-year-old son Bobby. Six of Bobby's classmates placed their white carnation boutonnieres on the coffin. Bobby's young niece threw herself on the coffin and sobbed brokenly. Several in the large crowd also cried. Bobby's father silently shook his head a couple of times as though he had been struck, then moved woodenly with his wife toward the green limousine at the head of the long cortege.

In the same cemetery Mrs. Harry Rosebrough watched dry-eyed as her son was buried. He had died on his 16th birthday. Pamela Engstrom, wearing a blue-and-white gingham dress—a gift from her mother—had died the day after her 18th birthday. The victims also included twins Carlene and Sharlene Engle, 18, who loved to sing songs composed by their mother, "Wake and Smile in the Sunshine" and "Take Pride in America." After the funeral, Sharlene's dusty Ford station wagon was parked across the street from her home. A FOR SALE sign was in the window.

So it was as 15,000 citizens mourned their dead. A bus bearing 53 members of the local high school choir and chaperon Christina Estabrook had ripped through 72 feet of guardrail as it turned onto an exit ramp. The bus plunged 21 1/2 feet to the ground. It landed on its top, wheels still spinning and roof crushed down to the seats.

Blood dripped on scattered sheets of choir music. "I heard someone scream 'Oh my God' from the front of the bus," sobbed Kim Kenyon, a 16-year-old junior whose girl friend was killed in the seat beside him. Added Perry Martin, 18, the choir's chief tenor: "Everything was a tangle of weeping and moaning and of scattered arms and legs." The final toll: 29 dead and 25 injured.

The boys and girls had gone through junior high school together. They had all performed together in *Fiddler on the Roof* earlier this year. Only three weeks from graduation, many of them had gone to their prom on the previous Saturday. Now their friends dazedly shuffled through Yuba City High School, pausing disconsolately from time to time at the principal's window to read the daily notice that listed the condition of the injured. Said Karen Hess, 18, president of the student body: "This is the first time that most of us have ever had close friends die."[1]

Why Yuba City?

Why not Salina, Kansas . . . or Clarkston, Georgia . . . or Ridgewood, New Jersey?

Why the high-school choir? Why not the band, or the debate team, or the football team?

It was a normal, everyday traffic accident—more fatalities than most, perhaps, but nothing like the devastation of a California earthquake, a flood in Pakistan, or a ferry boat accident in Manila. Nevertheless, an ordinary tragedy like the Yuba City bus wreck brings questions snarling to the surface.

Why did those twenty-nine kids deserve a grisly mass highway death? Was God trying to tell them something? Or was he sending a warning to their parents and friends? If you were a teenager in Yuba City High School, you couldn't avoid those questions. And if you survived the bus accident as a passenger, the rest of your life you would wonder why you had lived when so many friends died.

Does God reach down, slightly twist the wheels of school buses, and watch them career through guardrails? Does he draw a red pencil line through a map of Indiana to plot the exact path of a tornado? There, hit that house, kill that six-year-old, but skip over this next house. Does God program the earth like a video game, constantly experimenting with tidal waves, seismic temblors, and hurricanes? Is that how he rewards and punishes us, his helpless victims?

Posing the questions so brazenly may sound sacrilegious. But they've long haunted me, and in various forms have been tossed at me like spears by agnostic friends. Wondering about God is an almost universal part of the experience of suffering. I have a book on my shelf, *Theories of Illness,* that surveys 139 tribal groups from around the world; all but four of them perceive illness as a sign of God's (or the gods') disapproval.

Pain has value in protecting physical bodies—almost everyone grants that. Suffering has some moral value in exposing our needful state as mortal creatures on a Groaning Planet; most Christians, at least, take that further step, accepting that God speaks to the human race in general through the megaphone of pain. But pain never comes to us *in general.* It comes in specific: in a synaptic firestorm of nerves and spinal cord, or in an emotional cloud of sorrow and grief.

I once watched a television interview with a famous Hollywood actress whose lover had drowned in a harbor near Los Angeles. The police investigation revealed he had rolled off a yacht in a drunken stupor. The actress looked at the camera, her beautiful features contorted by grief, and asked, bizarrely, "How could a loving God let this happen?"

That actress probably had not thought about God for months, or years. But suddenly, faced with suffering, she lashed out in anger against God. For her and for nearly everyone, doubt follows pain quickly and surely, like a reflex action. Suffering calls our most basic beliefs about God into question. When it strikes, I cannot help wondering: what is God trying to tell me by this strep throat? By my friend's death? Does he have a specific message for me?

At a banquet, a guest at my table referred to a recent earthquake in South America. "Did you know that a much lower percentage of Christians than non-Christians died in the earthquake?" he asked with utter sincerity. I wondered about the Christians who did not survive—what had they done to deserve being cast in with the vulnerable pagans? And I wondered about the hint of smugness in his remark—like the old Colosseum scores: Christians 4, Gladiators 3.

I also thought about occasional tragedies that seem to target Christians: the Armenian massacres, a bus accident involving a church choir, a flash flood that ravaged a Campus Crusade campground in Estes Park, Colorado, a dam break at Toccoa Falls Bible College. Faith in God offers no insurance against tragedy.

Nor does it offer insurance against feelings of doubt and betrayal. If anything, being a Christian complicates the issue. If you believe in a world of pure chance, what difference does it make whether a bus from Yuba City or one from Salina crashes? But if you believe in a world ruled by a powerful God who loves you tenderly, then it makes an awful difference.

What the Bible Says

Much of the mental turmoil about pain and suffering hinges, I think, on the important issue of cause. If God is truly in charge, somehow connected to all the world's suffering, why is he so capricious, unfair? Is he the cosmic Sadist who delights in watching us squirm, who stamps out human beings like cigarette butts?

If you scour the Bible for an answer to the question, "Who did it?" you will come away with mixed answers. To illustrate this, I have sometimes handed out Bibles to individuals within a group, asking them to read a passage and comment on what answer it gives to the "cause" question.

Genesis 38:7. Quite clearly, God is portrayed as the direct cause of Er's suffering. He "was wicked in the Lord's sight; so the Lord put him to death."

Luke 13:10–16. Satan, or at least "a spirit" was the direct cause of this woman's infirmity, a condition that had crippled her for eighteen years. The apostle Paul also called his affliction, the thorn in his flesh, "a messenger of Satan."

Job 2:4–7. Job offers a combination of the two causes: Satan inflicts the pain, but only after obtaining God's permission.

Proverbs 26:27. This verse, typical of Proverbs, stresses the natural consequences of a person's actions: follow an evil pattern and you will one day suffer because of it.

As I explained in the first chapter, this book came about because of my friendship with Claudia Claxton and my concern over the muddled advice she received from fellow Christians. In view of these Bible passages, is there any wonder people have such confused words of advice? I could list dozens of passages that offer various explanations for the cause of specific suffering, but I have yet to find in the Bible any grand unifying theory of causation.

The Old Testament, in particular, presents many situations—the ten plagues on Egypt, for example—in which God supernaturally intervened in human history in order to punish evil. I have studied each of these instances in detail, and though I cannot propose a grand unifying theory, I can offer two overall observations.

(1) Many Old Testament passages warn against painful consequences that will follow specific actions. The German biblical scholar Klaus Kloch persuasively shows that Psalms, Proverbs, and most other Old Testament books present this notion of "wrong choices lead to painful consequences."[2]

Proverbs is full of such advice: "Laziness brings on deep sleep, and the shiftless man goes hungry" (19:15). As those authors saw it, God set up human beings and human society to operate according to fixed principles. Honesty, truthfulness, and compassion yield good results; cheating, lying, and greed yield just the opposite.

(2) Some Old Testament passages show God causing human suffering as punishment for wrong behavior. The prophetic books bristle with dire warnings of judgment to come. But look closer. Their predictions of doom usually follow a long, explicit forewarning. Amos, Jeremiah, Isaiah, Habakkuk, Hosea, and Ezekiel all spell out impressive lists of sin and wickedness that will provoke the punishment.

In almost every case, the prophets also hold out the hope that God will restrain himself if Israel repents and turns back to God. If she continues in rebellion, she will be crushed. Thus the judgment clearly comes from God, but is in no way capricious or unjust. Old Testament punishment was consistent with God's "covenant," or contract, with Israel, and came after much warning.

I agree that the Old Testament is replete with reward/punishment type of thinking, and presents life in terms of this principle: "Do good, get rewarded; do bad, get punished." However, I do not believe the principle applies in precisely the same way today. In the book *Disappointment with God,* I argue that the "rules" governing God's contract relationship with the Israelites expressed a unique relationship that we cannot, nor should we expect to, emulate.

Consider the principles from the Old Testament in light of the kinds of questions people raise today. "Why me?" we ask almost instinctively when tragedy hits. Claudia Claxton asked that question, as did the grieving friends and relatives in Yuba City, and even the actress who lost her lover. Two thousand cars were driving in the rain on the expressway—why did mine skid into a bridge? Lift lines were crowded with skiers all day—why was I the one to break a leg and ruin my vacation? A rare type of cancer strikes only one in a hundred people—why did my father have to be among the victims?

Suffering people torment themselves with such questions, and the biblical examples offer some guidance. As to the first overall observation, that certain actions may lead to painful consequences, that principle applies in full force today. A person who skis beyond a boundary, toward avalanche country and ungroomed slopes, puts her life in peril. A person who speeds on rain-slick highways courts the danger of hydroplaning. A person who eats all fried foods and Twinkies exposes his body to certain health risks.

The book of Proverbs goes further than these simple examples, making clear that our actions have a moral dimension that will affect our health and comfort on earth. Our modern versions—smoking, promiscuous sex, doing drugs, abusing the environment, gluttony—all have direct and painful consequences. Scientists recognize the connections and advertise them widely. The principles, built into creation, apply to Christians and non-Christians alike. Actuarial tables demonstrate this fact beyond dispute: Utah, home of health-conscious Mormons, has one of the lowest rates of heart disease while its neighbor Nevada, home of loose living, has one of the highest.

What of the second principle, that God sometimes intervenes directly, to punish people for wrong behavior? I have been astonished at how commonly and unthinkingly Christians apply that principle today. They visit the hospital room bearing gifts of guilt ("You must have done something to deserve this") and accusation ("You must not be praying hard enough").

But there is a huge difference between the suffering most of us encounter—a skiing injury, a rare form of cancer, the bus accident—and the suffering-as-punishment described in the Old Testament. There, punishment follows repeated warnings against specific behavior. To be effective, in fact, punishment requires a clear tie to behavior. Think of a parent who punishes a young child. It would do little good for that parent to sneak up at odd times during a day and whack the child with no explanation. Such tactics would produce a neurotic, not an obedient, child.

The people of Israel knew why they were being punished; the prophets had warned them in excruciating detail. The Pharaoh of Egypt knew exactly why the ten plagues were unleashed against his land: God had predicted them, told him why, and described what change of heart could forestall them. Biblical examples of suffering-as-punishment, then, tend to fit a pattern. The pain comes after much warning, and no one sits around afterward asking, "Why?" They know very well why they are suffering.

Does that pattern resemble what happens to most of us today? Do we get a direct revelation from God warning us of a coming catastrophe? Does personal suffering come packaged with a clear explanation from God? If not, I must question whether the pains most of us feel—cancer, a traffic mishap—are indeed punishments from God. If suffering does come as punishment, we are getting confusing messages indeed, for the occurrence of disease and pain seems random, unrelated to any pattern of virtue or vice.

Frankly, I believe that unless God distinctly reveals otherwise, we would do better to look to other biblical models. And the Bible contains some stories of people who suffered but definitely were not being punished by God.

What Jesus Says

Christians believe that with the coming of Jesus, God fully entered human history. He was no longer "out there," sometimes dipping into history to change things. Now he resided in the body of a human being on earth, making himself subject to the physical laws and limitations of this planet. Therefore, the best clue we have into how God feels about human pain is to look at Jesus' response.

Jesus never gave a poor or suffering person a

speech about "accepting your lot in life," or "taking the medicine that God has given you." He seemed unusually sensitive to the groans of suffering people, and set about remedying them. And he used his supernatural powers to heal, never to punish.

Miracles of healing were great crowd pleasers, of course, but even so Jesus refused to make them the centerpiece of his ministry. More than anything, he used physical healings as "signs" of some deeper truth. At times Jesus seemed almost reluctant to intervene, telling his followers he performed the signs only because they had need of them. Often he hushed up the spreading rumors about his miracles. On certain occasions Jesus deliberately elected not to intervene in the natural order of things, for example, by not calling on angels to deliver him from his most painful hour.

Was Jesus saying to us that it is not good for God to intervene in our world on a day-to-day basis? The important thing, the kingdom of heaven—isn't that a kingdom of the spirit to be worked out inside hearts and minds, not by an external, spectacular display of God's power? At the least, Jesus declined to make radical changes in the natural laws governing the planet. Rather than, say, rewiring the nervous system to make some design improvement, he himself took on the pain network with all its undesirable features. And when he faced suffering personally, he reacted much as we do: with fear and dread.

How did Jesus deal with the question "Who is responsible for suffering?" The clearest insight into that question appears in Luke 13. Again, just as in the Old Testament, there are several answers. For example, in verse 16 Jesus declares that Satan caused the pain of a woman bound in disease for eighteen years. And at the end of the chapter, Jesus grieves over the future of Jerusalem: like the Old Testament prophets, he could see that her actions of stubborn rebellion would bring about much suffering.

But early on in that same chapter, Jesus is asked about two "current events" that had evidently prompted much local discussion. One was an act of political oppression, in which Roman soldiers slaughtered members of a religious minority; the other, a construction accident that killed eighteen people. As I study the Bible, I can find no other situation more parallel to the kinds of suffering that bother most of us. Those first-century Jews were asking about their equivalents to the Yuba City bus accident, or the collapse of a stadium roof.

Jesus' response is at once enigmatic and brilliant. He does not fully answer the question most on their mind, the question of cause. Jesus never explains, "Here's why those two tragedies occurred." But he makes one thing clear: they did not occur as a result of specific wrongdoing: "Do you think that these Galileans were worse sinners than all the other Galileans because they suffered this way? I tell you, no! . . . Or those eighteen who died when the tower in Siloam fell on them—do you think they were more guilty than all the others living in Jerusalem? I tell you, no!"

No grieving relative need stand around wondering what brought about the calamity; Jesus makes plain that the victims had done nothing unusual to deserve their fates. They were the same as other persons. He doesn't say so, but perhaps the tower simply fell because it was built poorly. I believe Jesus would have replied similarly to the Yuba City tragedy: "Do you think they were worse sinners than other teenagers?" Perhaps the bus crashed because of driver error or mechanical failure.

But Jesus does not stop there. He uses both tragedies to point to eternal truths relevant to everyone ("Unless you repent, you too will all perish") and follows with a parable about God's restraining mercy. He implies that we "bystanders" of catastrophe have as much to learn from the event as do the victims. A tragedy should alert us to make ourselves ready in case we are the next victim of a falling tower, or an act of political terrorism. Catastrophe thus joins together victim and bystander in a call to repentance, by abruptly reminding us of the brevity of life.

Is God the Cause?

I once attended a funeral service for a teenage girl killed in a car accident. Her mother wailed, "The Lord took her home. He must have had some purpose. . . . Thank you, Lord." I have been with sick Christian people who agonize over the question, "What is God trying to teach me?" Or, they may plead, "How can I find enough faith to get rid of this illness? How can I get God to rescue me?"

Maybe such people have it all wrong. Maybe God isn't trying to tell us anything specific each time we hurt. Pain and suffering are part and parcel of our planet, and Christians are not exempt. Half the time we know why we get sick: too little exercise, a poor diet, contact with a germ. Do we really expect God to go around protecting us whenever we encounter something dangerous?

As I understand it, the approach Jesus takes corresponds exactly to what I have suggested about "pain, the megaphone of God." Suffering offers a general message of warning to all humanity that something is wrong with this planet, and that we need radical outside intervention ("Unless you repent. . . ."). But you cannot argue backward and link someone's specific pain to a direct act of God.

Another, similar story from the Gospels may clarify this approach even further. In John 9, Jesus refutes the traditional explanation of suffering. His followers point to a man born blind. Clucking with pity, they ask, "Who sinned, this man or his parents?" In other words, why did he deserve blindness? Jesus answers bluntly, "Neither this man nor his parents sinned, but this happened so that the work of God might be displayed in his life."

The disciples wanted to look backward, to find out "Why?" Jesus redirected their attention. Consistently, he points forward, answering a different question: "To what end?" And that, I believe, offers a neat summary of the Bible's approach to the problem of pain. To backward-looking questions of cause, to the "Why?" questions, it gives no definitive answer. But it does hold out hope for the future, that even suffering can be transformed or "redeemed." A human tragedy, like blindness, can be used to display God's work.

Sometimes, as with the man born blind, the work of God is manifest through dramatic miracle. Sometimes it is not. But in every case, suffering offers an opportunity for us to display God's work.

7

Why Are We Here?

It was only when I lay there on rotting prison straw
that I sensed within myself the first stirrings of good.
Gradually, it was disclosed to me that the line sepa-
rating good and evil passes not through states, nor
between classes, nor between political parties either—but right through every human heart—and
through all human hearts . . . I nourished my soul
there, and I say without hesitation: Bless you,
prison, for having been in my life.

Alexander Solzhenitsyn
The Gulag Archipelago

The Bible may seem to give mixed signals on
the question of cause. But its most exhaus-
tive treatment of the topic of suffering has
an unmistakable message. It appears in the book of
Job, smack in the middle of the Old Testament.

One of the oldest stories in the Bible, Job nevertheless reads like the most modern, for it faces
head-on the problem of pain that so bedevils our
century. In recent times, such authors as Robert
Frost, Archibald MacLeish, and Muriel Spark have
all tried their hands at retelling the story of Job.

Job, the most upright, spiritual man of his day, loves God with all his heart. Indeed, God handpicks him to demonstrate to Satan how faithful some humans can be. If anyone does not deserve suffering for his actions, it is Job.

But what happens? Incredibly, a series of wretched calamities descend upon Job, any one of which would suffice to crush most people. Raiders, fire, bandits, and a great wind ravage his ranch and destroy all his possessions. Of Job's large family only his wife survives, and she is scant comfort. Then, in a second phase of trials, Job breaks out in ulcerous boils.

Thus in a matter of hours all the terrors of hell are poured out on poor Job, utterly reversing his fortune and his health. He scratches his sores and moans. The pain he can somehow put up with. What bothers him more is the sense of betrayal. Until now he has always believed in a loving, fair God. But the facts simply don't add up. He asks anguished questions, the same questions asked by nearly everyone in great pain. Why me? What did I do wrong? What is God trying to tell me?

In that setting, Job and his friends discuss the mystery of suffering. The friends, devout and reverent men, fill the air with erudition. Boiled down, their arguments are virtually identical. Job, God is trying to tell you something. No one suffers without cause. Common sense and all reason tell us that a just God will treat people fairly. Those who obey and remain faithful, he rewards. Those who sin, he punishes. Therefore, confess your sin, and God will relieve your misery.

Job's wife suggests one more alternative: Curse God and die. Job, however, can't accept that choice either. Although what has happened to him does not correspond to justice, he simply can't bring himself to deny God. Where is the answer for Job? In desperation, he even toys with the notion of God as a Sadist who "mocks the despair of the innocent" (9:23).

In the face of his friends' verbal assaults Job wavers, contradicts himself, and sometimes even agrees with them. But as he reflects on life, he also recognizes other signs of unfairness. Thieves grow fat and prosper, while some holy men live in poverty and pain. Evidently, evil and good are not always punished and rewarded in this life.

Job's own uncontrolled outbursts contrast with the calm reason of his friends. But as he mulls over his particular case, he concludes they are wrong. Against all evidence, he holds on to two seemingly contradictory beliefs: he, Job, does not deserve his tragedy, but still God deserves his loyalty. Job holds firm in the face of such jabs as "Are you more righteous than God?"

Perhaps the most unsettling aspect of the book is that the arguments of Job's friends sound suspiciously like those offered by Christians today. One must search hard for a defense of suffering, in this book or any other, that does not appear somewhere in their speeches. And yet, in a wonderful ironic twist at the end of the book, God dismisses all their high-sounding theories with a scowl. "I am angry with you and your two friends," God said to one, "because you have not spoken of me what is right, as my servant Job has" (42:7).

Thus even in the Old Testament, where suffering is so frequently identified with God's punishment, Job's example shines brightly. The book of Job should nail a coffin lid over the idea that every time we suffer it's because God is punishing us or trying to tell us something. Although the Bible supports the general principle that "a man reaps what he sows" even in this life (see Psalms 1:3; 37:25), the book of Job proves that other people have no right to apply that general principle to a particular person. Nobody deserved suffering less than Job, and yet few have suffered more.

A Perfectly Fair World

On the surface, the book of Job centers around the problem of suffering, the same problem I have been discussing in this book. Underneath, a different issue is at stake: the doctrine of human freedom. Job had to endure undeserved suffering in order to demonstrate that God is ultimately interested in freely given love.

It is a hard truth, one at which great minds have stumbled. C. G. Jung, for example, went to strange lengths to account for God's behavior in the book of Job. He taught that God decided on the Incarnation and Jesus' death as a guilt response to the way he had treated Job. God entered the world in Jesus so that he could grow in moral consciousness.[1]

Jung may be underestimating the premium God

places on freely given love. The trials of Job stemmed from a debate in heaven over the question, "Are human beings truly free?" In the first two chapters of Job, Satan reveals himself as the first great behaviorist. He claimed that faith is merely a product of environment and circumstances. Job was conditioned to love God. Take away the positive rewards, Satan challenged, and watch Job's faith crumble. Poor Job, oblivious, was selected for the cosmic contest to determine this crucial matter of human freedom.

The contest posed between Satan and God was no trivial exercise. Satan's accusation that Job loved God only because "you have put a hedge around him," stands as an attack on God's character. It implies that God is not worthy of love in himself; faithful people like Job follow him only because they are "bribed" to do so. Job's response when all the props of faith were removed would prove or disprove Satan's challenge.

To understand this issue of human freedom, it helps me to imagine a world in which everyone truly does get what he or she deserves. What would a world of perfect fairness look like?

In a perfectly fair world, morality would operate according to fixed laws, just like the laws of nature. Punishment for wrongdoing would work like physical pain. If you touch a flame, you are "punished" instantly with a pain warning; a fair world would punish sin just that swiftly and surely. Extend your hand to shoplift, and you'd get an electrical shock. Likewise, a fair world would reward good behavior:

Fill out an IRS form honestly, and you'd earn a pleasure sensation, like a trained seal given a fish.

That imaginary world has a certain appeal. It would be just and consistent, and everyone would clearly know what God expected. Fairness would reign. There is, however, one huge problem with such a tidy world: it's not at all what God wants to accomplish on earth. He wants from us love, freely given love, and we dare not underestimate the premium God places on that love. Freely given love is so important to God that he allows our planet to be a cancer of evil in his universe—for a time.

If this world ran according to fixed, perfectly fair rules, there would be no true freedom. We would act rightly because of our own immediate gain, and selfish motives would taint every act of goodness. We would love God because of a programmed, inborn hunger, not because of a deliberate choice in the face of attractive alternatives. It would be a B. F. Skinner, automaton world of action/response, action/response. In contrast, the Christian virtues described in the Bible develop when we choose God and his ways in spite of temptation or impulses to do otherwise.

Throughout the Bible, an analogy that illustrates the relationship between God and his people keeps surfacing. God, the husband, is pictured as wooing the bride to himself. He wants her love. If the world were constructed so that every sin earned a punishment and every good deed a reward, the parallel would not hold. The closest analogue to that relationship would be a kept woman, who is pampered and bribed and locked away in a room so that the lover can be sure of her faithfulness. God does not "keep" his people. He loves us, gives himself to us, and eagerly awaits our free response.

God wants us to choose to love him freely, even when that choice involves pain, because we are committed to him, not to our own good feelings and rewards. He wants us to cleave to him, as Job did, even when we have every reason to deny him hotly. That, I believe, is the central message of Job. Satan had taunted God with the accusation that humans are not truly free. Was Job being faithful simply because God had allowed him a prosperous life? Job's fiery trials proved the answer beyond doubt. Job clung to God's justice when he was the best example in history of God's apparent injustice. He did not seek the Giver because of his gifts; when all gifts were removed he still sought the Giver.

Vale of Soul-Making

If a world of perfect fairness would not produce what God wants from us, our freely given love, neither would it produce what God wants for us. In the first few chapters I used the example of leprosy to demonstrate that pain is valuable, even essential, for life on this planet. In a related way, suffering can become a valuable instrument in accomplishing God's goals for human beings.

I have said that the megaphone of pain makes it difficult to accept that we have been placed on this "groaning" planet to pursue hedonistic pleasure. But if our happiness is not God's goal, what, then, does God intend for this world? Why bother with us at all?

To help understand, think of an illustration from a human family. A father determined to exclude all pain from his beloved daughter's life would never allow her to take a step. She might fall down! Instead, he picks her up and carries her wherever she goes or pushes her in a carriage. Over time such a pampered child will become an invalid, unable to take a step, totally dependent on her father.

Such a father, no matter how loving, would end up failing in his most important task: to nurture an independent person into adulthood. It would be far better for the daughter herself if her father stands back and lets her walk, even if it means allowing her to stumble. Apply the analogy directly to Job who, by standing on his own in the midst of suffering, without the benefit of soothing answers, gained powerful new strength. As Rabbi Abraham Heschel has said, "Faith like Job's cannot be shaken because it is the result of having been shaken."

C. S. Lewis expands on this idea in *The Problem of Pain*, where he says in part:

> We want not so much a father in heaven as a grandfather in heaven—whose plan for the universe was such that it might be said at the end of each day, "A good time was had by all."
>
> I should very much like to live in a universe which was governed on such lines, but since it is abundantly clear that I don't, and since I have reason to believe nevertheless that God is love,

I conclude that my conception of love needs correction. . . .

Over a sketch made idly to amuse a child, an artist may not take much trouble: he may be content to let it go even though it is not exactly as he meant it to be. But over the great picture of his life—the work which he loves, though in a different fashion, as intensely as a man loves a woman or a mother a child—he will take endless trouble—and would, doubtless, thereby give endless trouble to the picture if it were sentient. One can imagine a sentient picture, after being rubbed and scraped and re-commenced for the tenth time, wishing that it were only a thumbnail sketch whose making was over in a minute. In the same way, it is natural for us to wish that God had designed for us a less glorious and less arduous destiny; but then we are wishing not for more love but for less.[2]

Once again, these issues trace back to the most basic questions of human existence. Why are we here? The presence of suffering puzzles or even enrages those people who assume that human beings are fully formed creatures who need a suitable home. In the Christian view, though, as Professor John Hick has summarized it in the book *Philosophy of Religion*, God is dealing with incomplete creatures. The environment of earth should therefore primarily nurture the process of "soul-making."

We have already seen some advantages of a world of fixed laws and human freedom, even though humans can abuse the freedom and harm one another. John Hick explores another alternative, envisioning a Utopian world designed to protect us from all pain and evil, and concludes that a world free of mistakes would actually abort God's purpose for us.

Suppose, contrary to fact, that this world were a paradise from which all possibility of pain and suffering were excluded. The consequences would be very far-reaching. For example, no one could ever injure anyone else: the murderer's knife would turn to paper or his bullets to thin air; the bank safe, robbed of a million dollars, would miraculously become filled with another million dollars (without this device, on however large a scale, proving inflationary); fraud, deceit, conspiracy, and treason would somehow always leave the fabric of society undamaged. Again, no one would ever be injured by accident: the mountain-climber, steeple-jack, or playing child falling from a height would float unharmed to the ground; the reckless driver would never meet with disaster. There would be no need to work; there would be no call to be concerned for others in time of need or danger, for in such a world there could be no real needs or dangers.

To make possible this continual series of individual adjustments, nature would have to work "special providences" instead of running according to general laws which men must learn to respect on penalty of pain and death. The laws of nature would have to be extremely flexible: sometimes an object would be hard and solid, sometimes soft. . . .

One can at least begin to imagine such a world. It is evident that our present ethical concepts would have no meaning in it. If, for example, the notion of harming someone is an essential element in the concept of wrong action, in our hedonistic paradise there could be no wrong actions—nor any right actions in distinction from wrong. Courage and fortitude would have no point in an environment in which there is, by definition, no danger or difficulty. Generosity, kindness, the *agape* aspect of love, prudence, unselfishness, and all other ethical notions which presuppose life in a stable environment, could not even be formed. Consequently, such a world, however well it might promote pleasure, would be very ill adapted for the development of the moral qualities of human personality. In relation to this purpose it would be the worst of all possible worlds.

It would seem, then, that an environment intended to make possible the growth in free beings of the finest characteristics of personal life, must have a good deal in common with our present world. It must operate according to general and dependable laws; and it must involve real dangers, difficulties, problems, obstacles, and possibilities of pain, failure, sorrow, frustration, and defeat. If it did not contain the particular trials and perils which—subtracting man's own very considerable contribution—our world contains it would have to contain others instead.

To realize this is . . . to understand that this world, with all its "heartaches and the thousand natural shocks that flesh is heir to," an environment so manifestly not designed for the maximization of human pleasure and the minimization of human pain, may be rather well adapted to the quite different purpose of "soul-making."[3]

In some ways it would be easier for God to step in, to have faith for us, to help us in extraordinary ways. But he has instead chosen to stand before us, arms extended, while he asks us to walk, to participate in our own soul-making. That process always involves struggle, and often involves suffering.

To What End?

The notion of earth as a "vale of soul-making" (the poet John Keats's phrase) sheds light on some of the most difficult passages in the Bible. Although the Bible remains vague on the cause of specific sufferings, it does give many examples, as in this verse from Amos, of God using pain for a purpose: "'I gave you empty stomachs in every city and lack of bread in every town, yet you have not returned to me,' declares the Lord" (Amos 4:6). On almost every page the Hebrew prophets warned Israelites that they would face calamity if they continued to flout God's laws.

Most of us operate on a different scale of values than God. We would rank life as the greatest value (and thus murder as the greatest crime). "Life, liberty, and the pursuit of happiness" is how the founding fathers of the United States defined the highest values a government should strive to protect. But clearly God operates from a different perspective. He indeed values human life, so much so that he declared it "sacred," meaning he alone, and no human being, has the right to take life. But in Noah's day, for example, God did not hesitate to exercise that right; numerous times in the Old Testament he took human life in order to halt the spread of evil.

Similarly, many Bible passages show that some things are more awful to God than the pain of his children. Consider the sufferings of Job, or Jeremiah, or Hosea. God did not even exempt himself from suffering: consider the awesome pain involved in himself becoming a man and dying on a cross. Do these show God's lack of compassion? Or do they, rather, demonstrate that some things are more important to God than a suffering-free life for even his most loyal followers?

As I have said, the Bible consistently changes the questions we bring to the problem of pain. It rarely, or ambiguously, answers the backward-looking question "Why?" Instead, it raises the very different, forward-looking question, "To what end?" We are not put on earth merely to satisfy our desires, to pursue life, liberty, and happiness. We are here to be changed, to be made more like God in order to prepare us for a lifetime with him. And that process may be served by the mysterious pattern of all creation:

pleasure sometimes emerges against a background of pain, evil may be transformed into good, and suffering may produce something of value.

Is God speaking to us through our sufferings? It is dangerous and perhaps even unscriptural to torture ourselves by looking for his message in a specific throb of pain, a specific instance of suffering. The message may simply be that we live in a world with fixed laws, like everyone else. But from the larger view, from the view of all history, yes, God speaks to us through suffering—or perhaps in spite of suffering. The symphony he is composing includes minor chords, dissonance, and tiresome fugal passages. But those of us who follow his conducting through early movements will, with renewed strength, someday burst into song.

Two Great Errors

Discussions about the problem of pain tend to drift toward the abstract and philosophical. Phrases like "the best of all possible worlds," "the advantages of human freedom," and "vale of soul-making" creep in, and these can deflect attention away from the actual problems of people in pain. Yet I have felt it necessary to explore some of these issues because I believe they have a direct and practical effect on our response to suffering.

In fact, I believe Christians walk a mental tightrope and are in constant danger of falling in one of two directions. On this subject, errors in thinking can have tragic results.

The first error comes when we attribute all suffering to God, seeing it as his punishment for human mistakes; the second error does just the opposite, assuming that life with God will never include suffering.

I have already mentioned one unfortunate consequence of the first error. I have interviewed many Christians with life-threatening illnesses, and every one without exception has told me how damaging it can be to have a visitor plant the thought, "You must have done something to deserve this punishment." At the very moment when they most need hope and strength to battle the illness, they get instead a frosty dose of guilt and self-doubt. I'm glad the author of Job took such care to record the rambling conversations of Job's friends: that book serves as a permanent reminder to me that I have no right to stand beside a suffering person and pronounce, "This is the will of God," no matter how I cloak that sentiment in pious phrases.

The error of attributing all suffering to God's punishment has far-reaching consequences, as the history of the church has grievously shown. During the late Middle Ages, women were burned at the stake for the heretical act of taking pain-relieving medicines for childbirth. "In sorrow shalt thou bring forth children," priests admonished as they condemned the women to death.[4] And after Edward Jenner had perfected the smallpox vaccine he faced his strongest opposition from clergy, who opposed any interference with the will of God. Even today some religious sects reject modern medical treatment.

Secular writers have seized on this weakness. In his novel *The Plague*, Albert Camus portrays a Catholic priest, Father Paneloux, torn by a dilemma. Should he devote his energy to fighting the plague or to teaching his parishioners to accept it as from God? He grapples with this issue in a sermon: "Paneloux assured those present that it was not easy to say what he was about to say—since it was God's will, we, too, should will it. Thus and thus only the Christian could face the problem squarely. . . . The sufferings of children were our bread of affliction, but without this bread our souls would die of spiritual hunger." Father Paneloux preaches this, but cannot quite believe it: later in the novel he abandons his faith after watching a small child die horribly of the plague.[5]

If the Bible were not so pronounced in denying that all suffering results from specific sins, if it did not paint Job's predicament in such sweeping terms, if it did not show the Son of God spending his days on earth healing diseases and not inflicting them, then the dilemma that Camus posed would be unresolvable. For, if we accept that suffering comes from God as a lesson to us (as, for example, Islam does), the next logical step would be a resigned fatalism. Polio, AIDS, malaria, bubonic plague, cancer, yellow fever—why should a person fight any of these if they are God's agents sent to teach us a lesson?

When the Black Death hit England in the seventeenth century, some street prophets delighted in pronouncing the plague a judgment from God. But other believers, among them doctors and clergy, chose to stay in London to fight the disease. One sacrificial rector gathered the 350 villagers of Eyam around him and got them to agree to a self-imposed quarantine as a health measure to keep the plague among them from spreading to surrounding villages. In all, 259 villagers died, but in the process they ministered to each other in their illness and prevented further contamination.

In his *Journal of the Plague Year*, Daniel Defoe contrasted the Christians' response with the Mohammedans'. When plague struck the Middle East, the religious fatalists there did not alter their behavior in the least, but continued going out in public at will. A much higher percentage among them died than among the Londoners who took precautions.[6]

In modern times, some Christians still lean dangerously toward a fatalism that more befits Islam or Hinduism than Christianity. Several years ago researchers studied why Southerners in the U.S. tended to suffer a higher frequency of tornado-related deaths than Midwesterners. After taking into account such factors as differences in building materials, the researchers concluded that some Southerners, being more religious, had developed a fatalistic attitude toward disaster: "If it hits, it hits, and there's nothing I can do to stop it." In contrast, Midwesterners were more likely to listen to weather reports, secure loose equipment, and take shelter.[7]

If the researchers' conclusions are accurate, I take that trend as a dangerous perversion of Christian dogma. Southerners should listen to the weather service and take precautions. Father

Paneloux should have been on the front lines, arms linked with doctors, battling the plague. Jesus himself spent his life on earth fighting disease and despair. Not once did he hint at fatalism or a resigned acceptance of suffering.

We the inhabitants of this "groaning" planet have the right, even the obligation, to fight against human suffering. Anyone who thinks otherwise should reread the parable of the Good Samaritan in Luke 10, and the parable of the sheep and the goats in Matthew 25.

Health and Wealth Theology

In recent times, some parts of the church have tilted in a very different direction, toward the second great error. They teach that life with God will never include suffering. Such a "health and wealth theology" could only spring up in times of affluence, in a society well-stocked with pain-relieving aids.

Christians in Iran, say, or Cambodia could hardly come up with such a smiley-face theology. As one East European Christian observed, "You Western Christians often seem to consider material prosperity to be the only sign of God's blessing. On the other hand, you often seem to perceive poverty, discomfort, and suffering as signs of God's disfavor. In some ways we in the East understand suffering from the opposite perspective. We believe that suffering may be a sign of God's favor and trust in the Christians to whom the trial is permitted to come."[8]

Nowadays we reserve our shiniest merit badges for those who have been miraculously healed, featuring them in magazine articles and television specials, holding out the unreserved promise that healing is available to everyone if only they would claim it.

In no way do I mean to discount the wonderfulness of physical healing. But obviously miracles do not offer a permanent solution for the problem of suffering because the eventual mortality rate is exactly the same for Christians and non-Christians alike—100 percent. We all have eyes subject to the need for corrective lenses, bones subject to breaking, and soft tissue subject to destruction from auto accidents and terrorist bombs. Christians get cancer too; they fully share the sorrow of this world.

The modern emphasis on miraculous healing has the frequent side effect of causing unhealed ones to feel as though God has passed them by. Recently I watched a televised call-in healing program. The biggest applause came when a caller reported his leg had been healed just one week before he was scheduled for amputation. The audience yelled, and the emcee burbled, "This is the best miracle we've had tonight!" I couldn't help wondering how many amputees were watching, forlornly wondering where their faith had failed.

Unlike many television evangelists, the apostle Paul seemed to expect from the Christian life not health and wealth, but a measure of suffering. He told Timothy, "In fact, everyone who wants to live a godly life in Christ Jesus will be persecuted" (2 Timothy 3:12). A sick person is not unspiritual. And Christian faith does not magically equip us with a germ-free, hermetically sealed space suit to protect against the dangers of earth. That would insulate us from complete identification with the world—a luxury God did not allow his own Son.

To hold out the inducement that becoming a Christian will guarantee you health and prosperity—why, that is the very argument advanced by Satan in the book of Job, and decisively refuted.

To restore balance to this issue, we would do well to relearn the lessons about faith taught in the Bible's greatest chapter on the subject, Hebrews 11. The author compiles a list of faithful persons through the centuries. Most of the saints listed in the first part of the chapter received miraculous deliverance: Isaac, Joseph, Moses, Rahab, Gideon, David. But the latter part of the chapter mentions others who were tortured and chained, stoned, and sawed in two.

Hebrews 11 gives vivid details about the second group: they went about in sheepskins and goatskins, were destitute, wandered in deserts and mountains, and lived in holes in the ground. The chapter offers the blunt assessment, "These were all commended for their faith, yet none of them received what had been promised." It adds, though, God's own appraisal of these sojourners on earth who placed their hopes in a better, heavenly country: "Therefore God is not ashamed to be called their God, for he has prepared a city for them."

I thought about this list of "God's favorites" recently as I read through *Fear No Evil*, the last book written by David Watson, a well-known English preacher and writer. Struck down with colon cancer at the height of his career, Watson rallied his Christian friends around him and began a desperate journey of faith. He had gained prominence in the charismatic movement, and Watson and most of his friends were convinced that God would solve the cancer through a miraculous healing.

Over time, as Watson grew sicker and weaker, he had to reach for another kind of faith, the kind cultivated by the saints mentioned in the latter part of Hebrews 11. He needed the faith that sustained Job, barely, in his darkest days, and his book tells how he attained that faith.

David Watson wrote the last words of his book in January, and died in February. Many people received his book with a touch of disappointment; they had hoped rather for an account of supernatural healing. But J. I. Packer, who wrote the foreword after Watson's death, saw it as recovering an ancient tradition of Christian books on the "art of dying." Until recently, a good death was seen as a godly man's crowning achievement, the climax of his good life.

Packer gives this assessment:

> The fact that David, right to his last page, hopes for supernatural healing that never comes is not important. In the providence of God, who does not always show his servants the true point of the books he stirs them to write, the theme of *Fear No Evil* is the conquest of death—not by looking away from it, nor by being shielded from it, but by facing it squarely and going down into

it knowing that for a believer it is the vestibule of glory.

David's theology led him to believe, right to the end, that God wanted to heal his body. Mine leads me rather to say that God evidently wanted David home, and healed his whole person by taking him to glory in the way that he will one day heal us all. Health and life, I would say, in the full and final sense of those words, are not what we die *out of*, but what we die *into*.[9]

8

Arms Too Short to Box with God

Some say that to the gods we are like flies that boys idly swat on a summer day. Others say that not a feather from a sparrow falls to the ground without the will of the Heavenly Father.

Thornton Wilder
The Bridge of San Luis Rey

You are lying in a hospital bed, kept alive artificially by tubes of plastic spilling from your arm and nose. A killer tornado has destroyed everything you own. All you've worked for—your house, car, savings account—has disappeared forever. Your family decimated, you have no visitors except some rather cranky neighbors. You are barely hanging on to life.

You move through the usual stages of grief, your prayers and questions tinged with bitterness. If only God would visit me personally and give some answers, you say to yourself. I want to believe him, but how can I? What has happened contradicts everything I know about a loving God. If I could just see him once and hear him explain why I must go through this hard time, then I could endure.

One person in very similar straits to these got his wish. Job, the prototype of innocent suffering, received a personal visit from God himself, who answered him out of a whirlwind. God's reply to Job comprises one of his longest single speeches in the Bible, and because it appears at the end of the Bible's most complete treatise on suffering it merits a close-up look. Perhaps God has already recorded what he would say directly to us.

First, recall the setting. What could God say to Job? He might have laid a gentle hand on Job's head and told him how much he would grow in personhood through the time of trial. He might have expressed a little pride in Job, who had just won for him a decisive victory: "Job, I know you've had unfair treatment, but you came through. You don't know what this means to me and even to the universe." God might have delivered a lecture on the necessity of preserving human freedom, or on the tragic results of the Fall. (He might even have enlightened Job on the value of pain, explaining how much worse his life would be with leprosy!)

A few kind phrases, a smile of compassion, a brief explanation of what went on—any of these would have helped Job. God did nothing of the kind. To the contrary, he turned the tables on Job, rushing in aggressively,

> Who is this that darkens my counsel
> with words without knowledge?

Brace yourself like a man;
>> I will question you,
>> and you shall answer me. (38:2–3)

From there, God proceeded to sweep Job off his feet with a series of questions—not answers—that virtually ignore thirty-five chapters' worth of debates on the problem of pain.

A Nature Lesson

Much has been made about God's magnificent speech in Job 38–41. In a passage that could be addressed to the Sierra Club or Audubon Society, God took Job on a verbal tour of all the wonders of nature. I, too, marvel at the splendid imagery, but along with my marvel comes a nagging sense of bewilderment. Why this speech, at this moment?

Readers who quote admiringly from God's speech, or needlepoint its beautiful poetry into slogans for wall plaques, may have lost sight of the context in which Job heard those majestic words: he was homeless, friendless, naked, ulcerous, in despair. What a time for a nature-appreciation course! Why did God sidestep the very questions that had been tormenting poor Job?

Before a thoroughly dejected audience, God sang out with peals of divine glee. He called to mind:

Sunrise. "Have you ever given orders to the morning, or shown the dawn its place . . .?"
Rain and snow. "Have you entered the storehouses of the snow or seen the storehouses of

the hail? . . . From whose womb comes the ice? . . . Who can tip over the water jars of the heavens when the dust becomes hard and the clods of earth stick together?"

Thunderstorms. "Who cuts a channel for the torrents of rain, and a path for the thunderstorm? . . . Do you send the lightning bolts on their way? Do they report to you, 'Here we are'?"

Lions. "Do you hunt the prey for the lioness and satisfy the hunger of the lions when they crouch in their dens or lie in wait in a thicket?"

Mountain goats. "Do you know when the mountain goats give birth? Do you watch when the doe bears her fawn?"

Wild donkeys. "Who let the wild donkey go free? Who untied his ropes? I gave him the wasteland as his home, the salt flats as his habitat. He laughs at the commotion in the town; he does not hear a driver's shout."

The ostrich. "The wings of the ostrich flap joyfully, but they cannot compare with the pinions and feathers of the stork. . . . God did not endow her with wisdom or give her a share of good sense. Yet when she spreads her feathers to run, she laughs at horse and rider."

The horse. "Do you give the horse his strength or clothe his neck with a flowing mane?

Do you make him leap like a locust,
striking terror with his proud snorting?"
Birds of prey. "Does the hawk take flight by your
wisdom and spread his wings toward the
south? Does the eagle soar at your command and build his nest on high?" (from
Job 38–39)

Stalking lionesses, soaring eagles, streaks of
lightning, crocodiles, wild oxen—God summoned
up these and other images for Job with the satisfaction and delight of a proud artist. After each description, he either stated or implied, "Job, are you
powerful enough to duplicate these feats? Are you
wise enough to run the world? . . . Do you have an
arm like God's, and can your voice thunder like
his?" God even employed sarcasm in 38:21: "Surely
you know, for you were already born! You have
lived so many years!"

God's words hit Job with devastating power,
prompting an overwhelmed, repentant surrender. "I
know that you can do all things; no plan of yours
can be thwarted. . . . Surely I spoke of things I did
not understand, things too wonderful for me to
know" (42:2–3).

Did God answer Job's questions about suffering
and unfairness? Not really. He seemed deliberately
to avoid a logical, point-by-point explanation. (I
find it ironic that so many people have written
books attempting to defend God's reputation as it
regards this messy problem of pain when God himself saw no need for self-defense.) Why, then, the

combative tone? What did God want from Job?

God wanted, simply, an admission of trust. The message looming behind the splendid poetry reduces down to this: Until you know a little more about running the physical universe, Job, don't tell me how to run the moral universe.

If we, like Job, are so ignorant about the wonders of the world we live in, a world we can see and touch, who are we to sit in judgment of God's moral government of the universe? Until we are wise enough to orchestrate a blizzard—or even manufacture a single perfect snowflake—we have no grounds to sue God. Let him who is about to accuse God consider the greatness of the God accused.

A God wise enough to rule the universe is wise enough to watch over his child Job, regardless of how things seem in the bleakest moments. A God wise enough to create me and the world I live in is wise enough to watch out for me.

A Best-seller's Oversight

God's speech at the end of Job is one of the central reasons I cannot agree with the conclusions of a well-written popular book on the problem of pain, *When Bad Things Happen to Good People*. Rabbi Harold Kushner wrote it after watching his son battle the cruel disease progeria, which bizarrely speeds up the aging process so that the young boy grew bald, wrinkled, and weak, then finally died.

In the book, which became a surprise best-seller, Kushner explains that he learned to accept God's love but question God's power. He came to believe that God is good, and hates to see us suffer, but simply is not powerful enough to straighten out the problems of this world—problems such as children with progeria. Suffering exists on this planet because "even God has a hard time keeping chaos in check," and God is "a God of justice and not of power."[1] In other words, God is as outraged by the suffering on this planet as anyone, but his hands are tied.

Kushner's book became a best-seller because people found it comforting. The rabbi had voiced for them what they had wanted to believe all along: that God desires to help, but cannot. When we call on him to solve our problems, we are simply expecting too much of God. Kushner's ideas sound like something we may want to be true. But are they true?

If Kushner has discovered hidden truths about God, why didn't God reveal these same truths in his speech to Job? That biblical book could conveniently be subtitled "When the Worst Things Happened to One of the Best People." The final climactic scene offered God a perfect platform from which to discuss his lack of power, if that indeed was the problem. Surely Job would have welcomed these words from God: "Job, I'm sorry about what's happening. I hope you realize I had nothing to do with the way things have turned out. I wish I could help, Job, but I really can't."

Instead, Job 38–41 contains as impressive a description of God's power as you'll find anywhere in the Bible. God never once apologized to Job for his lack of power; rather his verbal fugues about ostriches, wild oxen, snowstorms, and constellations all served to underscore it.

If God is less-than-powerful, why did he choose the worst possible situation, when his power was most called into question, to boast about his power? Elie Wiesel might have had the most perceptive comment on the God portrayed by Rabbi Kushner: If that's who God is, I think he ought to resign and let someone more competent take his place.

Response, Not Cause

Although God's speech resolved Job's questions, it may not resolve ours. (Looking back, we may have trouble understanding why Job felt so satisfied with a seemingly evasive answer, but, then, we didn't hear God speak out of a whirlwind either.) In the end, it was God's presence that filled the void. But what lessons apply to the rest of us, those of us who did not have the privilege of hearing God's speech in person?

In my view the book of Job reinforces the pattern followed by Jesus in Luke 13 and John 9. Suffering involves two main issues: (1) cause —Why am I suffering? Who did it?—and (2) response. By instinct, most of us want to figure out the cause of our pain before we decide how to respond. But God does not allow Job that option. He deflects attention from the issue of cause to the issue of Job's response.

It's as if God has walled off two areas of responsibility. He fully accepts responsibility for running the universe, with all its attendant problems. To someone like Job, who focuses on those problems,

God has one word of advice: "Stop your whining. You have no idea what you're talking about." Or, as Frederick Buechner puts it, "God doesn't explain. He explodes. He asks Job who he thinks he is anyway. He says that to try to explain the kind of things Job wants explained would be like trying to explain Einstein to a little-neck clam. . . . God doesn't reveal his grand design. He reveals himself."[2]

As for Job, he had only one thing to worry about: his response. God never explained the origin of Job's suffering, but rather moved the focus to the future. Once the tragedy has happened—now what will you do? Casting about for blame would get him nowhere; he needed to exercise responsibility in his response, the one area he, and not God, had control over.

This biblical pattern is so consistent that I must conclude the important issue facing Christians who suffer is not "Is God responsible?" but "How should I react now that this terrible thing has happened?" For that very reason, I will shift my main focus in this book away from the theoretical questions about suffering. Instead, I will direct attention to personal examples of actual people who respond to pain.

In the Bible, at least, the problem of pain is less a philosophical riddle than a test of human response and faithfulness. As Florida pastor Stephen Brown expressed it, in a statement not to be taken too literally, every time a non-Christian gets cancer, God allows a Christian to get cancer as well, so the world can see the difference.

What difference? What response is best? The

Bible replies often, with an unwavering but disturbing answer:

> Consider it pure *joy*, my brothers, whenever you face trials of many kinds, because you know that the testing of your faith develops perseverance. Perseverance must finish its work so that you may be mature and complete, not lacking anything. (James 1:2–4)
>
> Dear friends, do not be surprised at the painful trial you are suffering, as though something strange were happening to you. But *rejoice* that you participate in the sufferings of Christ, so that you may be overjoyed when his glory is revealed. (1 Peter 4:12–13)
>
> In this you greatly *rejoice*, though now for a little while you may have had to suffer grief in all kinds of trials. (1 Peter 1:6–7)

One of the best expressions of the Bible's ideal attitude toward suffering emerges from a rift between Paul and the Christians in Corinth. In a fit of pique, Paul had sent a strongly worded letter. Reflecting on it later, he writes, "I am no longer sorry that I sent that letter to you, though I was very sorry for a time, realizing how painful it would be to you. But it hurt you only for a little while. Now I am glad I sent it, not because it hurt you, but because the pain turned you to God. It was a good kind of sorrow you felt, the kind of sorrow God wants his people to have. . . ." (2 Corinthians 7:8–9 LB).

"Pain turned you to God"—Paul's succinct

phrase serves as an accurate summary of the role of suffering. It underscores the Bible's emphasis on response, not cause. It also fits the lesson that Jesus applied from the two tragedies in his day (Luke 13): "Don't you realize that you also will perish unless you leave your evil ways and *turn to God?*"

Something Produced

"Rejoice!" "Be glad!" How do these suggestions differ from the insensitive hospital visitor who brings a smile and a "Look on the bright side!" pep talk? Read further in each biblical passage, for every such admonition leads to a discussion of productive results. Suffering produces something. It has value; it changes us.

By using words like "Rejoice!" the apostles were not advocating a spirit of grin-and-bear-it or act-tough-like-nothing-happened. No trace of those attitudes can be found in Christ's response to suffering, or in Paul's. If those attitudes were desirable, self-sufficiency would be the goal, not childlike trust in God.

Nor is there any masochistic hint of enjoying pain. "Rejoicing in suffering" does not mean Christians should act happy about tragedy and pain when they feel like crying. Rather, the Bible aims the spotlight on the end result, the productive use God can make of suffering in our lives. To achieve that result, however, he first needs our commitment of trust, and the process of giving him that commitment can be described as rejoicing.

Romans 5:3–5 breaks down the process into stages: "We also rejoice in our sufferings, because we know that suffering produces perseverance; perseverance, character; and character, hope. And hope does not disappoint us, because God has poured out his love into our hearts by the Holy Spirit, whom he has given us." Quite simply, a quality like perseverance will *only* develop in the midst of trying circumstances. Think about it: a person who always gets what he or she wants has no chance to learn perseverance, or patience. Suffering can be one of the tools to help fashion those good qualities.

Seen in this light, the apostles' command to "Rejoice!" makes sense. James does not say, "Rejoice in the trials you are facing," but rather "Count it pure joy when you face trials. . . ." The difference in wording is significant. One celebrates the fact of pain; the other celebrates the opportunity for growth introduced by pain. We rejoice not in the fact that we are suffering, but in our confidence that the pain can be transformed. The value lies not in the pain itself, but in what we can make of it. The pain need not be meaningless, and therefore we rejoice in the object of our faith, a God who can effect that transformation.

A few chapters after his step-by-step analysis in Romans 5, Paul makes a grand, sweeping statement, "And we know that in all things God works for the good of those who love him. . . ." That statement is sometimes twisted and made to imply that "Only good things will happen to those who love God." Paul meant just the opposite. The remainder of chapter 8 defines what kind of "things" he had in mind: trouble, hardship, persecution, famine, nakedness, danger, sword—all pages from Paul's autobiography. Yet, as the apostle's life well illustrates, God used even those things to advance his will in and through Paul. It would be more accurate to say that God was working in Paul through harsh circumstances than to say he was at work in the circumstances themselves.

Does God introduce suffering into our lives so that these good results will come about? Remember the pattern established at the end of Job. Questions about cause lie within God's domain; we cannot expect to understand those answers. We have no right to speculate, "Some relatives came to Christ at the funeral—that must be why God took him home." Instead, response is our assignment. Paul and other New Testament authors insist that if we respond with trust God will, without doubt, work in us for good. As Job himself said so presciently, ". . . those who suffer he delivers in their suffering; he speaks to them in their affliction" (36:15).

The notion of suffering as productive brings a new dimension to our experience of pain. Human beings undergo goal-directed suffering quite willingly, as athletes and pregnant women can attest. According to the Bible, a proper Christian response to suffering gives similar hope to the person on the hospital bed. As we rely on God, and trust his Spirit to mold us in his image, true hope takes shape within us, "a hope that does not disappoint." We can literally become better persons because of suffering. Pain, however meaningless it may seem at the time, can be transformed.

Where is God when it hurts? He is in *us*—not

in the things that hurt—helping to transform bad into good. We can safely say that God can bring good out of evil; we cannot say that God brings about the evil in hopes of producing good.

Mary's Journey

Once Dr. Paul Brand and I were discussing individual Christians who had undergone great suffering. After he had related several personal stories, I asked whether the pain had turned those people toward God or away from God. He thought at length, and concluded that there was no common response. Some grew closer to God, some drifted bitterly away. The main difference seemed to lie in their focus of attention. Those obsessed with questions about cause ("What did I do to deserve this? What is God trying to tell me? Am I being punished?") often turned against God. In contrast, the triumphant sufferers took individual responsibility for their own responses and trusted God despite the discomfort.

Then Dr. Brand told me about one of his most famous patients, Mary Verghese.*

Mary was not a leprosy patient. Rather, she worked as a medical resident at Brand's leprosy hospital in India. One day she went on a picnic outing in a station wagon driven by a young student out to demonstrate his bravery. After following a poky school bus for several miles the driver, thoroughly exasperated, jerked the car into the passing lane and

---

*Mary's story is told in *Take My Hands* by Dorothy Clarke Wilson.

floored the accelerator. When he saw another car coming head-on, he instinctively stomped on the brake pedal—but hit the gas instead. The station wagon veered over a bridge and tumbled down a steep embankment.

Mary Verghese, promising young physician, lay motionless at the bottom of the bank. Her face was slit in a deep gash from cheekbone to chin. Her lower limbs dangled uselessly, like two sticks of wood.

Mary's next few months were almost unbearable. As summer temperatures reached 110 degrees outside, Mary lay in her sweltering hospital room, in traction, wrapped in a perspex jacket and plastic brace. She faced agonizing hours of therapy. Each week nurses would test her for sensation, and each week she would fail, never feeling the pinpricks on her legs.

After observing her downward spiral of despair, Dr. Brand stopped by her room for a visit. "Mary," he began, "I think it's time to begin thinking of your professional future as a doctor." At first she thought he was joking, but he went on to suggest that she might bring to other patients unique qualities of sympathy and understanding. She pondered his suggestion a long time, doubting whether she would ever recover sufficient use of her limbs to function as a doctor.

Gradually, Mary began to work with the leprosy patients. The hospital staff noticed that patients' self-pity, hopelessness, and sullenness seemed to fade when Mary Verghese was around. Leprosy patients whispered among themselves about the wheelchair doctor (the first in India) who was more disabled than they were, whose face, like theirs, bore scars. Before long Mary Verghese began assisting at surgery—tedious, exhausting work for her in a sitting position.

One day Dr. Brand met Mary rolling her wheelchair between buildings of the hospital and asked how she was doing. "At first the threads seemed so tangled and broken," she replied, "but I'm beginning to think life may have a pattern after all."

Mary's recovery was to involve many excruciating hours of therapy, as well as major surgery on her spine. She remained incontinent for life and fought constantly against pressure sores. But she now had a glimmer of hope. She began to understand that the disability was not a punishment sent by God to entrap her in a life of misery. Rather, it could be transformed into her greatest asset as a doctor. In her wheelchair, with her crooked smile, she had immediate rapport with disabled patients.

Eventually Mary learned to walk with braces. She worked under scholarship in New York's Institute of Physical Medicine and Rehabilitation, and ultimately headed up a new department at the Physiotherapy School in Vellore, India.

Mary stands as an outstanding example of a person who got nowhere asking why a tragedy happened. But as she turned toward God and asked to what end, she learned to trust him to weave a new design for her life. In doing so, Mary Verghese has probably achieved far more than she would have had the accident not occurred.

Mary Verghese offers a great contrast to people I know who have turned away from God because of their suffering. They talk about their illness, often hypochondriacally, as if it's the only part of their lives. They give full vent to the self-pity that smolders beneath the surface in each of us.

The suffering person faces choices. She can recoil in anger and despair against God. Or she can accept the trial as an opportunity for joy. I do not mean to imply that God loves one type of sufferer and rejects the other, or even that one is more "spiritual" than the other. I believe God understands those people who kick and struggle and scream as well as those who learn that suffering can be a means of grace, of transformation. (Remember, God had far more sympathy for Job's honest ravings than for his friends' pieties.)

God does not need our good responses for himself, to satisfy some jealous parental hunger. He directs attention from cause to response for our sakes, not his. Indeed, the path of joyful acceptance is self-healing: an attitude of joy and gratitude will reduce stress, calm nerves, allay fears, help mobilize bodily defenses.

Would it really help us to know exactly why God permits a specific instance of suffering? Such awareness may engender even more bitterness. But it does help our actual condition when we turn to him in trust. It can break down self-sufficiency and create in us a profound new level of faith in God. It can transform our suffering into qualities of lasting, even eternal, value.

I ask you neither for health nor for sickness, for life nor for death; but that you may dispose of my health and my sickness, my life and my death, for your glory. . . . You alone know what is expedient for me; you are the sovereign master; do with me according to your will. Give to me, or take away from me, only conform my will to yours. I know but one thing, Lord, that it is good to follow you, and bad to offend you. Apart from that, I know not what is good or bad in anything. I know not which is most profitable to me, health or sickness, wealth or poverty, nor anything else in the world. That discernment is beyond the power of men or angels, and is hidden among the secrets of your Providence, which I adore, but do not seek to fathom.

—a prayer by Blaise Pascal[3]

PART 3

How People Respond
to Suffering

9

⇐◦◦◦⇒

After the Fall

Pain that cannot forget
falls drop by drop
upon the heart
until in our despair
there comes wisdom
through the awful grace of God.

Aeschylus

Notions about the productive value of suffering and the crucial role of a person's response may sound fine in theory, but few people concern themselves with theoretical suffering. The important question is, Do these principles work out in actual life situations?

To learn more, I visited two Christians who fight daily battles against pain, physical and psychological, that sometimes rages out of control. Both were cut down in the prime of life; in many ways their identities ever since have been defined by the misfortune they met. Yet the two, Brian Sternberg and Joni Eareckson Tada, have given contrasting human responses. Their experience with suffering has been so all-consuming that each deserves a full chapter.

*   *   *

On July 2, 1963, Brian Sternberg fell ten feet, and that one-second fall completely altered his life, as well as that of his family. In high school Brian had devoted himself to the uncommon sport of pole-vaulting. He liked the experience of fashioning a single graceful event from many different parts—the mad dash down the runway, the jarring thrust of the pole plant, the leap of recoiled strength like a cougar's, the feet-first propulsion, the slight hesitation of weightlessness at the top of the bar, the quick, scary descent like a high dive into air cushions.

For Brian it was not enough to excel at vaulting technique. Knowing the slight edge some extra refinement could give his body, he took up gymnastics as well. A ballet of strength, gymnastics is perhaps sport's highest claim to art. Nearly every day after high school classes Brian would head to the gym to practice his vault approaches, leaps, and falls on the trampoline. He learned to twist and loop and turn flips high in the air, exulting in the sheer pleasure of his bodily mastery. Vaulting required rigorous control and discipline; gymnastics set him free.

As a freshman at the University of Washington, Brian established a national collegiate freshman mark of 15'8". The following year track magazines ranked him the number-one pole-vaulter in the world. The year was 1963. John Kennedy was president, and beating the Russians a national pastime.

It looked as if the U.S. had a winner in Brian Sternberg, and world attention focused on the nineteen-year-old.

In 1963 Brian made sports headlines nearly every week. Undefeated in outdoor competition, he set an American record in indoor competition. Then he set his first world mark with a vault of 16'5". In quick succession Brian racked up new records of 16'7" and 16'8", capturing both the NCAA and AAU titles. Other elite vaulters reached a plateau; Brian kept climbing.

Those were happy days for the Sternbergs. They all knew the glory was fleeting, for track stars fade quickly. But it was fun for the whole family to pile into the car and drive to see Brian single-handedly pack out a field house and bring the crowd wildly to its feet.

Everything changed on July 2, three weeks after Brian's last world record. Now, several decades later, Brian Sternberg still competes, but in a far more lonely and desperate contest. There have been no more vaults.

The Accident

The ordeal began when he grabbed his sweater and yelled, "I'm going to limber up at the pavilion, Mom." He drove across the river to the University of Washington and began a gymnastics warm-up. The U.S. track team was preparing for a tour to the Soviet Union, and Brian's workouts were now indispensable. This is how Brian described what happened next:

If there is ever a frightening moment in trampolining, it is just as you leave the trampoline bed, on your way up. At that moment, even the most experienced gymnast sometimes gets a sensation of panic, for no good reason, that does not disappear until he is down safe on the bed again. It hit me as I took off. I got lost in midair and thought I was going to land on my hands and feet, as I had done several times before when the panic came. Instead I landed on my head.

I heard a crack in my neck, then everything was gone. My arms and legs were bounding around in front of my eyes, but I couldn't feel them moving. Even before the bouncing stopped, I was yelling, "I'm paralyzed," in as loud a voice as I could, which was pretty weak because I had practically no lung power. The paralysis was affecting my breathing.

There was nothing I could do. I couldn't move. It scared me at first, but then, for some reason, the panic disappeared. I told the people looking down at me, "Don't move me, especially don't move my neck." At one point, when I started losing my power to breathe and could feel myself passing out, I remember telling a buddy about mouth-to-mouth resuscitation: "Do everything, but don't tilt my head back."

Real anguish hit me a couple of times while we waited for the doctor. It was not physical pain: I just broke from the thought of what had happened to me. But at the time I was thinking only about the near future. I had not begun to think about the possibility of never walking again.[1]

Doctors know little about the spinal-cord system, because they can't easily study it without damaging the patient. For the first forty-eight hours they did not know whether Brian would survive. When he did, they could only guess at what range of movement might be restored to him.

For the next eight weeks Brian lay strapped onto a Foster frame, a steel-and-canvas device nicknamed "the canvas sandwich." Hinged at both ends, it allowed a nurse to flip Brian upside down every few hours, in order to prevent bedsores and other complications.

Once out of the Foster frame, he could move his head, although for a long time he wouldn't, because of the terrible memory of that snapping sound in his neck. He could also contract a few shoulder muscles. Superb shoulder development had always marked him as a vaulter; now those muscles too began to atrophy. To slow the deterioration, technicians would attach electrodes to his muscles and, by sending voltage through them, cause them to contract. Brain found it very strange to watch his own muscles twitch while he felt nothing.

For a while he had no pain. The sensations from his nervous system, in fact, offered no proof that he had legs or arms or a torso. He felt suspended, as if floating around the room. He couldn't even feel the mattress under him.

Lying in bed, a "head" and nothing more, Brian

began to experience tactile hallucinations. He developed an imaginary pair of legs and arms that he could command at will. He would concentrate hard on, say, "basketball," and somehow his subconscious would bring to his nerve center the exact memory of a basketball. The sensation felt exactly as if he was holding one between his hands. The games were fun at first, giving him hope that one day his tactile perceptions would reconnect to reality.

But before long the games began to turn against him. The basketball would stick to his imaginary fingers, and he couldn't let go. Or instead of a basketball, he'd feel a razor blade. Its sharp edges would slide across his hands, with an excruciating effect—imaginary, of course, but quite real to Brian's pain network. For a time he could not escape the illusion of having a metal nut screwed tightly to each fingertip.

At night came the nightmares: leering, haunted nightmares of himself stomping all over the walls and ceiling of his room, like a fly. Others had little shape or plot, just a formless, disembodied sense of terror. And always after the nightmares came the morning; that was far worse, because he could not awake from the nightmare of reality.

Fits of emotional depression, even more severe than the hallucinations, would overtake him without warning. He could see his athlete's body shriveling, adapting to inactivity. For hours Brian would look at the same walls and with the same desperate mental lunges try to make his muscles obey the brain's commands. And every time he worked hard and failed, he'd dig himself deeper into an emotional pit. He would cry out to the doctors, "I've had it. I don't know what I'm going to do. Nothing's happening; I can't stand lying tied up like this. I'm exhausted. I've tried to move for too long, and I just can't. . . ."[2] The tears and sobs would choke away his speeches.

When the depression hit in waves, like nausea, Brian had a few sources of comfort to cling to. His girlfriend and his family stood by him, and he heard from thousands of sympathizers, as far away as Japan and Finland. For an hour or so each day his parents would read the letters and cards aloud, until the emotions got too thick and they couldn't continue. One seventy-nine-year-old man wrote, "My body's not good, but my spinal cord is fine. I wish I could give it to you."

Support also poured in from the world athletic community. The Soviet Union struck an unprecedented special medal to honor Brian. Football's Kansas City Chiefs played a benefit game to help allay his medical expenses.

After a few weeks, however, nothing seemed to help the depression. Doctors could give little hope—no one with Brian's injury had ever walked again. What pulled him out of that pit was a phone hookup with delegates at a Fellowship of Christian Athletes conference in Ashland, Oregon. For more than an hour Brian spoke to the athletes and talked with coaches and sports people. In return the Christian athletes, expressing their faith in Brian's recovery, sparked his own search for faith.

Three months after the accident is when Brian dates his awakening as a Christian. He realized that apart from a miracle he would never walk again. No amount of straining could budge his limbs. Dead nerve fiber in his spinal cord would have to be re-made, and medicine could not do that. Yet he also recognized that faith in God was not a transaction: "You heal me, God, and I'll believe." He had to be-lieve because God was worthy of his faith. Brian took that risk.

He then began a prayer that has not ended. Scores, hundreds, thousands of times he's presented to God the same request. Everything about his life reminds him that the prayer has not been answered. He's prayed with bitterness, with pleading, with desperation, with fervent longing. Others too have prayed—churches, college students, small clusters of athletes. Always the same prayer, never the an-swer Brian desires and believes in.

Less than a year after the accident, Brian told a reporter from *Look* magazine, "Having faith is a necessary step toward one of two things. Being healed is one of them. Peace of mind, if healing doesn't come, is the other. Either one will suffice." But Brian has a different view now. To him there's only one option—complete healing.

Brian's World

In order to meet Brian, I had to fly to Seattle, leave a message, and wait until he felt well enough to see a visitor. The pain, he says, "oscillates from ridicu-lously high to excruciating."

What could anneal a faith to survive years of suffering and unanswered prayers? Over time, some who first sought physical healing for Brian have changed their prayers. But not the Sternbergs. Are they superhuman or merely stubborn? I wondered as I drove to their Seattle home the first time. Others had warned me: "It's strange—they just won't accept Brian's condition."

The Sternberg home perches on a ridge above Seattle Pacific University. It overlooks a steep street which cars slide down helplessly in severe rain or ice storms. The street was dry, and I made it up okay. Mrs. Helen Sternberg, Brian's trim, blonde mother, met me at the door. On the roof a friend of Brian's was adjusting a rotating radio antenna. Inside the house, the view of Seattle was spectacular through full-length windows. I watched the street and water traffic for twenty minutes while an orderly prepared Brian.

What strikes a visitor first is how totally Brian must depend on other people. If left alone for forty-eight hours, he would die. Orderlies from high schools and Seattle Pacific bathe him, give him medication, feed him, hold glasses of water for him. Brian has always resisted this dependence, but what choice does he have? His body lies exactly where the last orderly placed it.

Brian's head is of normal size, but the rest of his body has shrunk due to muscle atrophy. He has learned to control his shoulder muscles so that he can make some motions with his full arm. He can hit switches, turn knobs (with difficulty), and even type with the use of a special contraption that restrains all but one finger.

Brian's room, no larger than an average bedroom, fences in his life. He has no ten-speed bike or skis or ice skates in a garage. With his eyes he pointed out for me the various objects around him. An Adidas sports blanket hangs above his bed, a memento of the 1964 Tokyo Olympics Brian never attended. On one wall is a letter from John F. Kennedy, dated August 15, 1963. "I want you to know that you have been much in our thoughts during these past weeks and that we hope for continued improvement in the days ahead." The letter was read at the pro football benefit game, and Brian cried when he heard those words.

He showed the greatest enthusiasm, though, when demonstrating a complex assortment of ham radio equipment surrounding his bed. He has developed a consuming interest in amateur radio as a way of forming connections to the outside world.

Brian talked slowly and carefully about a variety of subjects. He loves to talk electronics. And he loves to tell stories of his role as area representative for the Fellowship of Christian Athletes. Speaking from his wheelchair, he has often addressed athletes in gyms, classrooms, and locker rooms.

I found it hard to leave Brian's room. Although much of what he said fascinated me, he seemed to lack the sense of balance and proportion that governs conversation. After a couple of hours, as I edged toward the door, he began talking louder, more urgently. He asked me to do certain favors for him. Long after I told him I must be going, he kept bringing up new topics of conversation.

When I finally broke away, an orderly explained that Brian often acted this way around visitors. Maybe it had something to do with the paralysis, he suggested. Unable to control his own body, Brian was subconsciously seeking control of others.

The Miracle That Won't Come

One fact did become clear in my visit with Brian: now more than ever, he refuses to accept his condition. He has one hope and one prayer—for total healing. He tells that to every visitor. Medically, he needs a miracle; time has done little, and his chances of natural recovery have steadily diminished.

The worst part is the pain. Brian lives with a constant state of bodily revolt. Originating from deep within, the pain spreads throughout his entire body, like the pain machine in Orwell's *1984* that tapped right into the central nervous system. Taken at a single jolt, the pain is enough to knock a strong man howling across the floor. To Brian, it's an unceasing daily routine.

Brian's family has shared the long pain and frustration close up. In the living room his parents told me of their struggle. Outside, lights of the city blinked as thousands of commuters snaked along the city's streets and bridges. That view, combined with the fire blazing in the fireplace, made the setting seem idyllic. Mrs. Sternberg leaned forward to speak of Brian's dilemma.

During the first six months after the accident,

the Sternbergs were flooded with genuine expressions of hope and support. Many Christians believed Brian would recover. It must be God's will, they said, for such a young, talented athlete to walk again. Brian met with famous Christians known for their healing ministry. At one point, leaders from seven different denominations gathered in his room to pray and anoint him with oil. Everyone felt stirred, everyone believed, but nothing changed.

For comfort and guidance the Sternbergs turned to the Bible. They had talked to pastors and theologians, and had read shelffuls of books on why God allows suffering. As they read the Bible, they became even more convinced Brian would be healed.

"What we found," Mrs. Sternberg told me, "was that God loves. No, it's more than that. God *is* love. All around us people were telling us to accept this tragedy as what God must want for us. But the Jesus we saw in the Bible came to bring healing. Where there was hurt, he touched and made well. He never cursed anyone or brought affliction.

"Jesus was God's language to man. What God is, Jesus lived. Has God's language changed? Does our son's condition contradict what God revealed as himself? I never read about Jesus saying to a blind man, 'Sorry, buddy, I wish I could help, but God is trying to teach you something, so get used to it.' When Jesus saw a blind man, he healed. And he taught us to pray for God's will to 'be done on earth as it is in heaven.'

"To put it bluntly, I don't think God is very pleased with Brian's condition. The Bible holds up

God's will as a full, abundant life. It represents wholeness and health—not the withered body Brian's trapped in. We must not use 'God's will' as a pious period to every question mark. We can't stop searching and grow fatalistic, saying, 'I know God's will has been done.'"

She paused. The words were strong, emerging against a background of pain few others have felt. Other Christians, like Mary Verghese, have found comfort in first accepting their condition. The Sternbergs aren't satisfied with acceptance.

She pressed her hands together and continued, "In this life, we don't know full answers to all questions. We take a lot on faith. My husband and I and Brian cling most strongly to God's love. If something—like the accident—doesn't tally with God's love, we look elsewhere. We know it's not from him. Where there is dis-ease between me and God, between me and myself, or between me and a fellow-man, this is disease, and it calls for healing.

"I don't know why Brian's not on his feet yet. I believe God is all-powerful, but I also believe he limits himself. Evil is strong. And I think it is greatly to Satan's advantage to incapacitate us. Anything to keep us from wholeness. He'll exploit our weakness, like a boxer jabbing again and again at a sore jaw or bloody eye. He doesn't quit."

As she talked of the battle between good and evil, my mind shifted to the life of Christ on earth, and attacks directed against him: a slaughter of babies, temptations, betrayal, and finally death. Yet God transformed seeming defeat, even the unimaginable death of his own Son, into victory. In smaller, more subtle ways he has used Brian Sternberg's tragedy, too. Yet, will he crash through with a resounding reversal, overpowering their family tragedy with a physical healing as he had overpowered death with a resurrection? The Sternbergs were staking everything on this hope.

Mrs. Sternberg continued, "No one in Brian's condition has ever walked. No one. Yet we still have faith. I have no idea when God will heal Brian. Conceivably, this particular battle will not be won here on earth. Some people you pray for are healed and some aren't, in this world. But that matter of timing doesn't change God's desire for our wholeness in body, mind, and spirit. We won't give up. We're like doctors searching for a cure; we won't stop investigating. We think it pleases God for us to persevere."

It was late, and our conversation had to end. Before I left the Sternberg home, though, I asked to see Brian's sports mementos. We went into a separate room crowded with trophies, plaques, and certificates. One named him the outstanding athlete of the continent for 1963.

A photo on one wall caught my eye. It showed Brian breaking his last world record at Compton, California. He was sailing against the sky, almost horizontally, with shoulders thrust back and arms outstretched, his hips barely clearing the bar. Every muscle in his body was rippling and tense. The action was frozen by electronic flash, and in a way it's been frozen ever since.

I felt a wash of sorrow—the body of the person I had met and held a conversation with was a pitiful shell of this superb body. Brian has grown, of course, emotionally, spiritually. But he has shrunk, too. Pain crushes. I couldn't get the two images out of my mind as I stepped out of the warmth into a chilly Seattle wind. The Brian of the photo. And Brian today—a twisted, helpless body on the bed where it will lie tomorrow, the next day . . . who knows how long?

Could I believe if that were me? Would I rationalize the suffering, or learn to accept it, or rebel against it? Would my faith in healing survive years, decades? Were the Sternbergs right in gambling everything on a miracle that has not come despite thousands of prayers? Were they unfairly dictating terms to God? Should they "praise the Lord anyhow" as some would suggest?

I had no answers. What stood out mainly was the fierce, fighting quality of their faith. As I drove away, I felt no pity for the Sternbergs. Pity implies weakness, and I had met great strength. Strength that would endure, even if the specifics never fell into line. "A spinal cord injury occurs in this country every thirty minutes," Mrs. Sternberg had told me. "Half a million people are in wheelchairs. So many of them have given up. We feel we can't. We intend to keep on hoping."

A Second Visit

I first visited the Sternbergs in 1972, still in the first decade after Brian's accident. The persistence of their faith impressed me then, and I wondered what I would find when I visited them again in 1987, fifteen years later. Brian was now a middle-aged man. The physical healing he had longed for, and longs for still, has not come. He has now spent more years paralyzed than with movement.

Seattle was in the full bloom of summer, and as I drove up the steep hill to their house, I found the entire family sitting in lawn chairs outdoors. Brian's parents had aged gracefully, and looked little different. Brian, however, had gained the paunch of middle age and his hair was liberally streaked with gray.

Over coffee, the Sternbergs brought me up to date. They had seen some slight physical improvement over the years. The line of paralysis on Brian's chest had crept down several inches, allowing his arms more range of motion. The pain was much more controlled. And sensation had returned to most of his body: although he could not move his legs, at least he was aware of them now. As a result, most of the tactile hallucinations had ceased.

The Sternbergs took pains to point out all the good things that had happened. "One real miracle," said Mr. Sternberg, "is that neither Helen nor I have gotten sick. In almost twenty-five years of caring for Brian, we've managed to keep our health."

For several years the Sternbergs prayed for a healing ministry that would encompass their broadened definition of disease. Finally one came into being: a monthly, Sunday-night prayer service in a Seattle church. People with hurts and needs are invited to come forward and spend a few silent minutes with the pastor, while all the rest direct their prayers to the one person's needs. The shared experience pulled the church together remarkably, and the practice spread far beyond Seattle.

In 1976 Brian nearly died. Pneumonia attacked his fragile lungs, and in the hospital he developed a staph infection. He lay in a coma for two weeks and suffered two cardiac arrests. Doctors installed a pacemaker, but he lingered near death for more than two months. He lost his voice for a long time, and lost some short-term memory.

This time, the prayers for healing were answered. Brian eventually regained all his faculties except what he had lost through the spinal cord injury. Something else seemed clear to me, as we sat around and talked: Brian's personality had changed as well. He was more mellow, and serene, and showed none of the symptoms of personality imbalance that had stood out before.

Gently, I asked the Sternbergs if their belief about physical healing had changed over the years. They said no. "Some people like to point to the good that has come about and interpret that as the reason for Brian's accident. We don't think so. We believe in a loving God, and we still believe God wants Brian whole. Our timing may be off. It looks less and less likely that Brian will have a whole body in this life. You know, in the book of Daniel there's a story about an angel dispatched to answer Daniel's prayer. It takes him three weeks to reach Daniel—but when he arrives he assures Daniel that

God heard the prayer the moment he prayed it."

As we talked, watching the afternoon sun slip behind the hills, I couldn't help comparing my two visits. It occurred to me as I listened to the Sternbergs that a slow, gradual miracle had been taking place, one they might have overlooked. An accident traumatic enough to crack most families apart had instead brought theirs together. They had resisted the easier path of consigning Brian to a nursing home or rehab hospital. For more than two decades they had been pouring selfless love into their son, and it seemed evident to me, as I watched Brian now, that their love had borne fruit. Against their will the Sternbergs, all of them, had come to terms with suffering.

An analogy used by Paul Tournier came to mind as I started the jerky, braking descent of their street. He said the Christian life resembles a trapeze act. You can swing on the bar, exercising and building muscles all you want. But if you want to improve and excel, you have to take risks. You have to let go, knowing that nothing is beneath you, and reach out for the next trapeze bar.

Brian would have liked that analogy, I thought. A long time ago the Sternbergs together let go of the props and announced to the world they would believe God, despite . . . anything. Brian sees that as his personal calling. Not as many spectators are standing around watching now, but the Sternbergs still believe. I drove away, inspired again by their tenacious belief.

10

On My Feet Dancing

He can be revealed only to the child; perfectly, to
the pure child only. All the discipline of the world
is to make men children, that God may be revealed
to them.

George MacDonald
Life Essential

Not long after my first visit with Brian
Sternberg, I traveled to Baltimore, Mary-
land, to interview a remarkable teenager
named Joni Eareckson. Of course, Joni has by now
become a familiar name because of her work as a
painter, author, and popular Christian speaker. But
when I met her nothing had yet been published, and
I had heard only bits and pieces of her story.

Joni's story had close parallels to Brian's: both
were teenage athletes cut down in their prime and
forced to adjust to life as quadriplegics. On the way
to the interview, I anticipated a mood similar to
what I had found at the Sternbergs, that of an un-
easy struggle mixed with tough, undying faith. But
when I arrived at Joni's house, the breadth of a con-

tinent removed from Brian's, I found a quite different atmosphere.

I reached Joni Eareckson's home by following one of the tranquil creeks west of Baltimore. In sharp curves and S-turns the road slithered around abrupt, lumpish hills. A stand of hardwood forest lined both sides of the roadway until the road climbed to the crest of the highest hill, where suddenly a sweeping panoramic landscape came into view. Joni's house was on that hill. It was a cottage made of large boulders and hand-hewn timber, painstakingly fitted together by Joni's father.

The full-length glass walls of Joni's art studio jutted out over the hill. A brown stallion was grazing in the valley, swishing his tail at flies. A Great Dane romped across the lawn. Many artists aspire to work in such a rustic setting, but Joni's professional life was different from most others. She can only go into her studio if someone pushes her, and she draws with a pen or brush held between her teeth.

As a teenager Joni used to ride her stallion through forest trails at breakneck speed, splash in the creek with the Great Dane, and slap basketballs against a backboard beside the cottage. Sometimes she would even join a fox hunt through the property.

But now her daily exercise consists of far subtler movements. With the aid of a biceps-and-shoulder brace she can move her arm enough to turn the pages of a book. And the act of drawing requires a long succession of meticulous, labored head nods. Slowly, a recognizable scene takes form.

A two-second mistake completely changed

Joni's life, but her buoyant optimism was not one of the things it changed. When I was introduced to her, I was mostly struck by the aliveness of her facial expression, and the brightness of her eyes. Her spirit was so effervescent that she faintly brought to mind all those "Think positive—love yourself!" courses taught by former Miss Americas. In contrast to most of them, however, Joni's spirit was formed by tragedy.

A Fateful Dive

The summer of 1967 was unusually hot and humid. July was stifling. In the morning I practiced with the horses, working up a sweat that only a dip in the Chesapeake Bay could cool. My sister Kathy and I rode to the beach and dove into the murky water.

I was never content to swim laps in a pool or splash around in the shallow part of the bay. I preferred free swimming, in the open water. A raft floating fifty or sixty yards offshore made a perfect goal, and Kathy and I raced to it. We were both athletic, and sometimes reckless.

When I reached the raft, I climbed on it and quickly dove off the side, almost without thinking. I first felt the familiar drag of the water, and then a stunning jolt—my head had crashed into a rock on the bottom. My limbs splayed out. I felt a loud buzzing, like an electric shock accompanied by intense vibration. Yet there was no pain.

I couldn't move! My face pressed hard into

the grinding sand on the bottom, but I couldn't pull away. My brain was directing my muscles to make swimming motions, but none of them responded. I held my breath, prayed, and waited, suspended facedown in the water.

After maybe a minute I heard Kathy calling me—a faint, muffled voice above the water surface. Her voice came closer and clearer, and then I saw her shadow right above me. "Did you dive in here? It's so shallow," I heard her say through the water.

Kathy bent down, tried to lift me, then stumbled. Oh, God. How much longer, I thought. Everything was going black.

Just as I was about to faint, my head broke through the surface and I choked in a great gulp of air. I tried to hold on to Kathy, but again my muscles would not respond. She draped me over her shoulders and began paddling to shore.

Feeling certain that my hands and legs were tied together around my chest, I noticed with a sudden shock of terror that instead they were dangling motionless across Kathy's back. I had lost touch with my body.

An ambulance rushed Joni from the solitude of the bay into a whirl of activity at Baltimore's City Hospital. She lay in a small room blocked off by privacy curtains. One nurse asked about her medical history. Another clipped off her brand-new swimming suit, leaving her feeling exposed and helpless. A doctor with a long metal pin kept asking "Do you feel this?" as he pressed it against her feet, her calves, her fingers, and her arms. Concentrating on the stimuli with all her might, Joni could honestly answer "Yes" only when he tested her shoulders.

After a hurried consultation of doctors, one named Dr. Sherrill chopped off Joni's flowing blonde hair with electric clippers, and a nurse shaved her head. As she began fading from consciousness, she thought she heard the high whine of an electric drill. Her last memory was of someone holding her head while the doctor drilled two neat holes, one on either side of her skull.

The Mirror

When Joni awoke, she found herself strapped into a Stryker frame (similar to Brian Sternberg's Foster frame). Metal tongs, inserted into the holes in her skull, were attached to a spring-like device that pulled her head away from her body. Her face poked through a small opening in the canvas sheet to which she was strapped. Every few hours a nurse would flip the frame. All day she alternated views: the floor, the ceiling.

Despite her lack of mobility and the depressing atmosphere of the intensive care unit, Joni survived the first few weeks in good spirits. The pain was slight, and doctors held out hope that some of the nerves might repair themselves. In those early days her room was crowded with visitors and flowers and gifts. Her sisters would spread out *Seventeen* magazines on the floor for her to read facedown.

After four weeks, once Joni had passed the critical stage, Dr. Sherrill performed a fusion procedure on her spine. Joni was jubilant, hoping that the surgery would solve her problems and put her on her feet again. The surgery was indeed successful, but that same day Dr. Sherrill leveled with her. "Joni," he said, "I'm sorry, but the injury is permanent. Fusion surgery did not change that. You'll never walk again, and your arms will have limited use."

For the first time since the accident, that harsh fact sank in. She had expected a few more months' treatment, then rehabilitation, then recovery. Suddenly she saw that her whole life would change. No more sports cars, horse shows, lacrosse matches. Maybe no more dates. Ever.

"I was devastated," she recalls. "My life had been so full. I was involved in as many school activities as I could squeeze in. And suddenly I found myself all alone, just a bare, immobile body between two sheets. My hobbies and possessions were meaningless to me. Those beautiful horses in the barn which I used to trick-ride, standing on their shoulders—I would never ride them again. I couldn't even feed myself. I could sleep and breathe; everything else someone did for me."

Strapped to the canvas facing downward, Joni watched hot, salty tears fall from her face and drip designs on the floor. Her nose ran, and she had to call for a nurse. She even needed help to cry.

Joni's spirits fell to greater depths a few days

later, when two friends from school visited her for the first time. Their image of Joni was of a vivacious, energetic athlete, and nothing had prepared them for the transformation. When they came to Joni's bedside, their mouths dropped. "Oh, my God," whispered one of the girls. They stood for a few seconds in awkward silence, then ran outside. Joni could hear one girl vomiting and one girl sobbing outside her hospital door. She wondered what could be so horrible to cause such a reaction.

A few days later, she found out. Joni asked a visitor named Jackie to bring her a mirror. When Jackie stalled, Joni insisted. Apprehensive, Jackie obeyed, finding a mirror and holding it before her nervously. Joni took one look in the glass and screamed, "Oh, God, how can you do this to me!"

The person in the mirror had eyes that were bloodshot and sunken into dark cavities far back into her skull. Her skin color had faded to a dull yellow, and her teeth were black from medication. Her head was still shaved, with metal clamps on either side. And her weight had shrunk from 125 to 80 pounds.

Joni sobbed uncontrollably. Finally she wailed, "Oh, Jackie, I need your help. Please do one thing for me. I can't face it any longer."

"What's that, Joni? I'll do anything for you."

"Help me die. Bring me some pills, or a razor blade even. I can't live inside a grotesque body like this. Help me die, Jackie."

Jackie could not bring herself to obey that request, regardless of Joni's condition. So Joni learned another cruel fact: she was too helpless even to die on her own.

Fullness

Millions of people have gotten acquainted with Joni since that awful day in City Hospital. She speaks at conferences around the world, appears on national television programs, records a daily radio broadcast, has acted out the role of her life in a Worldwide Pictures movie, and has been the subject of articles in numerous magazines like *People* and *Saturday Evening Post.* In addition to her life story, *Joni*, she has written numerous books and made best-selling recordings of her singing. Her artwork graces a line of cards, posters, and stationery.

Almost everyone who meets Joni Eareckson Tada today (she also got married along the way) comes away feeling happier, more hopeful. She is miles away from the shriveled, pitiable girl in the mirror. How has she done it?

"Once during those depressing days in the hospital, when my day consisted of pancake flips to ease the bedsores, a visitor tried to cheer me up," Joni remembers. "He quoted a Bible verse to me, a promise which Jesus left his followers: 'I have come to give you life in all its fullness.'

"I was so bitter and cynical then, the thought struck me as almost mockery. Life in all its fullness? If I struggled the rest of my life, the most I could foresee would be some pitiful, inferior half-life. No more tennis, no making love, or marriage, no real contribution to the world.

"But over the years, my outlook has changed. I awake every day grateful for what God has given me. Somehow—and it took me three years even to believe it might be possible—God has proven to me that I, too, can have a fullness of life."

Joni's first lesson was to overcome the barrier facing any disabled person by accepting her condition and its limitations. It was futile to waste energy moaning about her awful physical state. Wishing would not change the face in the mirror. She had to accept herself as a quadriplegic and search for new ways of coping.

The process was painful. When her boyfriend would put his arm around her and squeeze, she felt nothing. At these times and others she kept fighting a temptation to shut her eyes and fantasize, imagining what it would be like if she were well again. A fiancé, a sports car, long hikes in the woods, a place on a college lacrosse team—the possibilities were endless. But they were also worthless, and Joni realized that dwelling on them did not relieve her suffering and only delayed the process of self-acceptance.

Joni soon learned that "normal" people often feel uncomfortable around the disabled. When conversing with her, some people would lean over her wheelchair and speak loudly, using simple words, as if she were mentally deficient. Sometimes, as she was being pushed along a sidewalk, pedestrians would allow a five-foot berth, stepping off the curb to let the wheelchair pass, though the sidewalk was plenty wide enough. Joni came to realize why some disabled people in hospitals and nursing homes show no desire to leave for the outside world. Inside, they are the normal ones, and they live among professionals trained to understand.

Friends helped. Joni's most thrilling memory of those early days is of a crazy moment, about a year after her injury, when a friend raced her wheelchair across a sand beach and pushed her into the pounding Atlantic surf. Joni squealed with delight. She may never be able to body-surf on the breakers again, but at least she could let the waves lap against her legs and the salt spray brush her cheeks. She loved it when people treated her in that carefree spirit instead of always being gentle and cautious around her.

But even learning to sit in the wheelchair required agonizing therapy. After lying horizontal for months, Joni's body had to be gradually coaxed into a sitting position. The first time a nurse raised her to a forty-five-degree angle, she nearly collapsed from nausea and dizziness as her heart tried to adjust to the new demands.

Ugly bedsores kept developing. Around her tailbone and hips, sharp edges of bone would protrude through skin. To alleviate the pressures, doctors opened the skin further (with Joni fully conscious—she felt no pain and needed no anesthesia) and filed down sharp bones in her hips and tailbone. More weeks flat in bed followed, then a repeat of the grueling exercises before she could sit again.

In these difficult times, Joni leaned heavily on friends for emotional support. A cluster group of

Christian students would visit her faithfully. Once they surprised her by smuggling a puppy into her hospital room. Joni giggled as the puppy slathered her face with his tongue.

Forty-Year Delay

At first, Joni found it impossible to reconcile her condition with her belief in a loving God. It seemed that all God's gifts, the good things she had enjoyed as an active teenager, had been stolen from her. For what reason? What did she have left? The turning to God was very gradual. A melting in her attitude from bitterness to trust dragged out over three years of tears and violent questioning.

One night especially, Joni became convinced that God did understand. Pain was streaking through her back, causing the kind of torment that is unique to those with paralysis. Healthy persons can scratch an itch, massage an aching muscle, or flex a cramped foot. The paralyzed must lie still, as victims without defense against the pain.

Cindy, one of Joni's closest friends, was beside her bed, searching desperately for some way to bring encouragement. Finally, she clumsily blurted out, "Joni, you aren't the only one. Jesus knows how you feel—why, he was paralyzed too."

Joni glared at her. "What? What are you talking about?"

Cindy continued, "It's true. Remember, he was nailed on a cross. His back was raw from beatings, and he must have yearned for a way to move to change positions, or shift his weight. But he couldn't. He was paralyzed by the nails."

The thought intrigued Joni and, for a moment, took her mind off her own pain. It had never occurred to her that God might have felt the same piercing sensations that now racked her body. The realization was profoundly comforting.

God became incredibly close to me. I felt myself being transformed by the persistent love of my friends and family. And eventually I began to understand that, yes, God too loved me.

Few of us have the luxury—it took me forever to think of it as that—to come to ground zero with God. Before the accident, my questions had always been, "How will God fit into this situation? How will he affect my dating life? My career plans? The things I enjoy?" Many of those options were now gone. I had only a helpless body, and God. Maybe that's the kind of state the mystics strive for; I got mine unwillingly.

I had no other identity but God, and gradually he became enough. I became overwhelmed with the phenomenal possibility of a personal God, the same God who created the universe, living in my life. Perhaps he could make me attractive and worthwhile. I knew I could not do it without him.

The first months, even years, I was obsessed with the question of what God was trying to teach me. Secretly, I probably hoped that by figuring out God's ideas, I could learn my lesson and then he'd heal me.

I suppose every Christian with a similar experience goes back to the book of Job for answers. Here was a righteous man who suffered more than even I could imagine. But strangely, I could not find answers to the "Why?" of tragedies anywhere in the book of Job. What I found was that Job clung to God regardless, and God rewarded him.

"Is that what God wants?" I wondered. My focus changed from demanding an explanation from God to humbly depending on him. Okay, I am paralyzed. It's terrible. I don't like it. But can God still use me, paralyzed? Can I, paralyzed, still worship God and love him? He began to teach me that I could.

Maybe God's gift to me is dependence. I will never reach a place of self-sufficiency that crowds God out. I am aware of his grace every moment. My need for help is obvious every day when I wake up, flat on my back, waiting for someone to come dress me. I can't even comb my hair or blow my nose alone!

But I do have friends who care. I have the beauty of the scenery I paint. I can even support myself financially—the dream of every disabled person. Peace is internal, and God has lavished me with that peace.

There's one more thing. I have hope for the future now. The Bible speaks of our bodies being "glorified" in heaven. In high school that always seemed a hazy, foreign concept to me. But I now realize that I will be healed. I haven't

been cheated out of being a complete person—
I'm just going through a forty- or fifty-year de-
lay, and God stays with me even through that.

I now know the meaning of being "glorified." It's the time, after my death here, when
I'll be on my feet dancing.

It will be a while before Joni can dance again,
but after two years of rehabilitation, she did learn
to maneuver a motorized wheelchair well enough to
drag race down hospital hallways. Years later she
learned to drive, and now she has her own van, with
customized controls.

She eventually became a public speaker much in
demand, and with good reason. Joni captivates an
audience. She is immaculately dressed, with every
blonde hair neatly in place. As she speaks, she often retraces the events of the accident and her long
recovery. Her words flow articulately. Audiences
most appreciate Joni's zest for life and her enthusiasm. Her limbs stay motionless, but her eyes and
face sparkle with expression.

Joni moved to California some years ago, and
has added the spectacular scenery of the American
West to her repertoire of paintings. "Though I can
no longer splash in a creek and ride horses," she
says, "I can sit outside, and my senses are flooded
with smells and textures and beautiful sights." She
reproduces those scenes, sometimes before an audience, with her remarkable mouth-artistry.

In her talks, Joni sometimes refers to the massive barn that stood just outside her studio in Mary-

land. It was Joni's favorite building on the farm, for it housed her fondest memories: the sweet-smelling hay, the rustling sounds of restless horses, and the dark corners she explored as a child.

Joni describes its enchantment, its beauty, and her father's pride in its workmanship. But then she describes the nightmarish memory of a fire set by vandals that utterly destroyed the barn. That terrifying scene is etched in her mind: the wild screams of her pet horses, the smell of burning flesh, the frantic efforts of her family and neighbors to contain the fire.

The story does not end there, however. Her father, stooped and twisted from arthritis, began again the arduous task of reconstructing the barn by hand. The foundation remained, and on top of it he fitted new boulders, new beams, and new boards. The second barn, the re-created one, was even grander than the first.

"I am like that barn," Joni says. "I thought my life had been crushed beyond repair. But, with the help of God and my friends, it has been rebuilt. Now can you understand why I'm so happy? I've recovered what I thought would always elude me—life in all its fullness."

Two Who Suffer

Joni Eareckson Tada and Brian Sternberg represent those unfortunate persons for whom pain seems to be in revolt. Quadriplegics, cancer victims, parents of children with birth defects—these people of uncommon suffering may well cringe from a concept like "the gift of pain." To them, the phrase must sound hollow and sadistic; pain has left its natural cycle and become a Frankenstein.

One gained fame because of her suffering, the other lost fame because of his. After several decades, both are still incapacitated in body. Yet in their individual ways both Brian and Joni have found strength to continue, and even to grow, and their trust in God is an integral part of that process of healing wounded spirits.

Brian squarely faces the question of causation. Is God responsible? He and his parents are convinced that his condition is as abhorrent to God as it is to them. His conclusions run counter to some themes in this book, for he disallows such thoughts as the transforming value of suffering. Although he recognizes that God has providentially used his pain to bring good, he rejects the notion that God might allow such a condition to continue for the rest of his life. He has gambled his faith, and almost his theology, on the hope for healing.

Yet even that position, which seems more and more untenable to the Sternbergs' friends, signifies a turning toward God. Brian has held to a trust and belief in a loving, worthy God despite a level of torment that few will ever experience. In heaven, Brian will surely walk with the confident stride of a Job or a Habakkuk or a Jeremiah, who saw the world at its worst and still believed.

Joni Eareckson Tada's pain, except for brief flashes, has been mostly psychological, the pain of loss. Yet her life has been marked by a dominant grace note of triumph and joy. She wrestled with God, yes, but she did not turn away from him. She emerged with a spiritual depth and maturity that has brought inspiration to millions. I do not imply that every afflicted person can duplicate the success story of Joni Eareckson Tada. They cannot; Joni has unique and multiple gifts and talents. But in the way that she has used them, she has achieved something else: she has "dignified" suffering.

At first Joni received a flood of letters urging her to pray for healing, or berating her for lack of faith. She did pray for healing, of course. In the summer of 1972, after an intimate service of healing with about fifteen people present, she became convinced that in the next few weeks her spinal cord would miraculously regenerate. She even called friends and warned them, "Watch for me standing on your doorstep soon; I'm going to be healed."

It did not turn out that way. And in her books Joni explains why she was forced to the difficult conclusion that she would not receive physical healing. Joni now calls her accident a "glorious intruder," and claims it was the best thing that ever happened to her. God used it to get her attention and direct her thoughts toward him. Apart from the accident, she says, she probably would have lived a typical middle-class life: aimless, comfortable, with two divorces under her belt by now.

The injury changed all that. Over time God's grace in Joni's life became so evident that she now stands as an emblem strong enough to silence puerile arguments about faith. Does lack of healing mean lack of faith? But what about Joni Eareckson Tada? More, Joni became a striking demonstration of transformed or "redeemed" suffering. After succeeding admirably as an author, actress, singing star, and artist, she decided to devote herself instead to her area of greatest expertise: her disability. Today, Joni directs a ministry called "Joni and Friends" that sponsors conferences and seminars, and funds worthy projects for the disabled.

It is Joni's dream to awaken the church to the needs of the disabled, and to equip Christians to perform a healing role in all society. The crowds are smaller now. Far fewer people turn out to hear a seminar on helping the disabled than to hear a personal testimony. But, step by step, Joni is bringing hope to those who are disabled, and enlightenment to those who are not.

Thank God, very few of us will endure the trials of Joni or Brian. But in different ways, they have each lived out the truth of John 9: "Neither this man nor his parents sinned, but this happened so that the work of God might be displayed in his life." Following the pattern of the blind man of Jesus' day, two modern-day quadriplegics, one from Seattle and one from Baltimore, have brightly displayed the work of God.

Other Witnesses

It is by those who have suffered that the world has been advanced.

Leo Tolstoy

In his book *Creative Suffering* the Swiss physician and counselor Paul Tournier recalls his surprise upon reading an article entitled "Orphans Lead the World." The article, which appeared in a respected medical journal, surveyed the lives of 300 leaders who had had a great impact on world history. After searching for some common thread, the author discovered that all these leaders had grown up as orphans—either actually, through the death of or separation from parents, or emotionally, as a result of severe childhood deprivation. His list included such names as Alexander the Great, Julius Caesar, Robespierre, George Washington, Napoleon, Queen Victoria, Golda Meir, Hitler, Lenin, Stalin, and Castro.

"So there we are," writes Tournier, "giving lectures on how important it is for a child's development to have a father and a mother performing harmoniously together their respective roles towards him. And all at once we find that this is the very thing that those who have been most influential in world history have not had!"[1]

Tournier himself was an orphan, and he pondered the orphan phenomenon soon after the death of his wife, when he felt orphaned once again in old age. Previously, he had judged each major event of life, success or tragedy, as either good or evil. But now he began to perceive that circumstances, whether fortunate or unfortunate, are morally neutral. They simply are what they are; what matters is how we respond to them. Good and evil, in the moral sense, do not reside in things, but always in persons.

This insight changed the way Tournier approached medicine, and led to his theory of the whole person. "Only rarely are we the masters of events," he says, "but (along with those who help us) we are responsible for our reactions. . . . suffering is never beneficial in itself, and must always be fought against. What counts is the way a person reacts in the face of suffering. That is the real test of the person: What is our personal attitude to life and its changes and chances? Here is a man, sick or in the grip of some tragedy, who confides in me: What is he going to make of the grievous blow that has struck him? What is his personal reaction going to be? A positive, active, creative reaction which will develop his person, or a negative one that will stunt it? . . . The right help given at the right moment may determine the course of his life."[2]

In his medical practice, Tournier saw wounded people every day, and he was quick to admit that suffering may push a person toward brokenness and not toward personal growth. That, in fact, was why he moved away from the traditional pattern of diagnosis and treatment and began to address his patients' emotional and spiritual needs as well. He felt an obligation to help them channel suffering as a transforming agent.

Tournier used the analogy of a nutcracker. Unforeseen calamities apply force that can break through the hard outer shell of personal security. The act of breaking will cause pain, of course, but it need not destroy. To the contrary, in the right environment the disarray can lead to creative growth: when old routines and behavioral patterns no longer work, the patient, exposed and vulnerable, must seek new ones.

The role of the doctor, nurse, social worker, minister, or loving friend is simply this: to keep the nutcracker of circumstances from destroying, and to help the sufferer see that even the worst hardships open up the potential for growth and development.

A Movement of Creative Suffering

"What doesn't destroy me makes me stronger," Martin Luther King, Jr., used to say. In our calamitous century King, Gandhi, Solzhenitsyn, Sakharov, Tutu, Mandela, and many others have offered living demonstrations of Tournier's theory of creative suffering. Out of circumstances that should have merely destroyed, these courageous ones emerged with a strength that confounded whole nations.

Martin Luther King, Jr., for example, deliberately sought out the meanest southern sheriffs for his scenes of confrontation. He accepted beatings, jailings, and other brutalities because he believed a complacent nation would rally around his cause only when they saw the evil of racism in its ugliest extreme. "Christianity," he said, "has always insisted that the cross we bear precedes the crown we wear. To be a Christian one must take up his cross, with all its difficulties and agonizing and tension-packed content, and carry it until that very cross leaves its mark upon us and redeems us to that more excellent way which comes only through suffering."[3]

In the end that principle was what brought the civil rights movement the victory sought for so long. It was the sight of civil rights marchers being brutalized by policemen and sheriffs that finally aroused a nation. Just one week after the police assault on the bridge at Selma, Congress took up the Voting Rights Act of 1965. With each bloody confrontation King had become stronger, not weaker.

The principle that operates on large scale in someone like Martin Luther King, Jr., also pertains to the "little people" who followed him in the marches for freedom and justice. I think back to one unlikely hero in rural Mississippi, a man whose photo never appeared in newsmagazines. I interviewed Mr. Buckley in the early 1970s, a time when much of the South was still actively resisting the civil rights movement. When I left Mr. Buckley's house, I felt I had left the presence of a saint.

Mr. Buckley's house was the nicest black home I visited in Simpson County, Mississippi. It was brick on the outside and wood-paneled on the inside, and included four or five large rooms. At the age of ninety, though, Mr. Buckley seemed oblivious to his surroundings. He spent most of his time sitting in a wooden rocker by the kitchen fireplace, the way he used to sit around Home Comfort stoves in the one-room shacks of rural Mississippi. That's where I found him—rocking, reminiscing, scratching his close-cropped gray hair, and chuckling over how life used to be. His eyes were rheumy, his skin thick and leathery, burnt that way by nine decades of Mississippi sun.

In one interview, Mr. Buckley decided to recollect all his memories of childhood. After talking for three and a half hours into a cassette recorder, he paused and asked for a glass of water. He took a good long sip, swished it around in his mouth, and announced, "Well, that brings us up to 1901."

He was born one generation after slavery, and he grew up during the bitter days of Reconstruction. He lived through the fear-filled reign of the Ku Klux Klan, listening to their threats, watching crosses burn, hearing reports of lynchings and burnings. And after seventy-five years of being banned from white restaurants, white motels, white bathrooms, and white polling booths, Mr. Buckley joined the civil rights movement in the mid-1960s. Believing God could use him, he began working for the Rev. John Perkins in a voter registration drive.

In a county with over 5,000 black adults, only 50 were then registered to vote.

Federal marshals set up registration lines around the rear loading docks of the post office, and Mr. Buckley helped organize a caravan of buses and vans. Each name added to voter lists was carved out in fear. A hostile crowd of whites would sometimes appear, shouting insults and threats. Some blacks who registered lost their jobs. But still they came. Strong black men, bowed from carrying cotton sacks on their backs, formed a courageous line through downtown Mendenhall to ask for their vote. Eventually 2,300 were registered.

During his years as a leader in the black community near Mendenhall, Mr. Buckley walked with God, and the wounds he suffered for it made him a deeper, stronger person. He demonstrated to me how the poor and the oppressed could indeed, as Jesus said, be blessed. Faith in God was all he had when days were dark and nights were filled with sleepless fear. And in the end God resided in him with evident ease and familiarity.

Mr. Buckley's faith was tested most severely one night just after he and his wife moved into their new home. At last, in their eighties, the Buckleys had a comfortable home to live in, one that still smelled like fresh paint and looked neat and clean. But Mr. Buckley suddenly awoke at two o'clock in the morning, smelling smoke. He jumped out of bed just in time: The hallway of their house was ablaze, and flames were creeping along the baseboard to their bedroom. He and his wife escaped, barely, but lost all their possessions. The fire had been set by their neighbors.

Mr. Buckley told me, "Well, I reckon we been through a lot. I lost two of my three children, and I lost my first wife, and we almost got ourselves killed that night, fo' sure. But the Lord say he won't put more on us than we can stand. If we can't take it, he'll be right there beside us giving stren'th we didn't know we had."

Mr. Buckley died in 1986, at the age of ninety-seven. He spent his last years helping to found a new church in Mendenhall. He said, "I want a church where anyone is welcome, no matter their color, a church where people pray and expect answers to their prayers. I want a church where people are known by their love for one another." By his example, Mr. Buckley showed what kind of church he wanted.

The Great Reversal

"What doesn't destroy me makes me stronger," Martin Luther King, Jr., had said. Mr. Buckley's peaceful, wrinkled face seemed to prove it. Like a tough old oak that had weathered thunderstorms, blizzards, and forest fires, Mr. Buckley exuded a quality of strength such as most of us sheltered Americans will never experience. There's something unique about having only God to lean on in times of trial.

After the hours I spent with Mr. Buckley, I finally understood Jesus' strange, paradoxical words in the Beatitudes. I realized that I had always viewed the words "Blessed are the poor . . . those who mourn . . . the meek . . . the persecuted" as a kind of sop Jesus threw to the unfortunates. Well, since you aren't rich, and your health is bad, and your face is wet with tears, I'll toss out a few nice phrases and a promise of future rewards. Maybe you'll feel better. But some of the promises are expressed in present tense—"theirs *is* the kingdom"—and my meetings with poor blacks in Mississippi showed me how the poor and the oppressed can indeed be blessed. Mr. Buckley demonstrated a quality of life I had encountered in few other people. His faith was solid, aged, and worn.

The apostle Paul uses a strange phrase, "His [God's] strength is made perfect in weakness." It is a phrase misunderstood and sometimes ridiculed by those who denounce God for allowing pain and suffering in this world. But in representatives like Paul and like Mr. Buckley, the phrase has the ring of truth. Even of Jesus it was said, "He learned obedience from what he suffered" (Hebrews 5:8).

We who stand alongside, observing suffering people, expect to find anger and bitterness. We wait for them to turn on God and lash out against him for the inequities of life. Remarkably, they often find instead a solace in him that puts us to shame. It is no accident that some of the most inspiring stories of faith come from those often considered "losers" by the rest of the world.

Hesitantly, C. S. Lewis concludes: "I am not convinced that suffering . . . has any natural tendency to produce such evils [anger and cynicism].

I did not find the front-line trenches of the C.C.S. more full of hatred, selfishness, rebellion, and dishonesty than any other place. I have seen great beauty of spirit in some who were great sufferers. I have seen men, for the most part, grow better not worse with advancing years, and I have seen the last illness produce treasures of fortitude and meekness from most unpromising subjects . . . If the world is indeed a 'vale of soul-making,' it seems on the whole to be doing its work."[4]

What is there in the nature of suffering to cause this reversal whereby pain can fortify instead of destroy? Jesus plainly taught that the world as seen from God's viewpoint is tilted in favor of the poor and the oppressed. This teaching, sometimes called the "theology of reversal," emerges in the Sermon on the Mount and in other statements of Jesus: the first will be last (Matthew 19:30; Mark 10:31; Luke 13:30); he who humbles himself will be exalted (Luke 14:11; 18:14); the greatest among you should be like the youngest, and the one who rules like the one who serves (Luke 22:26). The parables of the Good Samaritan and the rich man and Lazarus also point to this reversal of the world's order.

But why? Why would God single out the poor and oppressed for special attention over any other groups? What makes the weak so deserving of God's concern?

I came across a thought-provoking list of "advantages" to being poor proposed by a Catholic nun named Monica Hellwig. I have adapted her list, broadening it to include all who suffer.[5]

1. Suffering, the great equalizer, brings us to a point where we may realize our urgent need for redemption.
2. Those who suffer know not only their dependence on God and on healthy people but also their interdependence with one another.
3. Those who suffer rest their security not on things, which often cannot be enjoyed and may soon be taken away, but rather on people.
4. Those who suffer have no exaggerated sense of their own importance, and no exaggerated need of privacy. Suffering humbles the proud.
5. Those who suffer expect little from competition and much from cooperation.
6. Suffering helps us distinguish between necessities and luxuries.
7. Suffering teaches patience, often a kind of dogged patience born of acknowledged dependence.
8. Suffering teaches the difference between valid fears and exaggerated fears.
9. To suffering people, the gospel sounds like good news and not like a threat or a scolding. It offers hope and comfort.
10. Those who suffer can respond to the call of the gospel with a certain abandonment and uncomplicated totality because they have so little to lose and are ready for anything.

Reading over this list, I began to realize why so many Christian saints have endured much suffering. Dependence, humility, simplicity, cooperation, abandon—these are qualities greatly prized in the spiritual life, but extremely elusive for people who live in comfort.

My understanding of the Beatitudes has undergone a radical change. I no longer see them as a sop thrown by Jesus to the unfortunates of the world. I view them not as patronizing slogans, but as profound insights into the mystery of human existence. The poor, the hungry, the mourners, and those who suffer truly are blessed. Not because of their miserable states, of course—Jesus spent much of his life trying to remedy those miseries. Rather, they are blessed because of an innate advantage they hold over people more comfortable and self-sufficient.

Self-sufficiency, which first reared its head in the Garden of Eden, is the most fatal sin because it pulls us as if by a magnet away from God. The suffering and the poor have the advantage that their lack of self-sufficiency is obvious to them every day. They must turn somewhere for strength, and sometimes they turn to God. People who are rich, successful, and beautiful may go through life relying on their natural gifts. But there's a chance, just a chance, that people who lack such natural advantages may cry out to God in their time of need.

In summary, through no choice of their own— they may urgently wish otherwise—suffering and oppressed people find themselves in a posture that befits the grace of God. They are needy, dependent, and dissatisfied with life; for that reason they may welcome God's free gift of love.

Poverty and suffering can serve as instruments

to teach us the value of dependence, and unless we learn dependence we will never experience grace. The apostle Paul gave the Corinthians an autobiographical example of this very principle. He battled against a "thorn in the flesh," an unidentified ailment for which many possibilities have been proposed: epilepsy, eye disease, chronic depression, malaria, sexual temptation. I am glad that Paul left the ailment vague, for the process he outlines in 2 Corinthians 12 applies to all of us with all our various thorns in the flesh.

At first Paul could see no benefit in his thorn in the flesh. Hardly able to "count it all joy," he instead resented the tormenting affliction. It interfered with his busy ministry schedule and caused him to question God. Three times he pleaded for a miracle of healing. Three times his request was refused. Finally, he received the lesson that God wanted him to learn through the affliction: "My grace is sufficient for you, for my power is made perfect in weakness."

The physical weakness was, in fact, being used for Paul's own benefit. The sins of spiritual pride, arrogance, and conceit represented far greater dangers, and this nagging physical weakness kept him relying on God, and not himself, for strength. When he finally saw that, Paul's attitude moved from one of resistance to one of transforming acceptance: instead of begging God to remove the thorn, he prayed that the pain would be redeemed or transformed to his benefit.

Once Paul had learned this lesson, in typical fashion he began shouting it to the world, "boasting" about his weaknesses. To the Corinthians, a sophisticated audience impressed by power and physical appearance, he bragged about God's pattern of choosing the lowly and despised people of the world to confound the wise, the weak to confound the strong. Paul had learned the lesson of the Beatitudes: poverty, affliction, sorrow, and weakness can actually be means of grace if we turn to God with a humble, dependent spirit. "For when I am weak, then I am strong," Paul concluded. The weaker we feel, the harder we may lean.

12

⊂●●●⊃

Extreme Cases

Sometimes I went so far as to thank destiny for the privilege of such loneliness [in Siberia], for only in solitude could I have scrutinized my past so carefully, or examined so closely my interior and outward life. What strong and strange new germs of hope were born in my soul during those memorable hours! I weighed and decided all sorts of issues, I entered into a compact with myself to avoid the errors of former years and the rocks on which I had been wrecked.

Fyodor Dostoyevski
The House of the Dead

Over the years I have read scores of accounts by survivors of concentration camps. They hold a certain fascination for me, perhaps because they present the issues of life at their most extreme. In the camps all marks of individuality are erased. Prisoners are given identical clothing and identical haircuts. They are addressed by number and not by name. They eat the same food and keep the same schedules. There are no differences of class. The barbed wire encloses humanity in its most basic, atavistic form.

In the hands of skilled—or sadistic—administrators, the concentration camps can become a laboratory of suffering. As Terrence Des Pres has pointed out, the aim of the camps was "to reduce inmates to mindless creatures whose behavior could be predicted and controlled absolutely. The camps have so far been the closest thing on earth to a perfect [B. F.] Skinner box. They were a closed, completely regulated environment, a 'total' world in the strict sense. Pain and death were the 'negative reinforcers,' food and life the 'positive reinforcers,' and all these forces were pulling and shoving twenty-four hours a day at the deepest stratum of human need."[1]

Yet if the accounts by Bettelheim, Frankl, Wiesel, Levi, Wiesenthal, Solzhenitsyn, Sharansky, and the like prove anything, they prove that the great behaviorist experiment failed. Stripped of all apparent dignity, these survivors nevertheless managed to emerge with their humanity intact while still possessing a sharply honed moral consciousness. To take just one example, a "rehabilitated" Solzhenitsyn cried out so loudly he was expelled from his homeland, but not before he had almost single-handedly dismantled the myth of Stalinism.

Similarly, if you attend a meeting of Jewish survivors of the Holocaust today, you will not find defeated, useless human beings who walk about like zombies. You will find politicians, doctors, lawyers, virtually a cross section of society in general. Children raised under a regime that approached absolute

evil yet matured into men and women who per-
sonify courage and compassion.

Taken together, the survivors demonstrate that
even suffering at its most diabolical extreme can be
transformed in the lives of individual human beings.
As Bruno Bettelheim summarized the lesson from
the camps: "Our experience did not teach us that
life is meaningless, that the world of the living is
but a whorehouse, that one ought to live by the
body's crude claims, disregarding the compulsions
of culture. It taught us that, miserable though the
world in which we live may be, the difference between it and the world of the concentration camps
is as great as that between night and day, hell and
salvation, death and life. It taught us that there is
meaning to life, difficult though that meaning may
be to fathom—a much deeper meaning than we had
thought possible before we became survivors."[2]

George Mangakis, who was tortured and sentenced to eighteen years' imprisonment by the military junta in Greece, ended up feeling pity for his
torturer, not himself.

> I have experienced the fate of a victim. I
> have seen the torturer's face at close quarters. It
> was in a worse condition than my own bleed-
> ing, livid face. The torturer's face was distorted
> by a kind of twitching that had nothing human
> about it. . . .
>
> In this situation, I turned out to be the lucky
> one. I was humiliated. I did not humiliate oth-
> ers. I was simply bearing a profoundly unhappy

humanity in my aching entrails. Whereas the men who humiliate you must first humiliate the notion of humanity within themselves. Never mind if they strut around in their uniforms, swollen with the knowledge that they can control the suffering, sleeplessness, hunger and despair of their fellow human beings, intoxicated with the power in their hands. Their intoxication is nothing other than the degradation of humanity. The ultimate degradation. They have had to pay very dearly for my torments.

I wasn't the one in the worst position. I was simply a man who moaned because he was in great pain. I prefer that. At this moment I am deprived of the joy of seeing children going to school or playing in the parks. Whereas they have to look their own children in the face.[3]

Dr. Viktor Frankl, a Jewish psychiatrist, learned through his own imprisonment that human life does have meaning and individuals have an inherent freedom that cannot be smothered even in the inhuman camp conditions. His conclusion summarizes the experience of many inmates:

The experiences of camp life show that man does have a choice of action. There were enough examples, often of a heroic nature, which proved that apathy could be overcome, irritability suppressed. Man *can* preserve a vestige of spiritual freedom, of independence of mind, even in such terrible conditions of psychic and physical stress

. . . everything can be taken from man but one thing: the last of human freedoms—to choose one's attitude in any given set of circumstances, to choose one's own way. . . .

In the final analysis it becomes clear that the sort of person the prisoner became was the result of an inner decision, and not the result of camp influences alone. Fundamentally, therefore, any man can, even under such circumstances, decide what shall become of him—mentally and spiritually.[4]

The Ultimate Question

If they answered certain basic questions about humanity, the concentration camps, and most notably Hitler's Holocaust against the Jews, prompted desperate questions about God. The question of this book, "Where is God when it hurts?" almost defined the Jewish experience during the Holocaust. How could he sit by, silent, and watch the immolation of six million of his chosen people? How could he let evil rule with such apparent sovereignty?

During the 1970s a man named Reeve Robert Brenner surveyed one thousand survivors of the Holocaust, inquiring especially about their religious faith. How had the experience of the Holocaust affected their beliefs about God? Somewhat astonishingly, almost half claimed that the Holocaust had no influence whatever on their beliefs about God. But the other half told a different story. Of the total number surveyed, eleven percent said they had rejected all belief in the existence of God as a direct result of their experience. After the war, they never regained faith. Analyzing their detailed responses, Brenner noted that their professed atheism seemed less a matter of theological belief and more an emotional reaction, an expression of deep hurt and anger against God for abandoning them.

Yet Brenner also discovered that a smaller number, about five percent of his overall sample, actually changed from atheists into believers because of the Holocaust. After living through such abominations, they simply had nowhere else to turn.[5]

Within a two-month period I read two poignant accounts by survivors of the Holocaust. These two authors, Elie Wiesel and Corrie ten Boom, typify the radically different responses of faith under such conditions. Their books, both best-sellers, are among the most readable works in the vast Holocaust literature.

Night, by Elie Wiesel, affected me as much as any book I have ever read. In a terse style, his sentences tightly packed with images, Wiesel describes the world in which he spent his teenage years. All the Jews in his village were first herded together into a ghetto, then stripped of possessions and loaded into cattle cars. Almost a third of them died in transit to the death camps.

The first night Wiesel's train pulled up at Birkenau, coils of ominous black smoke billowed from a massive oven, and for the first time in his life Elie smelled the scent of burning human flesh: "Never shall I forget that night, seven times cursed and seven times sealed. Never shall I forget that smoke. Never shall I forget the little faces of the children, whose bodies I saw turned into wreaths of smoke beneath a silent blue sky. Never shall I forget that nocturnal silence which deprived me, for all eternity, of the desire to live. Never shall I forget those moments which murdered my God and my soul and turned my dreams to dust. Never shall I forget these things, even if I am condemned to live as long as God Himself. Never."[6]

Wiesel saw his mother, a younger sister, and eventually all his family forced into an extermination oven. He saw babies pitchforked, children hanged, prisoners murdered by their cellmates over a piece of bread. Elie himself escaped death only on account of an administrative error. His books drum out different variations on the same story of senseless, hopeless tragedy.

In a foreword to *Night*, fellow Nobel laureate François Mauriac describes the meeting with Wiesel when he first heard his story.

> It was then that I understood what had first drawn me to the young Israeli: that look, as of a Lazarus risen from the dead, yet still a prisoner within the grim confines where he had strayed, stumbling among the shameful corpses. For him, Nietzsche's cry expressed an almost physical reality: God is dead, the God of love, of gentleness, of comfort, the God of Abraham, of Isaac, of Jacob, has vanished forevermore, beneath the gaze of this child, in the smoke of a human ho-

locaust exacted by Race, the most voracious of all idols. And how many pious Jews have experienced this death! . . .

Have we ever thought about the consequence of a horror that, though less apparent, less striking than the other outrages, is yet the worst of all to those of us who have faith: the death of God in the soul of a child who suddenly discovers absolute evil?[7]

A Deep Pit

I sometimes feel an aching desire to remain with Wiesel, overwhelmed by human tragedy. After undergoing such monstrosity, how can anyone begin living again? Can words like hope, happiness, and joy regain meaning? How can anyone speak of the character-building value of suffering?

After reading *Night* and several other books by Elie Wiesel, I read *The Hiding Place*, by Corrie ten Boom. The setting was by then familiar. Although not a Jew herself, Corrie was arrested in Holland for sheltering Jews and was transported to the death camps in Germany. She too felt the sting of a whip, saw prisoners disappear into the ovens, and watched her sister die. She too sensed the defilement of all virtue in a world of sovereign evil. Her books ask the same questions as Wiesel's, and sometimes her anger blazes against God.

But there is another element in *The Hiding Place*, the element of hope and victory. Woven throughout her story are the threads of small miracles, along with Bible studies, hymn-sings, and numerous acts of compassion and sacrifice. Throughout their ordeal, the two sisters continued to trust in a God who watched over them in love. As Corrie said, "However deep the pit, God's love is deeper still."

I must confess that, although my sympathies lie entirely with Corrie's view of life and I believe in her God of love, I had to fight thinking her book shallow compared to Wiesel's. Something dark and sonorous was tugging inside me, pulling me away from hope, toward despair.

Wiesel himself expressed his doubt as an act of liberation. "I was the accuser, and God the accused. My eyes were open and I was alone—terribly alone in a world without God and without man. Without love or mercy. I have ceased to be anything but ashes, yet I felt myself to be stronger than the Almighty, to whom my life had been tied for so long."[8] A force within urged me to stand proud beside Elie Wiesel as God's accuser and to throw off the confining shackles of belief.

One thing alone keeps me from standing as God's accuser. My reason for continuing to believe, ironically, is best expressed in a scene described by Wiesel himself, an episode that took place while he, at age fifteen, was imprisoned at Buna.

A cache of arms had been discovered at the Buna camp. They belonged to a Dutchman, who was immediately shipped away to Auschwitz. But the Dutchman also had a *pipel*, a young boy who served him, and the guards began torturing the young boy. The *pipel* had a refined and beautiful face that the camp had not yet ruined—the face, said Wiesel, "of a sad little angel."

When the *pipel* refused to cooperate with his interrogators, the SS sentenced him to death, along with two other prisoners who had been caught with arms.

> One day when we came back from work, we saw three gallows rearing up in the assembly place, three black crows. Roll call, SS all around us, machine guns trained: the traditional ceremony. Three victims in chains—and one of them the little servant, the sad-eyed angel.
>
> The SS seemed more preoccupied, more disturbed than usual. To hang a young boy in front of thousands of spectators was no light matter.
>
> The head of the camp read the verdict. All eyes were on the child. He was lividly pale, almost calm, biting his lips. The gallows threw its shadow over him.
>
> This time the *Lagerkapo* refused to act as executioner. Three SS replaced him.
>
> The three victims mounted together onto the chairs.
>
> The three necks were placed at the same moment within the nooses.
>
> "Long live liberty!" cried the two adults.
>
> But the child was silent.
>
> "Where is God? Where is He?" someone behind me asked.

At a sign from the head of the camp, the three chairs tipped over.

Total silence throughout the camp. On the horizon, the sun was setting.

"Bare your heads!" yelled the head of the camp. His voice was raucous. We were weeping.

"Cover your heads!"

Then the march past began. The two adults were no longer alive. Their tongues hung swollen, blue-tinged. But the third rope was still moving; being so light, the child was still alive. . . .

For more than half an hour he stayed there, struggling between life and death, dying in slow agony under our eyes. And we had to look him full in the face. He was still alive when I passed in front of him. His tongue was still red, his eyes not yet glazed.

Behind me, I heard the same man asking: "Where is God now?"

And I heard a voice within me answer him, "Where is He? Here He is—He is hanging here on this gallows. . . ."

That night the soup tasted of corpses.[9]

Wiesel lost his faith in God at that concentration camp. For him, God literally hung to death on the gallows, never to be resurrected. But in fact the image that Wiesel evokes so powerfully contains within it the answer to his question. Where was God? The voice within Elie Wiesel spoke truth: in a way, God did hang beside the young *pipel*. God did not exempt even himself from human suffering. He too hung on a gallows, at Calvary, and that alone is what keeps me believing in a God of love.

God does not, in the comfortable surroundings of heaven, turn a deaf ear to the sounds of suffering on this groaning planet. He joined us, choosing to live among an oppressed people—Wiesel's own race—in circumstances of poverty and great affliction. He too was an innocent victim of cruel, senseless torture. At that moment of black despair, the Son of God cried out, much like the believers in the camps, "God, why have you forsaken me?"

Jesus, the Son of God on earth, embodied all that I have been trying to say about pain. Like Job, an innocent sufferer who preceded him, he did not receive an answer to the questions of cause: "Why? . . . why?" he called out from the cross, and heard nothing but the silence of God. Even so, he responded with faithfulness, turning his attention to the good that his suffering could produce: ". . . for the joy set before him [Christ] endured the cross" (Hebrews 12:2). What joy? The transformation, or redemption, of humanity.

The Gospel writers stress that Jesus' suffering was not a matter of impotence; he could have called on a legion of angels. Somehow he had to go through it for fallen creation to be redeemed. God took the Great Pain of his own Son's death and used it to absorb into himself all the minor pains of earth. Suffering was the cost to God of forgiveness.

Human suffering remains meaningless and barren unless we have some assurance that God is sympathetic to our pain, and can somehow heal that pain. In Jesus, we have that assurance.

Thus the Christian message encompasses the full range of anger and despair and darkness expressed so eloquently in a book like *Night*. It offers a complete identification with the suffering world. But Christianity takes a further step as well. It is called the Resurrection, the moment of victory when the last enemy, death itself, is defeated. A seeming tragedy, Jesus' crucifixion, made possible the ultimate healing of the world.

Did God desire the Holocaust? Ask the question another way: Did God desire the death of his own Son? Obviously, because of his character he could not possibly desire such atrocities. And yet both happened, and the question then moves from the unanswerable "Why?" to another question, "To what end?"

At the instant of pain, it may seem impossible to imagine that good can come from tragedy. (It must have seemed so to Christ at Gethsemane.) We never know in advance exactly how suffering can be transformed into a cause for celebration. But that is what we are asked to believe. Faith means believing in advance what will only make sense in reverse.

The Chaplain of Dachau

Not long after reading the books by Elie Wiesel and Corrie ten Boom, I visited the site of one of the Nazi concentration camps. On the grounds of the Dachau camp near Munich, I met with a man who survived the Holocaust and who has taken on a life mission of announcing to the world that God's love is deeper than the sloughs of human depravity. He helped me understand how Corrie ten Boom's hopeful view of life was even possible in such a place.

The man, Christian Reger, spent four years as a prisoner in Dachau. His crime? He had belonged to the Confessing Church, the branch of the German state church which, under the leadership of Martin Niemöller and Dietrich Bonhoeffer, opposed Hitler. Reger, turned over to the authorities by his church organist, was arrested and shipped hundreds of miles away to Dachau.

Since liberation, Reger and other members of the International Dachau Committee have worked hard to restore the concentration camp as a lasting monument and lesson to all humanity. "Never Again" is their slogan. Nonetheless, the camp is difficult to find, since the locals are understandably reluctant to call attention to it.

The day I visited Dachau was gray, chill, and overcast. Morning fog hung low, close to the ground, and as I walked droplets of moisture gathered on my face and hands. Thirty barracks once stood on the site, and concrete foundation blocks a foot high mark out their location. One has been restored, and placards point out that sometimes 1,600 people were pressed into this barrack designed for a crowded 208. The cremation ovens are originals, left standing by the Allied liberators.

The fog, the pervasive grayness, and the unfinished ghost buildings added up to an eerie, solemn scene. A child was dancing along the foundation blocks of the barracks. Alongside the barbed wire fences, lilacs bloomed.

I found Christian Reger in the Protestant Chapel, which stands near a Catholic convent and a Jewish memorial. He wanders the grounds, searching out tourists to converse with in German, English, or French. He answers questions, and freely reminisces about his days there as an inmate.

During the final winter, when coal supplies ran low, the ovens were finally shut off. Prisoners no longer had to put up with the constant stench of burning comrades. Many died of exposure, however, and the bodies were stacked naked in the snow like cordwood, a number stenciled on each with a blue marker. Reger will tell such horror stories if you ask. But he never stops there. He goes on to share his faith, and how even at Dachau he was visited by a God of love.

"Nietzsche said a man can undergo torture if he knows the Why of his life," Reger told me. "But here at Dachau, I learned something far greater. I learned to know the Who of my life. He was enough to sustain me then, and is enough to sustain me still."

It was not always so. After his first month in Dachau, Reger, like Elie Wiesel, abandoned all hope in a loving God. From the perspective of a prisoner of the Nazis, the odds against God's existence seemed too great. Then, in July 1941, something happened to challenge his doubt.

Each prisoner was allowed only one letter a month, and exactly one month from the date of his incarceration Christian Reger received the first news from his wife. In the fragments of the letter, which had been carefully clipped into pieces by a censor, she chatted about the family and assured him of her love. At the very bottom Reger's wife printed a Bible reference: Acts 4:26–29.

Reger, who had smuggled in a Bible, looked up the verses, which formed part of a speech delivered by Peter and John just after their release from prison. "The kings of the earth take their stand, and the rulers gather together against the Lord and against his Anointed One. Indeed Herod and Pontius Pilate met together with the Gentiles and the people of Israel in this city to conspire against your holy servant Jesus, whom you anointed. They did what your power and will had decided beforehand should happen. Now, Lord, consider their threats and enable your servants to speak your word with great boldness."

That afternoon Reger was to undergo interrogation, the most terrifying experience in the camp. He would be called on to name other Christians in the Confessing Church outside. If he succumbed, those Christians would be captured and possibly killed. But if he refused to cooperate, there was a good chance he would be beaten with clubs or tortured with electricity. He knew firsthand about "rulers gathering together against the Lord," but other than that, the verses meant little to him. How could God possibly help him at a time like this?

Reger moved to the waiting area outside the interrogation room. He was trembling. The door opened, and a fellow minister whom Reger had never met came out. Without looking at Reger or changing the expression on his face, he walked over to him, slipped something into Reger's coat pocket, and walked away. Seconds later SS guards appeared and ushered Reger inside the room. The interrogations went well; they were surprisingly easy and involved no violence.

When Reger arrived back at the barracks, he was sweating despite the cold. He breathed deeply for several minutes, trying to calm himself, then crawled into his bunk, covered with straw. Suddenly he remembered the odd encounter with the other minister. He reached in his pocket and pulled out a matchbox. *Oh*, he thought, what a kind gesture. Matches are a priceless commodity in the barracks. He found no matches inside, however, just a folded slip of paper. Reger unfolded the paper, and his heart beat hard against his chest. Neatly printed on the paper was this reference: Acts 4:26–29.

To Reger, it was a miracle, a message directly from God. That minister could not possibly have seen the letter from Reger's wife—the man was a stranger. Had God arranged the event as a demonstration that he was still alive, still able to strengthen, still worthy of trust?

Christian Reger was transformed from that moment. It was a small miracle, as miracles go, but sufficient to anchor his faith in bedrock that could not be shaken, not even by the atrocities he would witness over the next four years in Dachau.

"God did not rescue me and make my suffering easier. He simply assured me that he was alive, and knew I was here. We Christians drew together. We formed a church here, among other convicted pastors and priests—a forced ecumenical movement, we called it. We found our identity as one flesh, as part of Christ's body.

"I can only speak for myself. Others turned from God because of Dachau. Who am I to judge them? I simply know that God met me. For me he was enough, even at Dachau."

As long as he has health, Christian Reger will stiffly pace the grounds of Dachau, speaking to tourists in his warm, thickly accented voice. He will tell them where God was during the long night at Dachau.

PART 4

How Can We Cope with Pain?

13

—◦◦◦—

Frontiers of Recovery

I do not ask the wounded person how he feels, I
myself become the wounded person.

Walt Whitman
Song of Myself

To learn about suffering, I have explored the
lives of people who are almost defined by
it: Brian Sternberg, Joni Eareckson Tada,
survivors of the Holocaust. For most of us, suffering comes for briefer periods and with less intensity. But one fact holds true of afflictions major and
minor: people respond differently.

I have known people with rheumatoid arthritis
who find it difficult to talk about anything else,
while others will only admit their pain after much
prodding and questioning. What makes the difference? Is there a way to predict a person's response
to pain and suffering? Can we learn how to prepare
for pain in such a way as to lessen its impact?

Pain itself, which may seem reflexive, does not
work like a simple cause-and-effect response. True,
neurons fire off whenever they sense a disturbance

that represents danger, but all such messages are filtered through and interpreted by the brain. A person's predisposition and understanding of pain can dramatically alter his or her experience of it. You will respond quite differently to a sudden blow to the face than will a professional boxer, who is paid a huge purse to undergo fifteen rounds of pummeling.

The medical community now freely admits that in a larger sense a person's attitude is one of the chief factors in determining the effect of all suffering. Dr. Robert Ader, a professor of psychiatry and psychology at Rochester School of Medicine, acknowledges that practically all illnesses have emotional factors. He concludes, "The germ theory simply can't account for why people get sick, because if it could—I don't know how big your office is, but if somebody gets the flu then I don't understand why everybody doesn't get it."[1]

Albert Schweitzer used to say that diseases tended to leave him rapidly because they found so little hospitality in his body. Or, as one observer commented less felicitously, "Sometimes it is more important to know what kind of fellah has a germ than what kind of germ has a fellah." Preparations, what we bring in advance, can have a decisive impact on our experience of pain and suffering. And knowing about them can teach us how to minister to others in pain when we ourselves are not suffering.

This book opened with the story of Claudia Claxton, my friend who suddenly found herself battling Hodgkin's disease. I asked Claudia and her husband John why that crisis seemed actually to pull them together, whereas more frequently a life-threatening crisis creates tension and pushes a couple apart.

"I was working as a chaplain's assistant in a hospital at the time," John replied. "I had seen sick and dying patients. In the movies, couples who have fought for years suddenly in the face of danger forget their differences and come together. But it doesn't work that way in real life.

"When a couple encounters a crisis, it magnifies what's already present in the relationship. Since Claudia and I happened to love each other deeply, and had worked on open communication, the crisis drove us to each other. Feelings of blame and anger against each other did not creep in. The crisis of her illness merely brought to the surface and intensified feelings already present."

According to John, the best way to prepare for suffering is to work on a strong, supportive life when you're healthy. You cannot suddenly fabricate foundations of strength; they must have been building all along.

The School of Suffering

The only people who can teach us about suffering—both for the sake of our own preparations and our attempts to comfort others—are the sufferers themselves. Yet someone else's sickness, especially terminal sickness, affronts our own health. It tends to bring out the worst in us: eyes averted out of fear, nervous twitches, empty promises ("Call me if you need anything"), conversation reduced to prattle.

What can we say? Is anything worth saying?

I confess that it is not easy for me to be around suffering people. I cannot imagine a less likely candidate for hospital visitation. I begin to clam up as soon as I open the extra-wide glass doors—because of the smell, I think. Smell has a direct sensory pathway into the brain, and those antiseptic odors trigger in me deep-seated memories of a childhood tonsillectomy. When a nurse in the hallway smiles and nods, I see a giant phantom nurse leaning over me with a plastic bag to smother me and steal my breath.

After several years of professional schizophrenia—writing and talking about pain while feeling personally helpless around it—I decided I should set aside my awkwardness and force myself to be near suffering people on a regular basis. About this time, a friend discovered he had one of the rarest, most severe forms of cancer. In medical history, the doctors told Jim, only twenty-seven people had been treated with his specific condition. The other twenty-six had all died. Jim was charting new territory, alone.

He was thirty-three years old, and had been married only ten months. Earlier that year he and his wife had spent their honeymoon sailing in the Caribbean. Jim cared primarily about his career, his passion for downhill skiing, and his young marriage. Suddenly, he faced the prospect of dying, and he needed help.

At Jim's invitation I began accompanying him to a therapy group at a nearby hospital. People join therapy groups for a variety of reasons: to improve self-image, to learn how to relate to others, to over-come an addiction. This therapy group, called Make Today Count, consisted of people who were dying. They used the euphemism "life-threatening illnesses" for their congeries of cancer, multiple sclerosis, hepatitis, muscular dystrophy, and other such diseases. Each member of the group knew that his or her life had boiled down to two issues: surviving and, failing that, preparing for death.

The first meeting was very hard for me. We met in an open waiting room area, sitting on cheap molded plastic chairs of a garish orange color doubtless chosen to create an atmosphere of institutional cheer. Bored-looking orderlies rolled stretchers up and down the hallways. Elevator doors opened and closed. I tried to ignore a nearby loud-speaker that periodically crackled with an announcement or a doctor's page.

Most people were in their thirties. That age group, usually so oblivious of death, seemed to have the deepest need to talk about its unexpected intrusion. The meeting began with each person "checking in." Someone had died in the month since the last meeting, and the social worker provided details of his last days and the funeral. Jim whispered to me that this was the one depressing aspect of the group: Its members were always disappearing.

I had expected a somber tone at the meeting, but found the opposite. Tears flowed freely, of course, but these people talked easily and comfortably about disease and death. The group served as the one place where they could talk so freely and still count on an empathetic response. They described the sad, almost bizarre manner in which most friends skirted the one thing that mattered most, the fact of their illness. Here in the group, they could lower all protective barriers.

Nancy showed off a new wig purchased to cover her baldness, a side effect of chemotherapy treatments. She joked that she had always wanted straight hair and now her brain tumor had finally given her an excuse to get it. Steve, a young black man, admitted he was terrified of what lay ahead. He had battled Hodgkin's disease as a teenager and had apparently won, but now, ten years later, symptoms were unexpectedly returning. He didn't know how to break the news to his fiancée. Lorraine, afflicted with tumors on her spinal cord, lay on the floor throughout the meeting and rarely talked. She had come to cry, she said, not to talk.

I was most affected by the one elderly person in the room, a handsome, gray-haired woman with the broad, bony face of an Eastern European immigrant. Speaking in simple declarative sentences wrapped in a thick accent, she expressed her loneliness. The group asked if she had any family. She replied that an only son was trying to get emergency leave from the Air Force in Germany. And her husband? She swallowed hard a few times and then said, "He came to see me just once. I was in the hospital. He brought me my bathrobe and a few things. The doctor stood in the hallway and told him about my leukemia." Her voice started to crack and she dabbed at her eyes before continuing. "He went home that night, packed up all his things, and left. I never saw him again."

"How long had you been married?" I asked after a pause. The group gasped aloud at her answer: "Thirty-seven years." (I later learned that some researchers report a seventy percent breakup rate in marriages in which one of the partners has a terminal illness. In this group of thirty people, no marriages remained intact longer than two years—including my friend Jim's.)

I met with that group for a year. Each person in it lived with the peculiar intensity that only death can bring. Certainly I cannot say I "enjoyed" the meetings; that would be the wrong word. Yet they became for me one of the most meaningful events of each month. In contrast to a party, where participants try to impress each other with signs of status and power and wit, in this group no one was trying to impress. Clothes, fashion, apartment furnishings, job titles, new cars—what do these things mean to people who are preparing to die?

The Make Today Count meetings seemed to confirm the "megaphone value" of suffering. More than any other people I had met, they concentrated on ultimate issues. They could not deny death, for every day they were, in Augustine's phrase, "deafened by the clanking chains of mortality." I found myself wishing that some of my shallow, hedonistic friends would attend a meeting.

Among these people, I, who had the audacity to write a book on the subject, felt ignorant. For a year I learned as a servant at the feet of teachers in the school of suffering. Most of what I will write in the next few chapters about preparing for suffering, and helping others, I gleaned from my experiences in that group.

What Helps Most

What can we do to help those who hurt? And who can help us when we suffer?

I begin with some discouraging good news. The discouraging aspect is that I cannot give you a magic formula. There is nothing much you can say to help suffering people. Some of the brightest minds in history have explored every angle of the problem of pain, asking why people hurt, yet still we find ourselves stammering out the same questions, unrelieved.

As I've mentioned, not even God attempted an explanation of cause or a rationale for suffering in his reply to Job. The great king David, the righteous man Job, and finally even the Son of God reacted to pain much the same as we do. They recoiled from it, thought it horrible, did their best to alleviate it, and finally cried out to God in despair because of it. Personally, I find it discouraging that we can come up with no final, satisfying answer for people in pain.

And yet viewed in another way that nonanswer is surprisingly good news. When I have asked suffering people, "Who helped you?" not one person has mentioned a Ph.D. from Yale Divinity School or a famous philosopher. The kingdom of suffering is a democracy, and we all stand in it or alongside it with nothing but our naked humanity. All of us have the same capacity to help, and that is good news.

No one can package or bottle "the appropriate response to suffering." And words intended for everyone will almost always prove worthless for one individual person. If you go to the sufferers themselves and ask for helpful words, you may find discord. Some recall a friend who cheerily helped distract them from the illness, while others think such an approach insulting. Some want honest, straightforward confrontation; others find such discussion unbearably depressing.

In short, there is no magic cure for a person in pain. Mainly, such a person needs love, for love instinctively detects what is needed. Jean Vanier, founder of l'Arche movement, says it well: "Wounded people who have been broken by suffering and sickness ask for only one thing: a heart that loves and commits itself to them, a heart full of hope for them."[2]

In fact, the answer to the question, "How do I help those who hurt?" is exactly the same as the answer to the question, "How do I love?" If you asked me for a Bible passage to teach you how to help suffering people, I would point to 1 Corinthians 13 and its eloquent depiction of love. That is what a suffering person needs: love, and not knowledge and wisdom. As is so often his pattern, God uses very ordinary people to bring about healing.

Nevertheless, love itself breaks down into specific and practical acts. We meet suffering people in every school, in every church, in every public building, as well as in every hospital. All of us will one day join them. As I've listened to what they have to say, I have come up with four "frontiers" where every suffering person will do battle: the frontiers of fear, helplessness, meaning, and hope. Our response to suffering depends largely on the outcome of our struggle in those frontiers.

14

———◦◦◦———

Fear

I have seen the moment of my greatness flicker,
And I have seen the eternal Footman hold my coat,
  and snicker,
And in short, I was afraid.

T. S. Eliot
The Love Song of J. Alfred Prufrock

Fear is the universal primal response to suffering. And yet beyond doubt it is also the single greatest "enemy of recovery."

John Donne knew fear well. He wrote his meditations in a day when waves of bubonic plague, the Black Death, were sweeping through his city of London. The last epidemic alone killed 40,000 people. Thousands more fled to the countryside, transforming whole neighborhoods into ghost towns. For six weeks Donne lay at the threshold of death, believing he had contracted the plague. The prescribed treatments were as vile as the illness: bleedings, strange poultices, the application of vipers and pigeons to remove evil vapors.

After noting signs of fear in his attending physician, Donne set down this description:

> Fear insinuates itself in every action or pas-
> sion of the mind, and as gas in the body will
> counterfeit any disease, and seem the stone, and
> seem the gout, so fear will counterfeit any dis-
> ease of the mind. . . . A man that is not afraid of
> a lion is afraid of a cat; not afraid of starving,
> and yet is afraid of some joint of meat at the
> table presented to feed him. . . . I know not what
> fear is, nor I know not what it is that I fear now;
> I fear not the hastening of my death, and yet I
> do fear the increase of the disease; I should be-
> lie nature if I should deny that I feared this.[1]

One would think that the advances in medicine
since John Donne's day would vastly reduce our
fears. Not so. Modern hospitals place patients in private rooms in which they lie all day with little to occupy their minds other than their unwell state. Sophisticated machines whir and hum, some with tentacles
probing inside the patient's own body. In the hallway
outside, physicians and nurses discuss a prognosis in
lowered voices, going over complex graphs and figures. The patient is poked and studied and bled and
charted, "for your own good," of course. All in all, a
perfect breeding ground for fear, which grows like a
staph infection in hospital corridors.

The Pain Augmenter
We speak of fear as an emotion, but actually it operates more like a reflex action, with immediate

physiological effects. Muscles tense up and contract involuntarily, often increasing pressure on damaged nerves and producing more pain. Blood pressure changes too, and we may go pale, or flush red. A very frightened person may even experience vascular collapse and faint. All animals sense fear—even an amoeba flees heat and pain—but humans seem especially susceptible. A spastic colon, for example, a common sign of human anxiety, is virtually unknown in other species.[2]

As the emotion of fear, based in the mind, filters down into the lower recesses of the body, it alters the perception of pain. A person with an exaggerated fear of hypodermic needles quite literally feels more pain from an injection than does a diabetic who has learned to take injections every day. The physiology is the same in both persons; fear makes the difference.

Asenath Petrie, a researcher at the University of Chicago, developed a system of classifying people into three categories according to their responses to pain (as discussed in her book, *The Individuality of Pain and Suffering*). "Augmenters" have a low threshold of pain and tend to exaggerate all pain. "Reducers," who demonstrate a higher threshold of pain, can tolerate much more without noticeable disturbance. "Moderates" fall in between. Petrie found that fear is the single factor that best describes the augmenters' approach toward pain.

During World War II Henry K. Beecher of the Harvard Medical School studied soldiers in Italy who had been wounded in battle. With astonishment

he observed that only one in three soldiers with severe wounds asked for morphine. Many said they
felt no pain, or the pain was minor. This pattern
contrasted sharply with what Beecher had seen as
an anesthesiologist in private practice: eighty percent of those patients, who had wounds very similar to the soldiers', begged for morphine or other
pain-killers.

Morphine works its magic primarily by reduc-
ing the patient's fear and anxiety levels. Evidently,
the soldiers' fears had been replaced, either by a
feeling of pride in the significance of the wound, or,
in some cases, by relief at being away from the
battlefield. Beecher concluded, "There is no simple
direct relationship between the wound per se and
the pain experienced. The pain is in very large part
determined by other factors."[3]

For most of us, the fears that accompany suffering are easy to identify. We fear the experience of
pain, and the unknown. We may also fear death. Am
I a burden? What am I missing out on? Do I have a
future? Will I ever be healthy again? Am I being
punished?

People who are suffering, whether from physical or psychological pain, often feel an oppressive
sense of aloneness. They feel abandoned, by God
and also by others, because they must bear the pain
alone and no one else quite understands. Loneliness
increases the fear, which in turn increases the pain,
and downward the spiral goes.

One night a member of the Make Today Count
group brought to the meeting a book filled with

drawings made by sick children. Their stick figures and simple words vividly expressed these primary fears. One boy drew a large, ugly military tank, bristling with weapons. Just in front of the tank, at the end of the gun barrel, he placed a tiny stick figure—himself—holding up a red stop sign.

Another boy drew an oversized hypodermic needle with a barbed fishhook on the end. An eight-year-old girl drew herself lying in a hospital bed, with the caption, "I'm lonely. I wish I was in my own bed. I don't like it in here. It smells funny." A few pages later, the same girl had another drawing, this time in the setting of a doctor's office. The chair, examining table, and filing cabinets were drawn on a giant scale. The girl portrayed herself as very small, sitting on the edge of the table. A balloon coming out of her mouth contained two words: "I'm scared."

Disarming Fear

In a sense, the entire first half of this book represents my own attempt to "disarm" fear. Knowledge about pain and an understanding of the role it plays in life help to diminish my fear. I now view pain not as an enemy I must overcome, but rather as a protective signal I must reach accommodation with. I marvel at the incredible design that went into the nervous system. I visualize pain not as a soiled spot I must somehow bleach out but as an example of my body talking to me about a subject of vital importance.

Pain is by far the most effective way for my body to get my attention. Thus I start by listening to my pain. Now that I understand its value, suffering is much less fearful. I have also found that along with such knowledge comes gratitude, one of my most effective emotional weapons in fighting fear.

At another level, the spiritual level, my study of the Bible has convinced me that the fact of suffering does not mean God is against me. Mainly through the example of Jesus, I have learned to see that God is on our side; Paul calls him, appropriately, "the Father of compassion and the God of all comfort" (2 Corinthians 1:3).

The Bible is a Christian's guidebook, and I believe its wisdom about suffering offers a great antidote to fear. "Perfect love drives out fear"—personal knowledge of the God of perfect love can conquer fear as light destroys darkness. I need not engage in frenzied efforts to "muster up faith." God is already full of loving concern, and I need not impress him with spiritual calisthenics.

The Christian has many resources available to help stave off fear. Just as the emotion of fear filters down from the mind to cause direct physiological changes, so the act of prayer can counter those same effects by fixing my attention away from my body to a consciousness of soul and spirit. Prayer cuts through the sensory overload and allows me to direct myself to God. As I do so my body grows still, and calm. Visceral muscles tightened by fear begin to relax. An inner peace replaces tension.

These same results can be achieved through meditation exercises, of course, but prayer to God offers additional benefits. It helps fight the isolation of pain by moving my focus away from my self and my own needs as I strive to consider the needs of others. Remember how the tolling of the bell prompted John Donne to think of his neighbor who had died of plague.

Donne's *Devotions*, in fact, offers a wonderful model of a Christian learning to disarm fear. As the quotation early in this chapter shows, Donne knew fear well. Most of the time he battled such fears alone, for in those days victims of contagious disease were subject to quarantine. As he lay on his bed he wondered if God, too, was participating in the quarantine. Where was God's promised presence?

Donne's real fear was not of the tinny clamor of pain cells all over his body; he feared God. He asked the "Why me?" question over and over again. Calvinism was still new then, and he wondered if God was behind the plague after all. Guilt from his spotted past lurked like a demon nearby. Perhaps he was indeed suffering as a result of some previous sin.

Donne never really resolves the "Why me?" questions in his book, but *Devotions* does record, step by step, how he came to resolve his fears. Obsessed, he reviews every biblical occurrence of the word "fear." As he does so, it dawns on him that life will always include circumstances that incite fear: if not illness, financial hardship, if not poverty, rejection, if not loneliness, failure. In such a world, Donne has a choice: to fear God, or to fear everything else.

In a passage reminiscent of Paul's litany in Romans 8 ("For I am convinced that neither death nor life, neither angels nor demons . . . will be able to separate us from the love of God. . . .”), Donne checks off his potential fears. Great enemies? They pose no threat, for God can vanquish any enemy. Famine? No, for God can supply. Death? Even that, the worst human fear, is no permanent barrier to those who fear God.

Donne determines that his best course is to cultivate a proper fear of the Lord, for that fear can supplant all others. Finally he prays, “. . . as thou hast given me a repentance, not to be repented of, so give me, O Lord, a fear, of which I may not be afraid.” In the most important sense, it did not matter whether his sickness was a chastening or merely a natural accident. In either case he would trust God, for in the end trust represents the proper fear of the Lord.

In *Devotions*, Donne likens the process to his changing attitude toward physicians. Initially, as they probed his body for new symptoms and discussed their findings in hushed tones outside his room, he could not help feeling afraid. But in time, seeing their compassionate concern, he became convinced that they deserved his trust. The same pattern applies to God. We often do not understand his methods or the reasons behind them. But the underlying issue is whether he is a trustworthy “physician.” Donne decided yes.

What is the right way to approach a God we fear? In answer, Donne holds up a phrase from Matthew’s story of the women who discovered Jesus’ empty tomb: they hurried away from the scene “with fear and yet great joy.” Donne sees in their "two legs of fear and joy" a pattern for himself.

Fear was surely in the air at the time of the Resurrection. How could they not fear a God of such awesome power? The women had, after all, met Jesus standing at the edge of the garden, alive again. Strange things were happening. They ran from the scene on legs of fear, yes, but also on legs of joy, for the strange happenings were signs of the best possible news: Jesus had conquered even death. And with that same hope John Donne found at last a fear of which he need not be afraid.

Availability

A different situation arises when it is not I who suffer, but someone else whom I want to help. What can I do to alleviate their fear? I have learned that simple availability is the most powerful force we can contribute to help calm the fears of others.

Instinctively, I shrink back from people who are in pain. Who can know whether they want to talk about their predicament or not? Do they want to be consoled, or cheered up? What good can my presence possibly do? My mind spins out these rationalizations and as a result I end up doing the worst thing possible: I stay away.

Again and again suffering people, especially my friends in Make Today Count, have stressed how much it means when healthy people make themselves available. It is not our words or our insights that they want most; it is our mere presence. By being alongside at a time of need we convey the same comfort that a parent gives a confused and wounded child: "It's all right, it's all right." The world will go on. I am with you in this scary time.

Tony Campolo tells the story of going to a funeral home to pay his respects to the family of an acquaintance. By mistake he ended up in the wrong parlor. It held the body of an elderly man, and his widow was the only mourner present. She seemed so lonely that Campolo decided to stay for the funeral. He even drove with her to the cemetery.

At the end of the graveside service, as he and the woman were driving away, Campolo finally confessed that he had not known her husband. "I thought as much," said the widow. "I didn't recognize you. But it doesn't really matter." She squeezed his arm so hard it hurt. "You'll never, ever, know what this means to me."

I have mentioned that no one offers the name of a philosopher when I ask the question, "Who helped you most?" Most often they answer by describing a quiet, unassuming person. Someone who was there whenever needed, who listened more than talked, who didn't keep glancing down at a watch, who hugged and touched, and cried. In short, someone who was available, and came on the sufferer's terms and not their own.

One woman, a cancer patient in the Make Today Count group, mentioned her grandmother. A rather shy lady, she had nothing to offer but time. She simply sat in a chair and knitted while her granddaughter slept. She was available to talk, or fetch a glass of water, or make a phone call. "She was the only person there on my terms," said the granddaughter. "When I woke up frightened, it would reassure me just to see her there."

We rightly disparage Job's three friends for their insensitive response to his suffering. But read the account again: When they came, they sat in silence beside Job for seven days and seven nights before opening their mouths. As it turned out, those were the most eloquent moments they spent with him.

Jewish people practice a custom called *shiva* after a death in the community. For eight days friends, neighbors, and relatives practically take over the house of the mourning person, bringing their own fruit crates to sit on. They provide food, clean up, carry on conversation, and, in short, force their presence on the griever. The grieving person who desires tranquillity or privacy may find the presence of so many guests irritating. But the message comes through loudly: We will not leave you alone. We will bear this pain with you. Fear, which thrives on loneliness, wilts away.

In one highly symbolic meal, the visitors feed the mourner like a baby, with their own forks and spoons. Wisdom of the ages has taught their culture this ritual of enforced availability, for the mourner needs the presence of others whether or not he or she acknowledges the need.

A story is told about the great composer Beethoven, a man not known for social grace. His deafness made conversation difficult and humiliating for him. When he learned of the death of a friend's son, Beethoven, overcome with grief, hurried to the griever's home. He had no words of comfort to offer. But he saw a piano in the room, and went to it. For the next half hour he played the piano, pouring out his emotions in the most expressive way he knew. After he had finished playing, he left. The friend later remarked that no one else's visit had meant so much.

God's Agents

Besides personal presence, what else can we offer? What does one say at such a time? Consistently I have gotten the same answer from suffering people: it matters little what we say—our concern and availability matter far more. If we can offer a listening ear, that may be the most appreciated gift of all.

Betsy Burnham, in a book written shortly before her death from cancer, told about one of the most meaningful letters she received during her illness:

> Dear Betsy,
> I am afraid and embarrassed. With the problems you are facing, what right do I have to tell you I am afraid? I have found one excuse after another for not coming to see you. With all my heart, I want to reach out and help you and your family. I want to be available and useful. Most of all, I want to say the words that will make you well. But the fact remains that I am afraid. I have never before written anything like this. I hope you will understand and forgive me.
>
> Love,
> Anne[4]

Anne could not find the personal strength needed to make herself available to her friend. But at least she shared her honest feelings with Betsy and made herself vulnerable. That too was a form of availability.

Another woman, reflecting on letters that she and her husband received in the midst of a family tragedy, told me that the letters' very clumsiness made them meaningful to her. Many writers would apologize for their ineptness in not knowing what to say. But to her the anguished groping for words was the whole point: their "sheer floundering confusion" best expressed what she and her family were feeling too.

The suffering person will probably expect from you the same kind of friendship you had before. Close relationships rarely develop between suffering people and strangers. Instead, the crisis forces them back to relationships they had built in health. Offer the same qualities you shared in healthy times. If you normally tell jokes, do so. If it would be natural for you to read the Bible and pray together, do that. If your previous relationship consisted of light conversation and a little gossip, start at that level until you feel comfortable to move on. Everything else has changed in a sick person's world; he or she needs assurance that friendship has not changed.

Time restrictions put limits on us, of course, and not all of us have the freedom to set aside other demands and offer large blocks of time. But we can all pray, a powerful form of availability. And we can offer regular, consistent tokens of our care. Suffering people say that fear and loneliness steal in at unexpected moments, and regularity is often more important than the quantity of time a person can give. Regularity becomes increasingly important with illnesses that tend to drag out over long periods of time, such as Parkinson's disease.

One man told me the most helpful person during his long illness was an office colleague who called every day, just to check. His visits, usually twice a week, never exceeded fifteen minutes, but the consistency of his calls and visits became a fixed point, something he could count on when everything else in his life seemed unstable.

There are limits, of course, on what mere friendship can accomplish. Out of self-pity, suffering people may erect barriers against you. "You'll never understand; you've never been through something like this," they may say. In such cases a person who has been through a similar experience may be best qualified to help, especially with the problem of fear.

Joni Eareckson Tada was jarred out of her self-pity by a hospital visit from a cheerful, radiant quadriplegic (she now continues the chain by ministering to others). Father Damien bore no fruit in his work among those with leprosy in Molokai, Hawaii, until he contracted the disease himself and could relate to them as a fellow-sufferer. Recognizing this principle, hospitals wisely cooperate with programs in which a woman facing a mastectomy, for example, can receive "friendship counseling" from another who has lived through the experience.

Make Today Count itself represents such a program. Its founder, Orville Kelly, realized that no one fully understood his fear except other cancer patients. As a result, he organized the first mutual support network for people with life-threatening illnesses. Now the American Cancer Society sponsors a twenty-four-hour-a-day phone line open for counseling cancer patients.

Still, those who stand alongside with no special skills at all need not feel useless. Nothing else—no learned "how-to" program, no expensive gift—is worth more to the sufferer than the comfortable assurance of your physical presence. Let me say this carefully, but say it nonetheless. I believe we in the body of Christ are called to show love when God seems not to.

Suffering people often have the sense that God has left them. No one expressed this better than C. S. Lewis in the poignant journal he kept after his wife's death (*A Grief Observed*). Lewis said that at the moment of his most profound need, God, who had always been available to him, suddenly seemed absent. Lewis felt fear, and abandonment, and in the end it was the community of other Christians who helped to restore him.

Remember, too, the Bible studies that saw Corrie ten Boom through Nazi concentration camps, and the stranger who slipped a simple word of encouragement to Christian Reger. God made his presence known to them through his agents, other hu-

man beings. Likewise, those of us who stand alongside must sometimes voice prayers that the suffering person cannot yet pray. In moments of extreme
suffering or grief, very often God's love is best perceived through the flesh of ordinary people like you
and me. In such a way we can indeed function as
the body of Jesus Christ.

15

——◦◦◦——

Helplessness

The doctor said: this-and-that indicates that this-and-that is wrong with you, but if an analysis of this-and-that does not confirm our diagnosis, we must suspect you of having this-and-that, then . . . and so on. There was only one question Ivan Ilyich wanted answered: was his condition dangerous or not? But the doctor ignored that question as irrelevant.

Leo Tolstoy
The Death of Ivan Ilyich

D r. Curt Richter, a psychologist from Johns Hopkins University, used two wild rats in a rather perverse experiment. He dropped Rat One, the "control" animal, into a tank of warm water and timed the reaction. Since rats are good swimmers, the creature paddled and thrashed around for sixty hours before it finally succumbed to exhaustion and drowned.

Richter added a step with Rat Two, holding the animal tightly in his hands for a few minutes until it ceased struggling. When he dropped it in the water, it reacted very differently. After splashing around for a few minutes, Rat Two passively sank to the bottom of the tank and died. Richter theorizes that it simply "gave up." The futility of the struggle in his hands had convinced the rat that its fate was hopeless even before it hit the water. In effect, Rat Two died of resigned helplessness.[1]

Other experiments demonstrate that the feeling of helplessness, like fear, can actually change physiology. Two different groups of rats are subjected to the same electrical shocks. The animals in Group One, which have a measure of control, soon learn to turn off the current by manipulating a lever. Group Two, however, has no lever. After a while, simply because of stress—the voltage is harmless—the immune system carried by their blood undergoes radical changes, and rats in the second group become much more vulnerable to disease.

Experiments on humans, not quite so perverse, likewise show that the feeling of helplessness alters not merely a person's psychological attitude but the actual perception of pain itself. The threshold of pain can be raised as much as forty-five percent by simple diversion tactics.

In one series of experiments, researchers tried to divert the subject's attention by ringing bells, repeatedly touching his hand, reading an adventure story aloud, and having the subject read a column of numbers. When the scientists used such tactics during a test of heat tolerance, they had to apply forty-five percent more heat for the preoccupied subject to notice the pain. The researchers were startled to see blisters swelling up unnoticed on their subjects' arms as those subjects concentrated on counting from fifty to one, backwards. On the other hand, if the subject had nothing to do but think about his pain (as is true in many hospitals and nursing homes), he showed much greater sensitivity.[2]

Losing a Sense of Place

People in my Make Today Count group talked about a syndrome they labeled "pre-mortem dying," in effect an advanced case of helplessness. It develops when well-intentioned relatives and friends try to make the dying person's last months more bearable. The syndrome starts with comments like these: "Oh, you mustn't do that! I know you have always taken out the garbage, but *really*, not in your condition. Let me do it." "Don't burden yourself with balancing the checkbook. It would just create an unnecessary worry for you. I'll take care of it from now on." "I think you'd better stay home. Your resistance is so low."

Gradually, inexorably, everything that has given a person a sense of place, a role in life, is taken away. A mother encourages her single daughter to sell her house and move back home. The daughter does so, but soon discovers that in the process of being helped she has also lost her independent identity. Feelings of worth and value, made precarious by the illness, slide further away. As one man told me, "All my life I've gotten feedback—grades in school, performance appraisals at work, pep talks from athletic coaches. Suddenly I have no way to measure my performance in life. If I have a to-do list, I'm the only one who cares whether it gets done."

Obviously, a very sick person must sometimes depend on others to help manage the practical matters of life. But as I learned from the group members, we bystanders can too easily slip into a pattern that, if unchecked, may eradicate everything that gives a person dignity. Dr. Eric Cassell, an internist at Cornell University, concluded about his patients, "If I had to pick the aspect of illness that is most destructive to the sick, I would choose the loss of control."[3]

Suffering people already have misgivings about their place in the world. Often they must stop working, and the fatigue brought on by illness or treatment makes every action more difficult and tedious. And yet, like all of us, they need to cling to some assurance that they have a place, that life would not go on without a bump if they simply disappeared, that the checkbook would go unbalanced except for their expert attention. Wise companions learn to seek out the delicate balance between offering help and offering too much help.

Modern society greatly compounds this problem of a sense of place, for it has no natural "place" for sick people. We put them out of sight, behind the institutional walls of hospitals and nursing homes. We make them lie in beds, with nothing to occupy them but the remote control devices that operate the television sets. They live according to other people's schedules, not their own: a nurse wakes them up, the hospital decides when to feed them, visitors drop by, a nurse turns out the light at night. (For this reason, many patients who welcome visitors prefer that they call first before dropping by—it gives them more a feeling of control over their schedule.)

I have made a kind of study of card racks, sometimes visiting new drug stores and card shops just to browse. The cards for sick people fall into distinct categories: schmaltzy cards with pictures of flowers and treacly poems, racy cards with messages about all the wild parties the recipient is missing, sincere cards with a solemn expression of sympathy, clever cards illustrated by *New Yorker* cartoonists. All have the same implicit message, expressed in their title: "get-well cards."

One card has on the cover, "Get well soon," and then inside, "otherwise somebody might steal your job." Another says, "Everybody hopes you feel better soon, except me," and inside, "I hope you feel better right now!" "This is no time to be sick," says one of Boynton's hippos from a hospital bed, "the weekend's coming up." What complaint could I have against these clever expressions of sympathy? The subtle, underlying message: You are out of commission, useless. You don't fit, at work, at parties. You are missing out. You are not OK. Only get well, and then you can rejoin life.

My friends in the Make Today Count group, none of whom will likely get well, impressed upon me that something as innocuous as a greeting card can deepen the devastating sense of feeling out of place, with no valid role in life.

I sometimes dream of producing my own line of get-well cards. I already have an idea for the first one. The cover would have huge letters, perhaps with fireworks in the background, spelling out CONGRATULATIONS!!! Inside, this message: ". . . to the 98 trillion cells in your body that are still working smoothly and efficiently."

I would look for ways to communicate the message that a sick person is not a *sick person,* but rather a person of worth and value who happens to have some bodily parts that are not functioning well. Perhaps the exercise of writing a series of cards like that would help me fight my own tendency of mentally labeling individuals as sick and disabled, thus complicating their battle against helplessness.

In an address to German deaconesses involved with disabled people, theologian Jürgen Moltmann attacked the modern distinction that tends to distance healthy people from the disabled or handicapped. In reality there is no such thing as a non-handicapped life, he said; only the ideal of health set up by a society of the capable condemns a certain group of people to be called handicapped. Our society arbitrarily defines health as the capacity for work and the capacity for enjoyment, but "true health is something quite different. True health is the strength to live, the strength to suffer, and the strength to die. Health is not a condition of my body; it is the power of my soul to cope with the varying condition of that body." In that respect, every human life is limited, vulnerable, and weak.[4]

Fighting Back

Norman Cousins, longtime editor of *Saturday Review,* waged a one-man crusade against modern health-care systems that foster helplessness. Hospitalized for a mysterious condition of creeping paralysis (diagnosed as ankylosing spondylitis, a degeneration of connective tissue in the spine), Cousins found that the hospital seemed perfectly designed to immobilize not only his body but his spirit. "The will to live is not a theoretical abstraction, but a physiological reality with therapeutic characteristics," he wrote in *Anatomy of an Illness.* But the hospital environment tended to stifle that will to live.

Medication fogged over his consciousness of reality. Confinement to bed made him restless and depressed. Nurses and doctors invaded his body orifices and stole away fluids. Unable to work and shut away from his most intimate relationships, he felt a gradual loss of control over his destiny.

Cousins sought to identify the obstacles facing him, as shown in this partial list:

> There was first of all the feeling of helplessness—a serious disease in itself.
> There was the subconscious fear of never being able to function normally again. . . .
> There was the reluctance to be thought a complainer.
> There was the desire not to add to the already great burden of apprehension felt by one's family; this added to the isolation.

There was the conflict between the terror of loneliness and the desire to be left alone.

There was the lack of self-esteem, the subconscious feeling perhaps that our illness was a manifestation of our inadequacy.

There was the fear that decisions were being made behind our backs, that not everything was made known that we wanted to know, yet dreaded knowing.

There was the morbid fear of intrusive technology, fear of being metabolized by a data base, never to regain our faces again.

There was resentment of strangers who came at us with needles and vials—some of which put supposedly magic substances in our veins, and others which took more of our blood than we thought we could afford to lose.

There was the distress of being wheeled through white corridors to laboratories for all sorts of strange encounters with compact machines and blinking lights and whirling discs.

And there was the utter void created by the longing—ineradicable, unremitting, pervasive—for warmth of human contact. A warm smile and an outstretched hand were valued even above the offerings of modern science, but the latter were far more accessible than the former.[5]

Norman Cousins knew that doctors could not "heal" him; at best they could harness the vitality that existed in his body's cells. But he felt that vitality ebbing away. In an attempt to regain control over his own destiny and revive his will to live, he launched an all-out campaign against helplessness. As his book records, he employed some rather unorthodox tactics.

First, Cousins posted a sign on his door limiting hospital personnel to one blood specimen every three days, which they had to share. They had been taking as many as four blood samples in a day, simply because it was more convenient for each hospital department to obtain their own samples. What seemed to hospital staff a case of patient revolt was to Cousins an important step in asserting control over his own body.

Cousins also borrowed a movie projector and scheduled time each day to watch movies by the Marx Brothers and Charlie Chaplin. He figured that since negative emotions demonstrably produce chemical changes in the body, perhaps positive emotions might counteract them. He made the "joyous discovery that ten minutes of genuine belly laughter would give me at least two hours of painfree sleep."

As soon as his health would permit, Cousins moved from his hospital room to a nearby hotel room. It cost one-third as much, provided a more serene (and more luxurious) environment, and allowed him to schedule meals and wake-up calls at his convenience, no one else's.

Although Norman Cousins warns against making his regimen a model for other people, his results were impressive indeed. At the onset, his doctor had given him one chance in five hundred of a full recovery; some paralysis seemed inevitable. But he recovered completely, extended his life by several more happy decades, and, long after the age most people retire, took up a new career of lecturing on health matters.

Helpless No More

The changes Norman Cousins suggests would call for a complete overhaul of modern health care systems, something that is unlikely to happen soon. But we can make small steps toward his goal of "humanizing" health care, helping ourselves as patients to feel less like a chip in a computer and more like a partner in recovery.

Some solutions are simple. In a 1984 study reported in *Science*, Roger S. Ulrich found that gallbladder patients who looked out over a cluster of trees instead of a brick wall had shorter post-operative stays and took fewer moderate painkillers. Ideally, he concluded, hospitals should be built next to public parks, or in a scenic environment. More and more architects today are taking account of such environmental factors as they design medical facilities.

In an attempt to recruit patients as partners in the battle against helplessness, some pain clinics negotiate "contracts" with their patients. First they get the patient to articulate his or her goals: to learn to walk, to lift an arm high without pain, to get a part-time job. Then they break down those goals into stages and assign weekly goals: standing for five minutes, then ten minutes; walking across the room with a cane, and then without a cane. Medical personnel chart each patient's weekly progress, and enthusiastically praise each new level of achievement.

Why must we rely on paid professionals for such encouragement? Friends and relatives can accomplish the very same thing by forming a "contract" with the recovering person and then rewarding any slight victory over helplessness.

We can also make certain the recovering patient has meaningful diversions. Just as the perception of pain increases in intensity when a research subject has no other diversions, the feeling of helplessness heightens when a patient lies alone, with nothing to do or think about except pain. I cannot imagine a more challenging place to combat pain than in a hospital room. Yet even in that sterile environment can be found sources for diversion.

In hospitals, so little happens that you must attend to small details. Instead of gulping from the paper cup, swallow slowly, with an awareness of the glottal muscles and of the texture and taste of water in your mouth. Stare at individual petals of the flowers in the room, searching for subtle patterns of design. Run your hands over sheets and bed and blankets to feel the textures.

A resilient human spirit can find extraordinary ways of combating isolation and deprivation. Benjamin Weir was a Presbyterian missionary in Beirut, Lebanon, kidnapped by Shiite Moslems. For sixteen months he was held in the most depressing of circumstances. He had no view of trees out a window; blindfolded most of the time, he had no view at all.

His hands manacled, he had no freedom to run his fingers over various textures.

Weir had no control over his schedule, his food, or anything else in his daily routine. And yet even in those circumstances he was able to call upon sufficient reserves of spirit to overcome the deadening sense of helplessness. He had no one to call on but God himself. This is his report on one of the early days of captivity.

I awoke refreshed by my nap. What other gifts would God show me in addition to sleep, a blanket, and a spirit of resistance and survival? Once again I lifted my blindfold and began examining the room. What was here that could bring me close to the sustaining presence of God? I let my imagination have total freedom.

Looking up, I examined an electric wire hanging from the ceiling. The bulb and socket had been removed so that it ended in an arc with three wires exposed. To me, those wires seemed like three fingers. I could see a hand and an arm reaching downward—like the Sistine Chapel in Rome, Michelangelo's fresco of God reaching out his hand and finger toward Adam, creating the first human being. Here God was reaching toward me, reminding me, saying, "You're alive. You are mine; I've made you and called you into being for a divine purpose."

What else? I began counting the horizontal slats of the shutters outside the French doors. There were 120. What could those horizontal pieces of wood stand for, so many of them? That's it! Many of them, a crowd! A cloud of witnesses past and present, who through times of trial have observed the faithfulness of God. . . . This recital of the basics of my faith sent a chill through me. What a message! I desperately needed it in my present setting.

Then my eyes lighted on two white circles near the ceiling, one on the right-hand wall, the other on the left. Everybody in Lebanon knows what they are, plastic covers for electrical connections. Yet what could they be for me? What comes in a pair? Ears! They were the ears of God. The Lord hears the groaning of the saints. So listen to me, dear God; I also surrender to your care and will.[6]

By the end of the day, Weir was humming the hymn, "Count your many blessings, name them one by one." He counted: health, life, food, mattress, pillow, blanket, his wife, his family, faith, hope, prayer, Jesus, Holy Spirit, Father's love. Thirty-three things in all. In the process of reviewing these blessings, he found that his feelings of fear and helplessness had melted away. As the light through the shutter faded, he relaxed and began to get ready for the night.

Reaching Out

In the frontier of helplessness, Norman Cousins fought his battle against an insensitive medical establishment. Benjamin Weir fought his more lonely, internal battle against isolation and despair. For people who have long-term disabilities, one of the best things we can do is to provide tools that allow them to resume "normal" activity.

With computer-driven devices, a fully paralyzed person can now operate a wheelchair, type, and turn on a TV or stereo, all by various combinations of sucking and blowing on an air tube. Such devices can spell the difference between feelings of help-lessness and hope, and even between recovery and defeat. Brian Sternberg's amateur radio hobby and Joni Eareckson Tada's artwork probably contribute more to their mental well-being than even the sup-port of caring friends.

Barbara Wolf wrote a book, *Living with Pain,* about her long struggle against chronic pain. She found that the only times in a day when she com-pletely forgot about the pain were the hours she spent teaching English. Then, her brain's active involve-ment drowned out all other sensations. She learned to channel that same concentration at other times. When a flash of pain hit in the middle of the night, she would organize her next day, work on a lecture, or plan an entire dinner, including all the recipes.

Sometimes going against her own nature, Wolf began forcing herself toward activities that re-quired complete concentration. Distraction, she found, was her single best weapon against pain. "Distraction is inexpensive and non-habit-forming; it does not require a doctor's prescription."[7] In ad-dition to her English teaching, she poured herself into hobbies that demanded her full attention:

parties, pets, sports, politics, writing.

Of the various avenues of distraction open to her, Wolf found that involvement with others was the most effective in quelling her pain. Often, suffering people find a most meaningful sense of place when they learn to reach out to others who hurt. Joni Eareckson Tada claims that the people who helped her most were other quadriplegics who devoted themselves to helping her through the roughest times.

A psychologist in Atlanta told me that he meets two kinds of people. The unhealthy ones go through life crying, "Please love me, please love me." The other group consists of people healthy enough to give, not just receive, love. He says that the best cure for the first group is to help them attain a place of wholeness where they can be lovers and helpers of others. If so, they will automatically fill the deep needs for attention and love inside them.

Similarly, counselors among the suffering strive to get their patients to view themselves as helpers and givers, instead of always being receivers. Joni Eareckson Tada described to me her surprise at learning that many disabled persons in her rehabilitation home stayed there voluntarily. It seemed easier than risking the "outside" world with all its prejudices and dangers. Joni became a leader to them, working at her exercises, inspiring hope, and wanting to be released. The very process of investing in their needs proved therapeutic. She became stronger as her self-concept improved and she stopped thinking of herself as an object of pity.

The French have a saying: "To suffer passes; to have suffered never passes." Too often we think about a ministry of helps as a one-way street in which I, the healthy person, reach out in compassion to assist the wounded. But people who have suffered are the very best equipped to help, and a person crosses the final barrier of helplessness when he or she learns to use the experience of suffering itself as a means of reaching out to others.

Rabbi Harold Kushner cites an old Chinese tale about a woman overwhelmed by grief after the death of her son. When she goes to the holy man for advice, he tells her, "Fetch me a mustard seed from a home that has never known sorrow. We will use it to drive the sorrow out of your life." The tale recounts how the woman goes from house to house, asking if the home has known sorrow. Each one has, of course, and the woman lingers to comfort her hosts until at last the act of ministering to others drives the sorrow from her life.

I know personally of two small-scale ministries, run out of private homes, that put this principle into practice. The first came into being when a woman in California discovered her son, the apple of her eye, was homosexual and was dying of AIDS. She found almost no sympathy and support from her church and community. She felt so alone and needy that she decided to start a newsletter that now joins together a network of parents of gay people. She offers little professional help, and promises no magic cures, but I have read scores of letters from other parents who see this courageous woman as a lifesaver. Having been through the sorrow and grief herself, she now seeks to be available for someone else.

Another woman, in Wisconsin, lost her only son in a Marine Corps helicopter crash. For the first time, she began noticing how frequently helicopter crashes were reported in the news. Now, whenever a military helicopter crashes, she sends a packet of letters and helpful materials to an officer in the Defense Department, who forwards the packet on to the affected families. About half the families strike up a regular correspondence, and in her retirement this Wisconsin woman leads her own "community of suffering." The activity has not solved the grief over her son, of course, but it has given her a sense of place, and she no longer feels helpless against that grief.

A wise sufferer will look not inward, but outward. There is no more effective healer than a wounded healer, and in the process the wounded healer's own scars may fade away.

16

——∞∞∞——

Meaning

It is not so much the suffering as the senselessness of it that is unendurable.

Friedrich Nietzsche

Merlin Olsen, former professional football player, has a well-defined philosophy of pain:

Man is an adaptable creature. One finds out what you can or cannot do. It's like walking into a barnyard. The first thing you smell is manure. Stand there for about five minutes and you don't smell it anymore. The same thing is true of a knee. You hurt that knee. You're conscious of it. But then you start to play at a different level. You change your run a little bit. Or you drive off a different leg. Maybe you alter your stance.

After surgery on my knee, I had to have the fluid drained weekly. Finally, the membrane got so thick they almost had to drive the needle in it with a hammer. I got to the point where I just said, "Damn it, get the needle in there, and get that stuff out."[1]

All participants in a sport like football are subjected to the same body checks, helmet spears, and pileups, and society lavishly rewards them for undergoing such pain. Thus pain from some sources— not only football, but also mountain climbing, a triathlon race, Marine Corps boot camp, torture by an enemy interrogator—individuals are willing to accept. In previous centuries some even honored self-inflicted pain as a sign of great devotion: the coarser the hair shirt and harsher the flagellation, the more pious the worshiper.

Even more remarkably, human beings deliberately inflict pain on themselves for the sake of simple vanity. For centuries Chinese women bound their feet injuriously in order to appear beautiful. Modern women, in addition to wearing too-narrow shoes, also pluck their eyebrows, expose themselves to harmful ultraviolet rays, and undergo plastic surgery on faces, breasts, and buttocks—all to meet cultural standards of beauty. We enhance personal prestige by enduring these voluntary pains, for society ascribes to them a certain meaning that makes them worth pursuing.

Compare two intense pains: the ordeal of a difficult breech delivery and the pain of kidney stones. Considering the number of nerve cells affected and the intensity and duration of pain, the two probably rank fairly close. For childbirth, however, meaning comes implicit in the event. "A woman giving birth to a child has pain because her time has come; but when her baby is born she forgets the anguish because of her joy that a child is born into the world," observed Jesus (John 16:21). A mother's pain produces something with meaning—a new life—and for that reason she can even contemplate repeating the experience. But for the person with kidney stones, what meaning is there?

More than any society in history, our modern one struggles with the meaning of suffering. We no longer view it as a judgment of the gods, but what is it? We grant a measure of meaning to lesser pains, such as those we take on voluntarily, but what meaning does a birth-defective child have? Or cystic fibrosis? Or mental retardation? For us, suffering is something to treat and get over with; but what about suffering that never goes away?

Mostly we see only a negative meaning in suffering: it interrupts health, and slams an unwelcome brake on our pursuit of life, liberty, and happiness. As I've mentioned, any card shop gives the message unmistakably. All that we can wish for suffering people is that they "Get well!" Yet, as one woman with terminal cancer told me, "None of those cards apply to the people in my ward. None of us will get well. We're all going to die here. To the rest of the world, that makes us invalids. Think about that word. Not valid."

What is the meaning of terminal cancer?

I received a letter from a pastor in the Midwest who recorded what happens when meaning begins to unravel. This man's suffering was emotional rather than physical. A "nervous breakdown" his doctors called it, but really it was more a breakdown in meaning.*

> The most painful part of it was the seeming silence of God. I prayed, I thought, to a silent darkness. I have thought a lot about this. He only *seemed* silent. The problem was partly my depression and partly the Christian community. For most Christians I was an embarrassment. Nothing they said dealt with what I endured. One pastor prayed for me in generalities and pieties that were utterly unrelated to the situation. They would not feel my pain.
>
> Other people just avoided me. Ironically, Job's friends were probably a help to him, psychologically. At least they forced out feelings, even if angry ones. Their pronouncements were useless, but they did deal with the questions and gave Job the impression that maybe God was around somewhere. No one in the Christian community, except my wife, helped me even to that degree.

Honoring Pain

One of the most important things we can do for a suffering person is to restore a sense of mean-

---

* Emotional pain, such as acute depression, represents a huge area of suffering that I cannot begin to mention in this book focusing on physical pain. I recommend *A Season of Suffering,* by John H. Timmerman (Multnomah Press, 1987) as a sensitive account of one family's struggle with depression.

ing or significance to the experience.

Actually, the problem is that we already convey meaning, though on a relative scale. When I give seminars on pain, I sometimes illustrate this by calling for audience participation. I ask for the Roman "thumbs up" or "thumbs down" signal: thumbs up if the pain I mention is acceptable, an affliction that attracts sympathy, and thumbs down if the pain is unacceptable and gets little sympathy. Typically, I get these responses:

Broken leg from skiing. Thumbs up all the way. What started out as a stumble on the rope tow ends up, after many retellings, as a double somersault free-fall off a cliff. Friends sign the cast with funny remarks, and the sufferer becomes a virtual hero. The attention is almost worth the pain.

Leprosy. Thumbs down. In my work with Dr. Paul Brand, I have gotten to know leprosy patients. They lobby strongly for the name "Hansen's disease" for one simple reason: the way people respond to the image of leprosy. Although the disease differs in virtually every respect from its stereotype, a person with leprosy still gets judgment and not sympathy. Loneliness is one of the disease's worst aspects.

Influenza. Mixed response. Some people hold thumbs down because no one really *likes* fevers, vomiting, and body aches. On the other hand, the flu, being universal, attracts much sympathy. We all know how it feels. "Take it easy," we say. "Stay at home a few extra days. Get your strength back."

Mumps. Response depends on the age you're

talking about. Children with mumps get plenty of sympathy. They're fawned over and indulged, perhaps granted extra television viewing time and ice cream. I still remember my childhood mumps experience with nostalgia. But an adult with mumps is something of a joke—even though to an adult mumps represents a far worse danger.

The list goes on. **Hemorrhoids:** a very painful condition, but socially a laughing matter. **AIDS:** what kind of response does an AIDS victim get? I know a few persons with AIDS, and they hear a very clear message from the church: "You get no sympathy from me. You deserve your suffering as God's punishment. Keep away." I cannot think of a more terrifying disease than AIDS, or one that provokes a less compassionate response.

Migraine headache, whiplash, cancer—each of these has a different "image," and in subtle and sometimes blatant ways we communicate to the sufferer an assessment of meaning that can make coping easier or harder.

I have come to believe that the chief contribution Christians can make is to keep people from suffering for the wrong reasons. We can "honor" pain. In the most important sense, all pain is pain; it does not matter whether the pain comes from migraine headaches or strep throat or acute depression. The first step in helping a suffering person (or in accepting our own pain) is to acknowledge that pain is valid, and worthy of a sympathetic response. In this way, we can begin to ascribe meaning to pain.

At a different level, Christians apply a further

set of values to suffering. Like the visitors to Claudia Claxton's bedside, we can heap coals of fire on the suffering. We can add guilt: "Haven't you prayed? Have you no faith that God will heal you?" Or confusion: "Is Satan causing this pain? Just natural providence? Or has God specially selected you as an example to others?" Pain is a foolproof producer of guilt, I have learned. We all do things we shouldn't, and when pain strikes, it's easy to blame ourselves for what has happened.

In a context of intense suffering, even well-intended comments may produce a harmful effect. "God must have loved your daughter very much to take her home so soon," we may be tempted to say, leaving the bereaved parents to wish that God had loved their daughter less. "God won't give you a burden heavier than you can bear"; the suffering person may wish for weaker faith that might merit a lighter burden.

I have interviewed enough suffering people to know that the pain caused by this kind of bedside response can exceed the pain of the illness itself. One woman well known in Christian circles poignantly described the agony caused by TMJ (temporomandibular joint dysfunction). The pain dominates her entire life. Yet, she says, it hurts far worse when Christians write her with judgmental comments based on their pet formulas of why God allows suffering. Perhaps the chief contribution a Christian can make is to keep people from suffering for the wrong reasons. We can "honor" their pain.

Buried Treasure

Following the biblical pattern, our search for meaning should move in a forward-looking direction, toward the results of suffering, rather than dwelling on its cause.

Frankly, to me much suffering would remain meaningless if we spent all our efforts on the unanswerable "Why?" questions. Why did Solzhenitsyn have to spend eight years in a hard labor camp just for making a casual criticism of Stalin in a letter to a friend? Why did millions of Jews have to die to fulfill the whims of a crazed dictator? Such suffering is meaningless in itself, and will remain so unless the sufferer, like a miner searching for diamonds in a vein of coal, finds in it a meaning.

Viktor Frankl, who spent time in one of Hitler's camps, said, "Despair is suffering without meaning." Frankl and Bruno Bettelheim extracted meaning from the senseless suffering of the Holocaust: observing the behavior of human beings in the extreme conditions of the camps gave them insights that formed the basis for all their later work. For Elie Wiesel and others, "bearing witness" became the meaning. They now devote themselves to honoring those who did not survive.

In prison Dostoyevski pored over the New Testament and the lives of the saints. Prison became, for him and later for his countryman Solzhenitsyn, a crucible of religious faith. Both describe a process in which, first, the blunt reality of human evil convinced them of the need for redemption. Then, through the living witness of believers in the camps, they saw the possibility of transformation. As Solzhenitsyn elegantly expressed it in his classic *One Day in the Life of Ivan Denisovich,* faith in God may not get you out of the camp, but it is enough to see you through each day.

Although my own suffering seems trivial in comparison with these pioneers, I too strive to extract meaning from it. I begin with the biblical promise that suffering can produce something worthwhile in me. I go through a list like that in Romans 5, where Paul mentions perseverance, character, hope, and confidence. "How does suffering accomplish these?" I ask myself. It produces perseverance, or steadiness, by slowing me down and forcing me to turn to God; it produces character by calling on my reserves of inner strength. I continue through the list, asking how God can be involved in bringing meaning to the suffering process.

John Donne spoke of suffering as a kind of "treasure in bullion." Because it is not coined into currency, the bullion does not always help us defray expenses here on earth. But as we get nearer and nearer our home, heaven, the treasure "that may lie in his bowels, as gold in a mine" takes on eternal value, a weight of glory.[2] If we turn to God in trust, the affliction itself can be redeemed, by helping to form our character in Christ's own image.

We might use a more contemporary analogy to express the same thought. Suffering can be what economists call a "frozen asset." It may not look remotely like an asset at the time, but gradually we can find meaning in it, an enduring meaning that will help to transform the pain.

Shared Meaning

Earlier in this chapter I quoted a letter from a pastor whose depression had brought on a breakdown in meaning. He could make no sense of his suffering, and the Christian community failed to help him in the process. Eventually that pastor had to commit himself to a mental institution for treatment. His family stood with him, though, and with their support and professional help, he finally climbed back to a place of health.

Years later that same pastor, with renewed mental health, faced another crisis. A week-old grandson died, plunging the extended family into confusion and grief. Now he was supposed to be the strong one for his children, and he didn't know if he could. The Sunday after the funeral, preaching in his new church, he began reading Psalm 145 from the pulpit. He tried to focus on the words before him, but concentration failed. His tongue got thick, his chin trembled, his tear ducts opened wide. He could not continue reading the serene words about God's goodness and fairness.

The pastor set aside his sermon notes and, with a choked voice, he told the silent congregation about his grandson's death. Even while he was speaking his mind flashed back to his time at the former church, to his feelings of helplessness and failure. He was afraid.

But this time was different. "As people left the

church," he remembers, "they said two important and helpful things:

"1. 'Thank you for sharing your pain with us.'

"2. 'I grieve with you.' This simple statement was the most helpful thing said. I did not feel alone. Unlike during the time of my depression before, I was not abandoned by God and his people. They embraced my grief."

Using very few words, and no special wisdom, that second congregation communicated to their pastor a sense of shared meaning. That his pain was important to them they demonstrated by taking it on themselves.

The search for meaning in suffering will always be a lonely search. No one but I can discern the meaning of my suffering. And yet by embracing grief and standing beside the hurting person, we can indeed aid another's search for meaning.

The skill of helping another person find meaning involves recognizing various stages along the path to healing. Sharon Fischer describes her own process in dealing with ovarian cancer:

> I needed time to digest what was happening in my life and to absorb the changes forced on my daily routine, my emotional stability and my plans for the future. Perhaps the greatest way to give suffering people time is being patient with them—giving them room to doubt, cry, question and work out strong and often extreme emotions.
>
> I found that not everything in my experi-

ence could be absorbed at once, and I needed to feel free to take the time I needed to work through feelings. Elisabeth Kübler-Ross has outlined five stages grieving people often pass through, either in facing their own deaths or in dealing with the death of a loved one. These stages—denial, anger, bargaining, depression and acceptance—are not always experienced in that sequence, and not everyone goes through all of them, but they exemplify the time it can take to process a traumatic experience. . . .

I am not by nature one who shares feelings easily. So it was not always easy for me to explain, even to those people closest to me, the complexity of my feelings and the depth of my reaction to the experience. But I needed good listeners—people willing to take an hour or two when I was ready to talk and just listen. Fortunately I had faithful friends, a neighbor who is a skilled counselor and family members who were available. I don't know what I would have done without people to listen.[3]

Fischer goes on to say that the least helpful people were those who came with suggested answers for her. One woman offered the opinion that diet—Sharon enjoyed hamburgers and chocolate chip ice cream—was the reason for Sharon's illness. Others urged her to rely less on medical treatment and more on prayer for healing.

I cannot emphasize too strongly how destructive such formulaic answers can be. "Rejoice with those who rejoice, and weep with those who weep," advised the apostle Paul (Romans 12:15), wise words that apply especially in times of crisis. The book of Proverbs is more blunt about inappropriate responses:

> Like one who takes away a garment on a cold day,
> or like vinegar poured on soda,
> is one who sings songs to a heavy heart. (25:20)

At the very time I was working on this book I received a phone call from a friend in another city who had just been diagnosed with AIDS. Wallowing in guilt over past sexual sins, he felt remorse, unworthiness, self-hatred, and rejection by God. He had lost all will to live. He needed help desperately.

Some people see AIDS as a direct punishment by God, a specific, targeted message of judgment. I do not. I see it, rather, as part of a general message, a principle of health: Just as abuse of alcohol and tobacco exposes the body to certain risks, so does sexual promiscuity. But, regardless, even if I am wrong and the disease has come as a direct punishment, what is my responsibility as his Christian friend?

My responsibility is to dispense grace, to show him how tenderly Jesus treated people with sexual sins, to assure him of God's love and forgiveness. In short, my role is to move his focus away from the backward glance and direct it forward. Even his guilt is a signal. He can lie in a hospital bed all day and grovel in his sins. Or he can bring that guilt to God, who has promised to put confessed sin behind him, "as far as the east is from the west."

The shared meaning of guilt is not judgment, but forgiveness. The shared meaning of suffering is restoration, and union with the sufferer.

God's Question Marks

Sometimes the only meaning we can offer a suffering person is the assurance that their suffering, which has no apparent meaning for them, has a meaning for us.

Henri Nouwen's slim book with the wonderful title *The Wounded Healer* poses the question of lonely, abandoned people. What possible meaning can one bring to their pain? He gives the example of a young minister who has no suggested meaning to offer an old man facing surgery—none but his own loving concern. "No man can stay alive when nobody is waiting for him," says Nouwen. "Everyone who returns from a long and difficult trip is looking for someone waiting for him at the station or the airport. Everyone wants to tell his story and share his moments of pain and exhilaration with someone who stayed home, waiting for him to come back."[4]

My wife works with some of the poorest people in the city of Chicago, directing a program of LaSalle Street Church, which intentionally seeks out lonely and abandoned senior citizens no one else cares for. Many times I have seen her pour herself into a senior citizen's life, trying to convince the senior that it matters whether he or she lives or dies. In such a way she "graces" their suffering.

One man Janet works with, ninety-year-old Mr. Kruider, refused cataract surgery for twenty years.

At age seventy he had decided that nothing much was worth looking at and, anyhow, God must have wanted him blind if he made him that way. Maybe it was God's punishment for looking at girls as a youngster, he said.

It took my wife two years of cajoling, arguing, persisting, and loving to convince Mr. Kruider to have cataract surgery. Finally, Mr. Kruider agreed, for one reason only: Janet impressed on him that it mattered to her, Janet, that he regain his sight. Mr. Kruider had given up on life; it held no meaning for him. But Janet transferred a meaning. It made a difference to someone that even at age ninety-two Mr. Kruider not give up. At long last the old man agreed to the surgery.

In a literal sense, Janet shared Mr. Kruider's suffering. By visiting so often she convinced him that someone cared, and that it mattered whether he lived or died or had sight or not. That principle of shared suffering is the thesis of Nouwen's book on the wounded healer, and perhaps the only sure contribution we can make to the meaning of suffering. In doing so, we follow God's pattern, for he too took on pain. He joined us and lived a life of more suffering and poverty than most of us will ever know. Suffering can never ultimately be meaningless, because God himself has shared it.

At times, though, despite our best efforts to honor others' pain, we encounter suffering that seems utterly devoid of meaning. I am thinking especially of a man with Alzheimer's disease; the daughter tries to tend to his needs, but every day her heart is broken by the sad shell of what used to be her father. Or I think of a severely disabled child with an IQ in the 30–40 range. The child may live a long life lying motionless in a crib, unable to talk, unable to comprehend, soaking up hours of expensive professional care.

Where is there meaning in such a senile adult and in such a child? I have received great help on this question from the compassionate work of Christians in East Germany. These people, who have grown up in a society more acquainted with suffering than ours in the West, have set an example to us all of reaching out to those least "valuable" or "useful" members of modern society.

"What is the point of their lives? Do their lives have any meaning?" asked Dr. Jürgen Trogisch, a pediatrician who works among the severely mentally handicapped. He could treat the externals, but what was going on inside, within such damaged brains?

For many years Dr. Trogisch could not answer the question of meaning. He performed his medical tasks anyway, but he had no answer. Then he ran an introductory course to train new helpers for the center, and at the end of the one-year training period, he asked the young helpers to fill out a survey. Among the questions was this one, "What changes have taken place in your life since you became totally involved with disabled people?" Here is a sampling of their answers:

—For the first time in my life I feel I am doing something really significant.

—I feel I can now do things I wouldn't have thought myself capable of before.

—During my time here I have won the affection of Sabine. Having had the opportunity to involve myself with a disabled person, I no longer think of her as disabled at all.

—I am more responsive now to human suffering and it arouses in me the desire to help.

—It's made me question what is really important in life.

—Work has assumed a new meaning and purpose. I feel I'm needed now.

—I've learned to be patient and to appreciate even the slightest sign of progress.

—In observing the disabled, I've discovered myself.

—I've become more tolerant. My own little problems don't seem so important any longer, and I've learned to accept myself with all my inadequacies. Above all I've learned to appreciate the little pleasures of life, and especially I thank God that he has shown me that love can achieve more than hate or force.

As Dr. Trogisch read over these and other responses, he realized with a start the answer to his question. The meaning of the suffering of those children was being worked out in the lives of others, his helpers, who were learning lessons that no sophisticated educational system could teach. He thought of two patients he had worked with for years, in whom he had seen little progress. "Could it be that Daniel and Monika have come into this world just for me? Are their deep and insistent questions perhaps God's questions to me? Are these two severely disabled children an answer—God's answer to me?"[5]

17

Hope

All that the downtrodden can do is go on hoping.
After every disappointment they must find fresh reason for hope.

Alexander Solzhenitsyn

Pharmaceuticals today are tested by the "double blind" method, meaning the administering doctors themselves do not know which is the true drug and which the inert, "control" drug. They must be tested that way for one simple reason: the power of human hope. Before double blind testing, virtually all new drugs showed spectacular results, regardless of their chemical content. Mystified researchers eventually found the doctor's demeanor to be the key factor in the new drugs' success: By smile, voice, and attitude, the doctor would unknowingly convey confidence and hope, convincing patients of the probability of improvement.

Dozens of studies have verified the healing power of hope—as well as the dangers of its opposite. The University of Rochester School of Medicine found that open heart surgery patients were far more likely to die after surgery if they showed signs of depression.[1] Another famous study, called "Broken Heart," surveyed the mortality rate of 4,500 widowers within six months of their wives' deaths. The widowers, most of them depressed, had a mortality rate forty percent higher than other men the same age.

Prisoner-of-war accounts indicate that some POWs may die for no apparent reason other than a loss of hope. Consider the experience of Major F. J. Harold Kushner, an army medical officer held by the Vietcong for five and a half years.

> Kushner got to know one POW, a tough young marine who had already survived two years of prison camp life. The marine was a model POW, keeping himself in good health and leading the camp's thought-reform group, mainly because the camp commander had promised to release those who cooperated. As time passed, however, the marine gradually discerned that his captors had lied to him. When the full realization of this fact sunk in, he became a zombie, refusing all work and rejecting all offers of food and encouragement. He simply lay on his cot sucking his thumb. In a matter of weeks he was dead.[2]

Writing about the young marine, Dr. Martin Seligman of the University of Pennsylvania says that a strictly medical explanation of his decline isn't adequate. "Hope of release sustained him," Seligman says. "When he gave up hope, when he believed that all his efforts had failed and would continue to fail, he died."

As the noted physiologist Harold G. Wolf puts it, "Hope, faith and a purpose in life, is medicinal. This is not merely a statement of belief but a conclusion proved by meticulously controlled scientific experiment."[3]

The Elusive Gift

At long-term care facilities the patients tend to divide into two categories: the "hopers," who endeavor to beat back their affliction and resume normal life, and the "defeatists." On a visit to the Menninger Clinic, pastor and author Bruce Larson asked the staff to identify the single most important ingredient in the treatment of the mentally disturbed. They were unanimous in singling out hope as the most important factor, but went on to confess they didn't really know how to "dispense" hope to a patient. It is a quality of the spirit, and thus an elusive gift. Yet they could tell right away when a patient turned the corner in treatment and for the first time believed that the future did not have to be the same as the troubled present.[4]

As the staff at the Menninger Clinic discovered, such courageous hope cannot be taught. But it can sometimes be caught. We can seek ways to awaken courage in suffering people.

The organization Amnesty International offers a good illustration of infectious hope. The founder, a political prisoner at the brink of despair, was given a matchbook with a single word written on it, "Courage!" That small gesture of shared humanity renewed his hope enough to keep him alive. When the man finally attained freedom, he devoted himself to building an organization based on the simplest principle imaginable. People in free countries write letters to prisoners who are being held and tortured for political reasons. For thousands of prisoners, the mere knowledge that someone else cares—even an unknown letter-writer—has kindled the flame of hope.

Sometimes hope seems irrational and pointless. It must have seemed so to inmates in concentration camps. Yet, as Solzhenitsyn insists in the quotation that heads this chapter, people without reasonable hope must still find a source for hope; like bread, it sustains life. For Solzhenitsyn, hope was a matter of choice, a mechanism of survival that fed his will to live. Later, he compiled the stories in *The Gulag Archipelago* both to honor and to bring hope to his fellow-prisoners. For Dostoyevski, hope of release, the sense of not being *"not at home,* but on a visit," became a parable for all of life, and helped convince him of an afterlife beyond this one.[5]

In his book *Experiences of God,* the theologian Jürgen Moltmann tells how hope kept him alive in a camp. Captured as a German war prisoner, he was shuffled among prisons in Belgium, Scotland, and England. Besides the normal hardships of prison life—no heat, little food, constant illness—he also had to deal with the despair that came from seeing his nation go down to defeat and learning of atrocities that had been committed in Germany's name. "I saw how other men collapsed inwardly, how they gave up all hope, sickening for the lack of it, some of them dying. The same thing almost happened to me. What kept me from it was a rebirth to new life thanks to a hope for which there was no evidence at all."[6]

That hope for Moltmann was a Christian hope. He had taken two books with him to war: Goethe's poems and the works of Nietzsche. Neither of these gave him any comfort. After experiencing the death of all the mainstays that had sustained his life up to then, he turned to a New Testament given him by a well-meaning army chaplain. The Psalms, printed at the back in an appendix, opened his eyes to "the God who is with those "that are of a broken heart.""

After his release in 1948, Moltmann abandoned his field of physics and went on to become a leading theologian, known best for his ground-breaking book *The Theology of Hope.*

The inspiring example of other people may represent the only way for a person to climb out of hopeless despair. Throughout this book I have used illustrations of people who have "successfully coped" with suffering. There are, of course, many contrary examples, of people destroyed by pain. But hope is such a crucial ingredient in coping with pain that I wonder if realistic "success stories" can ever be overemphasized. Someone in despair needs a person or an idea, something to grasp onto that may provide a lifeline out of the currents of gloom.

Healthy people may tire of the "disabled person finds happiness and usefulness" stories in *Reader's Digest* and *Guideposts*. But the disabled people I've talked with take those stories much more seriously. The survivors challenge their self-pitying tendencies. And some such stories—John Merrick (*The Elephant Man*), Helen Keller, Christy Brown (*My Left Foot*)—challenge all of us.

Hope means simply the belief that something good lies ahead. It is not the same as optimism or wishful thinking, for these imply a denial of reality. Often, I think, those of us who stand alongside suffering people tend to confuse hope and optimism. We look for signs of encouragement to administer like nostrums. "Yes, it's true that your memory is fading, Mother, but after all, what does memory matter?" "Your sight is failing, but you can still hear me OK. That's good, isn't it?" "I know this week has been hard for you, but perhaps the pain will go away next week."

My time among the people in the Make Today Count group taught me the limitations of optimism. Most of the above statements would strike dying people as insults, not grounds for hope. They need something beyond Pollyanna optimism. For them, hope resembles courage more than cheerfulness. It involves a leap, much like faith: ". . . hope that is seen is no hope at all" said the apostle Paul. "Who hopes for what he already has? But if we hope for what we do not yet have, we wait for it patiently" (Romans 8:24–25).

Yet hope saves us from pessimism also, the belief that the universe is a chaos without final meaning. True hope is honest. It allows a person to believe that even when she falls down and the worst has happened, still she has not reached the end of the road. She can stand up and continue.

Realistic hope permits a dying person to confront reality, but at the same time gives strength to go on living. Orville Kelly, the founder of Make Today Count, expressed this quality of courageous hope well: "I do not consider myself dying of cancer, but living despite it. I do not look upon each day as another day closer to death, but as another day of life, to be appreciated and enjoyed."

Long-suffering

The people in my hospital therapy group had long-term illnesses, the kind that will never go away, and such conditions call for a special kind of availability from the rest of us. In older days waves of typhoid, smallpox, or yellow fever would bring death quickly; nowadays the terminal illness is more likely to linger. People who struggle with long-term suffering report that a fatigue factor sets in. At first, no matter what the illness, they get a spurt of attention from well-wishers and friends. Cards fill their mailboxes, and flowers fight for space on the countertops. But over time, attention fades.

Many people are embarrassed and troubled by problems that do not go away. One Christian woman told me that with each successive reappearance of her cancer fewer visitors came to see her. As the illness dragged on she felt even more vulnerable and afraid, and she also felt more alone. Some Christians seemed resentful that their prayers for healing had gone unanswered, acting almost as if they blamed her. They lost faith and stayed away, leaving her with guilt and self-hatred to cope with in addition to her pain.

Parents of children with birth defects echo this woman's complaint. A flurry of sympathetic response follows the birth, but soon fades. Thus as the parents' needs and emotional difficulties increase, offers of help tend to decrease. Unlike a person facing a terminal illness, the parents of a severely disabled child have no end in sight. They accept the task of care-giving for life and, to complicate matters, they must also worry about how the child will manage after their own deaths.

In his list of fruits of the Spirit, Paul includes one that we translate with the archaic word "long-suffering." We would do well to revive that word, and concept, in its most literal form to apply to the problem of long-term pain.

Some Christians would far rather talk about miraculous healing than long-suffering, and I should mention why I have mostly avoided this important aspect of the problem of pain. I haven't emphasized miraculous healing in this book for two reasons. First, there are many good books available on miraculous healing, ranging from personal testimonies to theological treatises. Second, I'm writing about people who feel trapped in pain and who are questioning God. Healing is one way out of the dilemma, but in truth we must acknowledge that not everyone finds miraculous healing. Ask Brian Sternberg.

I don't mean to downplay physical healing. But as I have already mentioned, everyone who has been healed (and also those who have been used to heal others) eventually dies. So healing does not remove the problem of pain; it merely delays it.

The possibility of miraculous healing offers tremendous hope for the Christian. Yet if healing does not come, that dashed hope can be a great impediment to faith and can lead to feelings of betrayal and despair. Barbara Sanderville, a young paraplegic writer in Minnesota, described this process in a letter to me:

> Someone told me just after I became a Christian that God would heal me. This seemed too good to be true, and I didn't know if I dared believe it. But seeing nothing in the Bible that contradicted it, I began to hope, and then to believe. But my faith was shaky, and when Christians came along and said, "God doesn't heal everyone," or "Affliction is a cross we must bear," my faith would waver. Then last fall it just seemed to die. I gave up believing God would heal me.
>
> At that point in my life I knew I couldn't face spending the rest of my life in the wheelchair. Knowing that God had the power to heal me but wouldn't (or so I thought) made me very bitter. I would read Isaiah 53, and 1 Peter 2:24, and accuse God of holding the promise of heal-

ing before me like a piece of meat before a starving dog. He tempted me by showing the potential but never quite allowing me to reach it. This in turn produced deep guilt feelings because from the Bible I knew God was a loving God and answerable to no man. I had such a conflict in me that my mental state was precarious and I thought of suicide many times.

I began to take tranquilizers just to get through the day as my guilt and resentment built a higher and higher wall between God and me. About this time I began having headaches and problems with my eyes. An ophthalmologist could find no physical reason.

I was still praying because I knew God was alive, but I usually ended up crying and railing out at God. I'm afraid I experienced a lot of self-pity, which was very destructive. And over and over I asked God why He wouldn't heal me when it so plainly says that healing is a part of the redemption plan.

Barbara eventually found a mental healing that swept away the bitterness. She is still awaiting physical healing.

Because of experiences like Barbara's, I believe a hope for healing should be presented realistically. It is just that—a "hope," not a guarantee. If it comes, a joyous miracle has happened. If it doesn't come, God has not let you down. He can use even the infirmity to produce good. He does promise that, without fail.

Final Hope

As with the other frontiers of recovery—fear, help-lessness, meaning—the Christian has certain unique resources available in the struggle for hope. The last section of this book will deal with specific contributions that Christian faith can make. But I would be remiss if I did not mention in this chapter as well the final hope of resurrection, the hope for a new world in which the "problem of pain" will seem like a distant memory.

The Christian believes that, no matter how bleak things look at the present, something good really does lie ahead. Bruno Bettelheim, survivor of Hitler's camps, acknowledges that such belief translates into actual help: "It is a well-known fact of the concentration camps that those who had strong religious and moral convictions managed life there much better than the rest. Their beliefs, including belief in an afterlife, gave them a strength to endure which was far above that of most others."[7]

Joni Eareckson Tada tells of a time when she visited a home for the mentally retarded. Usually when she visits a care facility and recounts her life story, speaking from a wheelchair, she keeps her audience spellbound. These patients, however, of varying ages but all with undeveloped minds, had trouble with attention span. When Joni reached the part about imagining what heaven would be like, she could tell she had lost their interest entirely.

It was a warm day, and Joni could feel perspiration rolling down her body as she struggled to continue. Finally, in desperation, she said this, "And heaven will be the place where all of you will get new minds." As soon as the words came out, she regretted them—what if they sounded paternalistic, or cruel? But instantly the atmosphere in the room changed. Spontaneously, the patients started cheering, with loud applause.

Joni had tapped into their deepest hope. They, more than anyone, knew their minds were incomplete, unfulfilled. But she had held out the Christian promise of a place where such weaknesses would not carry over, a place of final healing. "But our citizenship is in heaven," Paul reminded the Philippians (3:20–21). "And we eagerly await a Savior from there, the Lord Jesus Christ, who, by the power that enables him to bring everything under his control, will transform our lowly bodies so that they will be like his glorious body."

We Western Christians in our increasing sophistication have, I think, grown a little ashamed of our faith's emphasis on immortality and rewards to come. I hear few sermons these days on the crown of life or crown of righteousness. Our culture announces to us that suffering is the reality and an afterlife of immortality is just a pipe dream.

But do we have any other sure hope to offer for the quadriplegic or the mother of a brain-damaged baby? And is the hope of an afterlife and eternal healing a worthy hope? To answer that question, I must tell you the story of Martha, one of the members of the Make Today Count group. In a sense, her story summarizes everything I learned about pain in my year with the group.

Martha caught my eye at the very first meeting. Other people there showed obvious symptoms of illness: thinning hair, a sallow complexion, a missing limb, an uncontrolled trembling. But Martha showed no such signs. She was twenty-six, and very attractive. I wondered if she, like me, was visiting with a friend.

When it was Martha's turn to speak, she said she had just contracted ALS, or Lou Gehrig's disease. Her father had died of the same disease a year before, and two years before that her uncle had died of it. ALS rarely shows hereditary connections, and very rarely attacks young women, but somehow she had cruelly defied the odds.

ALS destroys nerves. It first attacks voluntary movements, such as control over arms and legs, then hands and feet. It progresses on to involuntary movements, and finally inhibits breathing enough to cause death. Sometimes a person's body succumbs quickly, sometimes not. Martha's relatives had lived through two years of degeneration before death. Martha knew the disease's pattern in excruciating detail.

My first meeting with the group took place in March. In April, Martha arrived in a wheelchair. She could walk only with great difficulty, and because of that had just been fired from her job at a university library.

By May Martha had lost use of her right arm, and could no longer use crutches. A physical therapist had taught her to pick things up off the floor by using a broomstick-and-masking-tape contraption. She operated the manual wheelchair with great difficulty.

By June she had lost use of both arms and could barely move the hand controls on a new electric wheelchair. Needing round-the-clock care, she moved into a rehabilitation hospital.

I began visiting Martha at her rehabilitation hospital. I took her for short rides in her wheelchair, and sometimes picked her up for the group meetings. I learned about the indignity of her suffering. I learned to check her toes before putting on her shoes—if they were curled, they would jam painfully in the shoe—and to close her hand and guide it carefully into the sleeve of her jacket. I also had to watch for her dangling arms before setting her down on the car seat. It is not easy to position a 125-pound body of dead weight inside a compact car.

Martha needed help with every move: getting dressed, arranging her head on the pillow, cleaning her bedpan. When she cried, someone else had to wipe her tears and hold a tissue to her nose. Her body was in utter revolt against her will. It would not obey any of her commands.

Sometimes we talked about death and about hope. I confess to you readily that the great Christian hopes of eternal life, ultimate healing, and resurrection sounded hollow and frail and thin as smoke when held up to someone like Martha. She wanted not angel wings, but an arm that did not flop to the side, a mouth that did not drool, and lungs that would not collapse. I confess that eternity, even a pain-free eternity, seemed to have a strange irrelevance to the suffering Martha felt.

She thought about God, of course, but she could hardly think of him with love. She held out against any deathbed conversion, insisting that, as she put it, she would only turn to God out of love and not out of fear. And how could she love a God who did this to her?

It became clear around October that ALS would complete its horrible cycle quickly in Martha. She soon had to practice breathing with a toy-like plastic machine, blowing with all her might to make little blue balls rise in the pressure columns. Between gasps for breath, she talked about what she preferred losing first, her voice or her breath. Ultimately she decided she would rather her lungs quit first; she preferred dying to dying mute, unable to express herself.

Because of reduced oxygen supply to her brain, Martha tended to fall asleep in the middle of conversations. Sometimes at night she would awake in a panic, with a sensation like choking, and be unable to call for help.

Despite logistical difficulties, Martha managed to make one last trip to a favorite summer cabin in Michigan, and to her mother's home nearby. She was making final preparations, saying farewells.

In that process, Martha badly wanted at least two weeks back in her own apartment in Chicago as a time to invite friends over, one by one, in order to say good-bye and to come to terms with her death. But the two weeks in her apartment posed a huge problem. How could she stay at home in view of the need for round-the-clock care? Some government aid could be found to keep her in a hospital room, but not at home, not with the intensive service she needed just to stay alive.

Only one group in all of Chicago offered the free and loving personal care that Martha needed: Reba Place Fellowship, a Christian community in Evanston. Included among the members of Reba Place was a paraplegic named Sara who knew well the agony of living in a body that did not function properly. Partly due to Sara's influence, the entire community adopted Martha as a project and volunteered all that was necessary to fulfill her last wishes.

Sixteen women rearranged their lives for her. They divided into teams, adjusted their schedules, traded off baby-sitting duties for their own children, and moved into her apartment, one pair per shift. Seventeen other people signed on as a support team to pray for Martha and the care-givers. They prayed for her miraculous healing, but they also prayed for those who would minister to her if the disease continued its deadly course.

The sixteen women stayed with Martha, listened to her ravings and complaints, bathed her, helped her sit up, moved her, sat beside her all night to listen to her breathing, prayed for her, and loved her. They were available to calm her fears. They gave her a sense of place so that she no longer felt helpless, and gave meaning to her suffering. To Martha they were God's body.

The Reba Place women also explained to Martha the Christian hope. And finally Martha, seeing the love of God enfleshed in his body—at a time when God himself seemed to her uncompassionate, even cruel—came to that God in Christ. She presented herself in trust to the one who had died for her. She did not come to God in fear; she had found his love at last. In a very moving service in Evanston, she feebly gave a testimony and was baptized.

On the day before Thanksgiving of 1983, Martha died. Her body, crumpled, misshapen, atrophied, was a pathetic imitation of its former beauty. When it finally stopped functioning, Martha left it. But today Martha lives, in a new body, in wholeness and triumph. She lives because of the victory that Christ won and because of his body at Reba Place, who made that victory known to her. And if we do not believe that, and if our Christian hope, tempered by sophistication, does not allow us to offer that truth to a dying, convulsing world then we are indeed, as the apostle Paul said, of all men most miserable.

Part 5

How Does Faith Help?

18

———◁●◉●▷———

Seeing for Himself

God weeps with us so that we may one day laugh
with him.

Jürgen Moltmann

Every religion, whether Buddhist, Hindu,
Muslim, or New Age, must somehow address the problem of pain. Much of what I
have presented so far—pain's value to the human
body, how to prepare for and help one another
through suffering—applies to all people, regardless
of religious belief. But what difference does Christian faith make, specifically? What resources can
Christians fall back on?

By asking that we have, in a sense, circled back
to the opening question, "Where is God when it
hurts?" It is a question that C. S. Lewis asked, as did
Claudia Claxton, and the movie actress whose lover
rolled off a boat, and Joni Eareckson Tada and Brian
Sternberg, and the survivors of the concentration
camps. It is a question that every suffering person
eventually asks. Where is God? How does he feel
about my plight? Does he care?

> The lark's on the wing
> The snail's on the thorn
> God's in his heaven
> All's right with the world.

Robert Browning wrote those words in the mid-nineteenth century, an era of boundless optimism. But after two world wars and two atomic bomb attacks, the Holocaust, and numerous genocides and mass famines around the globe, few people would now dare to say, "All's right with the world." Worse, God seems to stay in his heaven despite all that's wrong with the world. Why doesn't he do something?

A Farmhand's Cry

Hear a modern-day complaint against God from the mouth of a migrant farmhand mother (as recorded by psychiatrist and author Robert Coles).

> Last year we went to a little church in New Jersey. . . . We had all our children there, the baby included. The Reverend Jackson was there, I can't forget his name, and he told us to be quiet, and he told us how glad we should be that we're in this country, because it's Christian, and not "godless."
> . . . Then my husband went and lost his temper; something happened to his nerves, I do believe. He got up and started shouting, yes sir. He went up to the Reverend Mr. Jackson and told him to shut up and never speak again—not to us, the migrant people. He told him to go back

to his church, wherever it is, and leave us alone and don't be standing up there looking like he was nice to be doing us a favor.

Then he did the worst thing he could do: He took the baby, Annie, and he held her right before his face, the minister's, and he screamed and shouted and hollered at him, that minister, like I've never seen anyone do. I don't remember what he said, the exact words, but he told him that here was our little Annie, and she's never been to a doctor, and the child is sick . . . and we've got no money, not for Annie or the other ones or ourselves.

Then he lifted Annie up, so she was higher than the reverend, and he said why doesn't he go and pray for Annie and pray that the growers will be punished for what they're doing to us, all the migrant people. . . . And then my husband began shouting about God and His neglecting us while He took such good care of the other people all over.

Then the reverend did answer—and that was his mistake, yes it was. He said we should be careful and not start blaming God and criticizing Him and complaining to Him and like that, because God wasn't supposed to be taking care of the way the growers behave and how we live, here on this earth. "God worries about your future"; that's what he said, and I tell you, my husband near exploded. He shouted about ten times to the reverend, "Future, future, future." Then he took Annie and near pushed her in the reverend's face and Annie, she started crying, poor child, and he asked the reverend about Annie's "future" and asked him what he'd do if he had to live like us, and if he had a "future" like ours.

Then he told the reverend he was like all the rest, making money off us, and held our Annie as high as he could, right near the cross, and told God He'd better stop having ministers speaking for Him, and He should come and see us for Himself, and not have the "preachers"— he kept calling them the "preachers"—speaking for Him.

. . . He stopped after he'd finished talking about the "preachers" and he came back to us, and there wasn't a sound in the church, no sir, not one you could hear—until a couple of other men said he was right, my husband was . . . and everyone clapped their hands and I felt real funny.[1]

This migrant family sums up the problem of suffering about as well as it can be expressed. Why does God allow a world of sick children and no money and no hope? Their dilemma is not abstract and philosophical, but intensely personal: their child Annie hurts, and they can see no solution. Does God even care?

Nothing that I can say in this or any book would solve the problems of this farmhand family. They cry out for a response of compassionate love, not a theoretical solution. But in his zeal the angry farmhand unwittingly pointed to Christianity's chief contribution to the problem of pain. Holding his child in front of the reverend's face, up near the cross, he demanded that God come down and see for himself what this world is like. It's not enough, he said, for God to keep having the preachers speak for him.

The fact is, God did come. He entered this world in human flesh, and saw and felt for himself what this world is like. Apart from the Incarnation, our faith would have little to say to the farmhand.

Keeping His Own Rules

Old Testament characters like Job and Jeremiah sometimes wondered aloud if God had "plugged his ears" to their cries of pain. Jesus put an abrupt and decisive end to such speculation. Not only had God not plugged his ears, he suddenly took on ears—literal, eardrum-ossicle-cochlea human ears. On the cracked and dusty plains of Palestine, God's Son heard firsthand the molecular vibrations of human groans: from the sick and the needy, and from others who groaned more from guilt than from pain.

Clear your mind and reflect for a moment on Jesus' life. He was the only person in history able to plan his own birth. Yet he humbled himself, trading in a perfect heavenly body for a frail body of blood and sinew and cartilage and nerve cells. The Bible says there is no temptation known to man that Jesus did not experience. He was lonely, tired, hungry, personally assaulted by Satan, besieged by leeching admirers, persecuted by powerful enemies.

As for physical appearance, there's only one description of Jesus in the Bible, one written hundreds of years in advance by the prophet Isaiah: "He had no beauty or majesty to attract us to him, nothing in his appearance that we should desire him. He was despised and rejected by men, a man of sorrows, and familiar with suffering. Like one from whom men hide their faces . . ." (Isaiah 53:2–3).

When Jesus first began his ministry, the people hooted, "Can anything good come from Nazareth?" An ancient ethnic joke: Jesus, the hick, the country bumpkin from Nazareth. In keeping with that reputation, he seemed to gravitate toward other rejects: those quarantined with leprosy, prostitutes, tax collectors, paralytics, notorious sinners.

Jesus' neighbors once ran him out of town and tried to kill him. His own family questioned his sanity. The leaders of the day proudly reported that not one authority or religious leader believed in him. His followers were a motley crew of fishermen and peasants, among whom the migrant farmhand would have felt comfortably at home. But in the end, even these forsook him when Jesus' countrymen traded his life for that of a terrorist.

No other religion—not Judaism, not Hinduism, not Buddhism or Islam—offers this unique contribution of an all-powerful God who willingly takes on the limitations and suffering of his creation. As Dorothy Sayers wrote,

> For whatever reason God chose to make man as he is—limited and suffering and subject to sorrows and death—He had the honesty and courage to take His own medicine. Whatever

game He is playing with His creation, He has kept His own rules and played fair. He can exact nothing from man that He has not exacted from Himself. He has Himself gone through the whole of human experience, from the trivial irritations of family life and the cramping restrictions of hard work and lack of money to the worst horrors of pain and humiliation, defeat, despair, and death. When He was a man, He played the man. He was born in poverty and died in disgrace and thought it well worthwhile.[2]

The fact that Jesus came to earth where he suffered and died does not remove pain from our lives. But it does show that God did not sit idly by and watch us suffer in isolation. He became one of us. Thus, in Jesus, God gives us an up-close and personal look at his response to human suffering. All our questions about God and suffering should, in fact, be filtered through what we know about Jesus.

How did God-on-earth respond to pain? When he met a person in pain, he was deeply moved with compassion (from the Latin words *pati* and *cum*, "to suffer with"). Not once did he say, "Endure your hunger! Swallow your grief!" When Jesus' friend Lazarus died, he wept. Very often, every time he was directly asked, he healed the pain. Sometimes he broke deep-rooted customs to do so, as when he touched a woman with a hemorrhage of blood, or when he touched outcasts, ignoring their cries of "Unclean!"

The pattern of Jesus' response should convince

us that God is not a God who enjoys seeing us suffer. I doubt that Jesus' disciples tormented themselves with questions like "Does God care?" They had visible evidence of his concern every day: they simply looked at Jesus' face.

And when Jesus himself faced suffering, he reacted much like any of us would. He recoiled from it, asking three times if there was any other way. There was no other way, and then Jesus experienced, perhaps for the first time, that most human sense of abandonment: "My God, my God, why have you forsaken me?" In the gospel accounts of Jesus' last night on earth, I detect a fierce struggle with fear, helplessness, and hope—the same frontiers all of us confront in our suffering.

The record of Jesus' life on earth should forever answer the question, How does God feel about our pain? In reply, God did not give us words or theories on the problem of pain. He gave us himself. A philosophy may explain difficult things, but has no power to change them. The gospel, the story of Jesus' life, promises change.

The Execution

> Love's as hard as nails
>   Love *is* nails:
> Blunt, thick, hammered through
> The medial nerves of One
> Who, having made us, knew
> The thing He had done,

Seeing (with all that is)
Our cross and his.
(C. S. Lewis, "Love's as Warm as Tears")

There is one central symbol by which we remember Jesus. Today that image is coated with gold and worn around the necks of athletes and beautiful women, an example of how we can gloss over the crude reality of history. The cross was, of course, a mode of execution. It would be no more bizarre if we made jewelry in the shape of tiny electric chairs, gas chambers, and hypodermic needles, the preferred modern modes of execution.

The cross, the most universal image in the Christian religion, offers proof that God cares about our suffering and pain. He died of it. That symbol stands unique among all the religions of the world. Many of them have gods, but only one has a God who cared enough to become a man and to die.

The scene, with the beatings and the sharp spikes and the slow torment of suffocation, has been recounted so often that we, who shrink from a news story on the death of a race horse or of baby seals, flinch not at all at its retelling. Unlike the quick, sterile executions we know today, this one stretched on for hours in front of a jeering crowd.

The promises Jesus made must have seemed especially empty to the people of his day. This man a king? A mock king if ever there was one, with his brier crown. Someone had thrown a fine purple robe over him, but blood from Pilate's beatings clotted on the cloth.

More unlikely—this man God? Even for his disciples, who had pursued him three years, it was too much to believe. They hung back in the crowd, afraid to be identified with the mock king. Their dreams of a powerful ruler who could banish all suffering turned into nightmares.

Jesus' death is the cornerstone of the Christian faith, the most important fact of his coming. The Gospels bulge with its details. He laid out a trail of hints and bald predictions throughout his ministry, predictions that were only understood after the thing had been done. What possible contribution to the problem of pain could come from a religion based on an event like the cross, where God himself succumbed to pain?

The apostle Paul called the cross a "stumbling block" to belief, and history has proved him out. Jewish rabbis question how a God who could not bear to see Abraham's son slain would allow his own Son to die. The Koran teaches that God, much too gentle to allow Jesus to go to the cross, substituted an evildoer in his place. Even today, U.S. television personality Phil Donahue explains his chief objection to Christianity: "How could an all-knowing, all-loving God allow His Son to be murdered on a cross in order to redeem my sins? If God the Father is so 'all-loving,' why didn't He come down and go to Calvary?"

All of these objectors have missed the main point of the gospel, that in some mysterious way it was God himself who came to earth and died. God was not "up there" watching the tragic events conspire "down here." God was in Christ, reconciling the world to himself. In Luther's phrase, the cross showed "God struggling with God." If Jesus was a mere man, his death would prove God's cruelty; the fact that he was God's Son proves instead that God fully identifies with suffering humanity. On the cross, God himself absorbed the awful pain of this world.

To some, the image of a pale body glimmering on a dark night whispers of defeat. What good is a God who does not control his Son's suffering? But another sound can be heard: the shout of a God crying out to human beings, "I LOVE YOU." Love was compressed for all history in that lonely figure on the cross, who said that he could call down angels at any moment on a rescue mission, but chose not to—because of us. At Calvary, God accepted his own unbreakable terms of justice.

And thus the cross, a stumbling block to some, became the cornerstone of Christian faith. Any discussion of how pain and suffering fit into God's scheme ultimately leads back to the cross.

At the end of the book of Job, God responded to questions about suffering by delivering a splendid lecture on his power. After Calvary, the emphasis shifts from power to love:

> For God so loved the world that he gave his one and only Son, that whoever believes in him shall not perish but have eternal life. (John 3:16)

> If God is for us, who can be against us? He who did not spare his own Son, but gave him up for us all—how will he not also, along with him, graciously give us all things? (Romans 8:31–32)

Why It Matters

I once talked with a priest who had just performed the funeral of an eight-year-old girl. His parish had prayed and wept and shared the family's agony for more than a year as the girl fought a futile battle against cancer. The funeral had strained the emotions, the energy, and even the faith of the priest. "What can I possibly say to her family?" he confided in me. "I have no solution to offer them. What can I say?" He paused for a moment, and added this, "I have no solution to their pain; I have only an answer. And Jesus Christ is that answer."

The death and resurrection of Jesus Christ provide more than an abstract theological answer to the problem of pain. They also offer us actual, practical help in our own struggles with suffering. I have identified at least four ways in which those events, now two millennia old, have a direct impact on my own suffering.

I learn to judge the present by the future.

A wise man named Joe Bayly once said, "Don't forget in the darkness what you have learned in the light." Yet sometimes the darkness descends so thickly that we can barely remember the light. Surely it seemed that way to Jesus' disciples.

In his most intimate encounter with them, during the meal known as the Last Supper, Jesus made the ringing declaration, "In this world you will have trouble. But take heart! I have overcome the world" (John 16:33). I can imagine the chill bumps on the backs of the eleven men who heard that assertion from the lips of God in flesh. At that moment, eleven of the twelve would gladly have given their lives for him; later that evening Simon Peter actually pulled a sword in Jesus' defense.

Yet by the next day all eleven had lost faith. Those triumphant words from the previous night must have cruelly haunted them as they watched him—safely, at a distance—anguish on the cross. It appeared as though the world had overcome God. All of them slipped away in the darkness. Peter swore with an oath he'd never known the man.

The disciples' problem, of course, was a matter of perspective. Yes, the memory of light from the past had been extinguished, but a few days later those same men would encounter the dazzling light of Easter. On that day, they learned that no darkness is too great for God. They learned what it means to judge the present by the future. Ignited by Easter hope, those former cowards went out and changed the world.

Today half the world celebrates the back-to-back holidays Good Friday and Easter. That darkest Friday is now called Good because of what happened on Easter Sunday; and because it happened Christians have hope that God will someday restore this planet to its proper place under his reign. The miracle of Easter will enlarge to cosmic scale.

It is a good thing to remember, when we encounter dark, disturbing times, that we live out our days on Easter Saturday. As the apostle Paul expressed it, "I consider that our present sufferings are not worth comparing with the glory that will be revealed in us" (Romans 8:18). It was no accident, I believe, that Jesus spoke his triumphant words, I HAVE OVERCOME THE WORLD, even as Roman soldiers were buckling on weapons for his arrest. He knew how to judge the present by the future.

I learn the pattern of transformed pain.

Christianity contains within it paradoxes that would make little sense apart from Jesus' life and death. Consider one paradox I have already alluded to in this book: although poverty and suffering are "bad things" that I rightly spend my life fighting against, yet at the same time they can be called "blessed." This pattern of bad transmuted into good finds its fullest expression in Jesus. By taking it on himself, Jesus dignified pain, showing us how it can be transformed. He gave us a pattern he wants to reproduce in us.

Jesus Christ offers the perfect example of all the biblical lessons about suffering. Because of Jesus, I can never say about a person, "She must be suffering because of some sin she committed"; Jesus, who did not sin, also felt pain. God has never promised that tornadoes will skip our houses on the way to our pagan neighbors' and that microbes will flee from Christian bodies. We are not exempt from the tragedies of this world, just as God himself was not exempt. Remember, Peter earned Jesus' strongest rebuke when he protested against the need for Christ to suffer (Matthew 16:23–25).

We feel pain as an outrage; Jesus did too, which is why he performed miracles of healing. In Gethsemane, he did not pray, "Thank you for this opportunity to suffer," but rather pled desperately for an escape. And yet he was willing to undergo suffering in service of a higher goal. In the end he left the hard questions ("if there be any other way . . .") to the will of the Father, and trusted that God could use even the outrage of his death for good.

As Cornelius Plantinga, Jr., has said, "We do not refer each other to the cross of Christ to explain evil. It is not as if in pondering Calvary we will at last understand throat cancer. We rather lift our eyes to the cross, whence comes our help, in order to see that God shares our lot and can therefore be *trusted*."[3] In the ultimate alchemy of all history, God took the worst thing that could possibly happen—the appalling execution of his innocent Son—and turned it into the final victory over evil and death. It was an act of unprecedented cunning, turning the design of evil into the service of good, an act that holds within it a promise for all of us. The unimaginable suffering of the cross was fully redeemed: it is by his *wounds* that we are healed (Isaiah 53:5), by his weakness that we are made strong.

How would the world be different if Jesus had come as a Superman figure, immune to all pain? What if he had not died, but merely ascended to heaven during his trial before Pilate? By not making himself exempt, but by deliberately taking on the worst the world has to offer, he gives us the hope that God can likewise transform the suffering each of us must face. Because of his death and resurrection, we can confidently assume that no trial—illness, divorce, unemployment, bankruptcy, grief—extends beyond the range of his transforming power.

The four gospels record only one instance of Jesus' disciples addressing him as God directly. It comes at the end of John, after Jesus' death and resurrection. All the disciples now believe in the risen Christ but one—doubting Thomas. An empiricist, Thomas insists that he will not be convinced unless he can put his fingers on the scars in Jesus' hands and side. Before long Jesus appears, despite the locked doors, and offers just that opportunity. "My Lord and my God!" Thomas cries out. The wounds were proof of a miracle beyond miracles.

I learn a new level of meaning to suffering.
In the Old Testament, faithful believers seemed shocked when suffering came their way. They expected God to reward their faithfulness with prosperity and comfort. But the New Testament shows a remarkable change—its authors expect just the opposite. As Peter advised suffering Christians, "This suffering is all part of the work God has given you. Christ, who suffered for you, is your example. Follow in his steps" (1 Peter 2:21 LB).

Other passages go further, using phrases I will not attempt to explain. Paul speaks of "sharing in his [Christ's] sufferings" and says he hopes to "fill up in my flesh what is still lacking in regards to Christ's afflictions." In context, all these passages show that suffering can gain meaning if we consider it as part of the "cross" we take on in following Jesus.

Although Christ does not always remove our pains, he fills them with meaning by absorbing them into his own suffering. We are helping to accomplish God's redemptive purposes in the world as co-participants with him in the battle to expel evil from this planet.

Harry Boer, who served four years as a chaplain during World War II, spent the final days of that war among marines in the Pacific Theater. "The Second Division saw much action, with great losses," he writes. "Yet I never met an enlisted man or an officer who doubted for a moment the outcome of the war. Nor did I ever meet a marine who asked why, if victory was so sure, we couldn't have it immediately. It was just a question of slogging through till the enemy gave up."[4]

I see a parallel situation in the veiled words about participating in Christ's sufferings. A far greater war is being fought on this planet, which will determine the destiny of all creation. And that war will involve certain casualties.

According to Paul, at the cross Christ triumphed over the cosmic powers—defeating them not with power but with self-giving love. The cross of Christ may have assured the final outcome, but battles remain for us to fight. Significantly, Paul prayed "to know Christ and the power of his resurrection and the fellowship of sharing in his sufferings"— embracing both the agony and the ecstasy of Christ's life on earth (Philippians 3:10).

It helps, though, to realize that the casualties we

sustain are wounds of honor that will one day be rewarded. We will never know, in this life, the full significance of our actions here, for much takes place invisible to us. Christ's cross offers a pattern for that too: what seemed very ordinary, one more dreary feat of colonial "justice" in a Roman outpost, made possible the salvation of the entire world.

When a pastor in South Africa goes to prison for his peaceful protest, when a social worker moves into an urban ghetto, when a couple refuses to give up on a difficult marriage, when a parent waits with undying hope and forgiveness for the return of an estranged child, when a young professional resists mounting temptations toward wealth and success— in all these sufferings, large and small, there is the assurance of a deeper level of meaning, of a sharing in Christ's own redemptive victory. "The creation waits in eager expectation for the sons of God to be revealed" (Romans 8:19).

I gain the confidence that God truly understands my pain.

Because of Jesus, I need never cry into the abyss, "Hey, you up there—do you even care?" The presence of suffering does not mean that God has forsaken me. To the contrary, by joining us on earth God gave solid, historical proof that he hears our groans, and even groans them with us. When we endure trials, he stands beside us, like the fourth man in the fiery furnace.

Why did Jesus have to suffer and die? The question deserves an entire book, and has prompted many books, but among the answers the Bible gives is this most mysterious answer: Suffering served as a kind of "learning experience" for God. Such words may seem faintly heretical, but I am merely following phraseology from the book of Hebrews.

Hebrews was written to a Jewish audience saturated in the Old Testament. The author strives to show that Jesus is "better"—a key word throughout the book. How is he better than the religious system they were used to? More powerful? More impressive? No, Hebrews emphasizes that Jesus is better because he has spanned the chasm between God and us. "Although he was a son, he learned obedience from what he suffered" (5:8). Elsewhere, that book tells us that the author of our salvation was made perfect through suffering (2:10).

These words, full of fathomless mystery, surely mean at least this: the Incarnation had meaning for God as well as for us. Human history revolves around not our experience of God, but his experience of us. On one level, of course, God understood physical pain, for he designed the marvelous nervous system that warns against harm. But had he, a Spirit, ever felt physical pain? Not until the Incarnation, the wrinkle in time when God himself experienced what it is like to be a human being.

In thirty-three years on earth Jesus learned about hardship and rejection and betrayal. And he learned too about pain: what it feels like to have an accuser leave the red imprint of his fingers on your face, to have a whip studded with metal lash across your back, to have a crude iron spike pounded through muscle, tendon, and bone. On earth, the Son of God learned all that.

In some incomprehensible way, because of Jesus, God hears our cries differently. The author of Hebrews marvels that whatever we are going through, God has himself gone through. "For we do not have a high priest who is unable to sympathize with our weaknesses, but we have one who has been tempted in every way, just as we are—yet was without sin" (4:15).

We have a high priest who, having graduated from the school of suffering, "is able to deal gently with those who are ignorant and are going astray, since he himself is subject to weakness" (5:2). Because of Jesus, God understands, truly understands, our pain. Our tears become his tears. We are not abandoned. The farmhand with the sick child, the swollen eight-year-old with leukemia, the grieving relatives in Yuba City, the leprosy patients in Louisiana—none has to suffer alone.

T. S. Eliot wrote in one of his *Four Quartets:*

> The wounded surgeon plies the steel
> That questions the distempered part;
> Beneath the bleeding hands we feel
> The sharp compassion of the healer's art
> Resolving the enigma of the fever chart.[5]

The surgery of life hurts. It helps me, though, to know that the surgeon himself, the Wounded Surgeon, has felt every stab of pain and every sorrow.

19

---❦---

The Rest of the Body

Those who have known pain profoundly are the ones most wary of uttering the clichés about suffering. Experience with the mystery takes one beyond the realm of ideas and produces finally a muteness or at least a reticence to express in words the solace that can only be expressed by an attitude of union with the sufferer.

John Howard Griffin

During three years of public ministry God's Son put his emotions on public display. Anyone could come to Jesus with problems of suffering. Anyone could follow him and, by observing his reactions to sick and needy people, go away with a clear answer to the question, "How does God feel about my pain?"

But of course Jesus did not stay on earth, and for nearly two thousand years the church has been without Christ's visible presence. We cannot now fly to Jerusalem, rent a car, and schedule a personal appointment with him at the King David Hotel. What about those of us who live today? How can we sense God's love?

Authors of the New Testament, still adjusting to the fact of Jesus' departure, addressed this issue with a certain urgency. They give two main suggestions.

Romans 8 contains one: "The Spirit helps us in our weakness. We do not know what we ought to pray for, but the Spirit himself intercedes for us with groans that words cannot express." The Gospels reveal the God alongside, a God who took on flesh and heard humanity's groans with human ears; the Epistles reveal the God within, an invisible Spirit who lives inside us and gives expression to our wordless pain.

Because I write about pain and disappointment, I get letters from people who pour out their private groans. I know well the helpless feeling of not knowing what I ought to pray, as I imagine every Christian sometimes does. How to pray for a dead-end marriage that seems to represent only stuntedness, not growth? Or for a parent of a child diagnosed with terminal cancer? Or for a Christian in Nepal imprisoned for her faith? What can we ask for? How can we pray?

Romans 8 announces the good news that we need not figure out how to pray. We need only groan. As I read Paul's words, an image comes to mind of a mother tuning in to her child's wordless cry. I know mothers who, through years of experience, have learned to distinguish a cry for food from a cry for attention, an earache cry from a stomach-ache cry. To me the sounds are identical, but not to the mother, who instinctively discerns the meaning of the helpless child's cry.

The Spirit of God has resources of sensitivity beyond those of even the wisest mother. Paul says that Spirit lives inside us, detecting needs we cannot articulate and expressing them in a language we cannot comprehend. When we don't know what to pray, he fills in the blanks. Evidently, it is our very helplessness that God, too, delights in. Our weakness gives opportunity for his strength.

For this reason—the new intimacy of a compassionate God living within—Jesus informed his disciples it was actually good that he was going away. "Unless I go away," he said, "the Counselor will not come to you" (John 16:7). Now the Holy Spirit lives inside us as a personal seal of God's presence. Elsewhere, he's called a "deposit," a guarantee of better times to come.

But the Holy Spirit is just that—a spirit: invisible, quick as the wind, inaccessible to human touch. And heaven lies off in the future somewhere. What about right now? What can reassure us physically and visibly of God's love here on earth?

The New Testament's second answer centers around "the body of Christ," a mysterious phrase used more than thirty times. Paul, especially, settled on that phrase as a summary image of the church. When Jesus left, he turned over his mission to flawed and bumbling men and women. He assumed the role of head of the church, leaving the tasks of arms, legs, ears, eyes, and voice to the erratic disciples—and to you and me. The French poet Paul Claudel expressed the change this way, "Since the incarnation, Jesus has only one desire: to recommence the human life he lived. That's why he wants additional human natures, people who'll let him start all over again."[1]

A careful reading of the four gospels shows that this new arrangement was what Jesus had in mind all along. He knew his time on earth was short, and he proclaimed a mission that went beyond even his death and resurrection. "I will build my church," he declared, "and the gates of hell will not prevail against it" (Matthew 16:18 KJV).

Jesus' decision to operate as the invisible head of a large body with many members affects our view of suffering. It means that he often relies on us to help one another cope. The phrase "the body of Christ," expresses well what we are called to do: to represent in flesh what Christ is like, especially to those in need.

The apostle Paul must have had something like that process in mind when he wrote these words: "[God] comforts us in all our troubles, so that we can comfort those in any trouble with the comfort we ourselves have received from God. For just as the sufferings of Christ flow over into our lives, so also through Christ our comfort overflows" (2 Corinthians 1:4–5). And all through his ministry Paul put that principle into practice, taking up collections for famine victims, dispatching assistants to go to troubled areas, acknowledging believers' gifts as gifts from God himself.

United by Pain

Nothing unites the individual parts of a body like the pain network. An infected toenail announces to me that the toe is important, it is mine, it needs attention. If you step on my toe, I may yell "That's me!" I know it's me, because your foot is at that moment resting on pain sensors. Pain defines me, gives me borders.

Wolves have been known to gnaw off one of their own hind legs once it has grown numb in the winter cold. The numbness interrupts the unity of the body; evidently they no longer perceive the leg as belonging to them.

Remember the baby who chewed off her own finger? Unable to feel pain, she had no acute sense that the finger was hers, and needed protection. Alcoholics and people with leprosy, diabetes, and other problems of insensitivity face a constant battle to keep in touch with their extremities.

In my work with Dr. Brand, especially, I have become aware of the body's vital need to sense pain. In the human body, blood cells and lymph cells rush pell-mell to the sight of any invasion. The body shuts down all nonessential activities and attends to the injury. And physical pain lies at the heart of this unified response.

Pain is the very mechanism that forces me to stop what I'm doing and pay attention to the hurting member. It makes me stop playing basketball if I sprain an ankle, change my shoes if they're too tight, go to the doctor if my stomach keeps hurting. In short, the healthiest body is the one that feels the pain of its weakest parts.

In the same way, we members of Christ's body should learn to attend to the pains of the rest of the body. In so doing we become an incarnation of Christ's risen body.

Dr. Paul Brand has developed this idea as a key part of his personal philosophy.

Individual cells had to give up their autonomy and learn to suffer with one another before effective multicellular organisms could be produced and survive. The same designer went on to create the human race with a new and higher purpose in mind. Not only would the cells within an individual cooperate with one another, but the individuals within the race would now move on to a new level of community responsibility, to a new kind of relationship with one another and with God.

As in the body, so in this new kind of relationship the key to success lies in the sensation of pain. All of us rejoice at the harmonious working of the human body. Yet we can but sorrow at the relationships between men and women. In human society we are suffering because we do not suffer enough.

So much of the sorrow in the world is due to the selfishness of one living organism that simply doesn't care when the next one suffers. In the body if one cell or group of cells grows and flourishes at the expense of the rest, we call it cancer and know that if it is allowed to spread the body is doomed. And yet, the only alternative to the cancer is absolute loyalty of every cell to the body, the head. God is calling us today to learn from the lower creation and move on to a higher level of evolution and to participate in this community which He is preparing for the salvation of the world.[2]

Cries and Whispers

It would be much easier for us to avoid people in need. Yet ministering to the needy is not an option for the Christian, but a command. We—you, I—are part of God's response to the massive suffering in this world. As Christ's body on earth we are compelled to move, as he did, toward those who hurt. That has been God's consistent movement in all history.

The Middle East, South Africa, Northern Ireland—these are loud cries of pain from the body of Christ. The scandals of some Christian leaders. Third World poverty. Do we listen to them, hear them, respond? Or do we grow numb and ignore the pain signals, in effect sacrificing a limb of the body of Christ? Not all cries of pain are so far away: there are some in every church and office. The unemployed, divorced, widowed, bedridden, homeless, aged—are we attending to them?

The Christian church, by all accounts, has done a mixed job of acting as Christ's body through the ages. Sometimes it has seemed to devour itself (the Inquisition, religious wars). Yet in his commitment to human freedom Christ still relies upon us to communicate his love to the world. And despite its failures the church has indeed responded in part. In every major city in the U.S., you can find hospitals with names like Lutheran General, Christ Hospital, St. Mary's, Good Samaritan, Baptist Hospital. These institutions, although often run as secular businesses, had their origins in a group of believers who believed healing was part of their calling as Christ's body.

In a nation like India, less than three percent of the population call themselves Christian, but Christians are responsible for more than eighteen percent of the health care. If you say the word "Christian" to an Indian peasant—who may never have heard of Jesus Christ—the first image to pop into his mind may well be that of a hospital, or of a medical van that stops by his village once a month to provide free, personal care in Christ's name. It's certainly not the whole of the gospel, but it's not a bad place to start.

In Western countries, much health care has been taken over by other sectors, but a new problem has arisen in major cities, that of homelessness. Will our society respond to the cries of pain from millions of homeless who spend the night in city parks, under expressway bridges, on heating grates? Once again, churches have been among the first to respond, organizing shelters and soup kitchens.

I received a copy of a letter from a woman in Grand Rapids who experienced the healing touch of the body of Christ on a smaller scale, one-on-one. For seven years she ministered to her husband, a well-known church musician afflicted with ALS, or Lou Gehrig's disease. He died, and on the first anniversary of his death, the widow sent out a letter of gratitude to her many friends at church. It read, in part:

Ever since the first symptoms of ALS appeared over eight years ago, you have surrounded us with love and support. You have cheered us with innumerable notes and letters and cards, some hilarious, some profound, some just warm and caring, but all greatly valued.

You visited and you phoned, often from faraway places. . . . Many of you prepared and brought marvelous food which nourished our spirits as well as our bodies. You shopped and ran errands for us and repaired our broken and out-of-order things while yours waited. You swept and shoveled our walks, brought our mail, dumped our trash. It was possible for us to be a part of our church services because you recorded them. And you brought gifts of love, too many to count, to brighten our hours.

You "doctored" . . . and even repaired a tooth right here in our home. You did ingenious things that made life easier for both of us, like the "coughing jacket" and signal switch that Norm was able to use until the last few days of his life. You shared Scripture verses with us and some of you made it your ministry to pray for those who came to our home regularly to give respiratory treatments. You made him feel like he was still a vital part of the music industry and of the church music ministry.

And how you prayed!!! Day after day, month after month, even year after year! Those prayers buoyed us up, lifted us through particularly hard places, gave us strength that would have been humanly impossible to have, and helped us to reach out on our own for God's resources. Someday we'll understand why Norm's perfect healing did not take place here. But we do know that he was with us much longer and in much better condition than is the norm for an ALS victim. Love is not a strong enough word to tell you how we feel about you!

I could go back through Part 4 ("How Can We Cope with Pain?") and show how this widow's fellow church members had, by instinct, done everything recommended in this book. They became the presence of God for her. Because of their loving concern, she was not tormented by doubts over whether God loved her. She could sense his love in the human touch of Christ's body, her local church.

Bearing Burdens
Listen to one who understands loyalty to the body: "Who makes a mistake and I do not feel his sadness? Who falls without my longing to help him? Who is spiritually hurt without my fury rising against the one who hurt him?" (2 Corinthians 11:29 LB). Or again: "Think too of all who suffer as if you shared their pain" (Hebrews 13:3 PHILLIPS).

Or yet another voice, that of John Donne:

The church is catholic, universal, so are all her actions; all that she does belongs to all. When she baptizes a child, that action concerns me; for that child is thereby connected to that body which is my head too, and ingrafted into that body whereof I am a member. And when she buries a man, that action concerns me: all mankind is of one author, and is one volume. . . .

No man is an island, entire of itself; every man is a piece of the continent, a part of the main. If a clod be washed away by the sea, Europe is the less, as well as if a promontory were, as well as if a manor of thy friend's or of thine own were; any man's death diminishes me, because I am involved in mankind, and therefore can never send to know for whom the bell tolls; it tolls for thee.[3]

Bear one another's burdens, the Bible says. It is a lesson about pain that we all can agree on. Some of us will not see pain as a gift; some will always accuse God of being unfair for allowing it. But, the fact is, pain and suffering are here among us, and we need to respond in some way. The response Jesus gave was to bear the burdens of those he touched. To live in the world as his body, his emotional incarnation, we must follow his example.

The image of the body accurately portrays how God is working in the world. Sometimes he does enter in, occasionally by performing miracles, and often by giving supernatural strength to those in need. But mainly he relies on us, his agents, to do his work in the world. We are asked to *live out* the life of Christ in the world, not just to refer back to it or describe it. We announce his message, work for justice, pray for mercy . . . and suffer with the sufferers.

Alan Paton, South African author of *Cry the Beloved Country,* holds up St. Francis of Assisi as a Christlike model of human response. One of the transforming moments of Francis Bernardone's life occurred when he was riding a horse as a young nobleman and came across a person with leprosy. Francis was bitter toward God at the time, and felt a certain revulsion at the diseased man. But something within him overcame both those reactions. He dismounted from his horse, walked over, and embraced the beggar, kissing him full on the lips.

St. Francis could have cursed either God or the man with leprosy, says Paton. He did neither. Rather than spending his energy in accusing God for allowing the wound to creation, he chose instead to make his life an instrument of God's peace. That act transformed both the giver and receiver: "What had seemed bitter to me was changed into sweetness of body and soul," said St. Francis.[4]

St. Francis's response was the very same response Alyosha gave to his brother Ivan in *The Brothers Karamazov.* He could not resolve Ivan's or his own questions about the problem of pain. But he chose to put himself beside the sufferers, and embrace them. And, pointedly, Dostoyevski portrayed Jesus giving that very same response to his enemy, the Grand Inquisitor.

If the church followed the pattern consistently, and responded to questions of suffering not with arguments but with love, perhaps those questions would not be asked with such troubled intensity. The united strength of Christ's body can be a powerful force on behalf of the lonely, suffering, and deprived. It can be like the tree in the gospel that grows so large that birds begin to nest in its branches.

In my visits in hospitals, I have been impressed by the huge difference between the measure of comfort that can be offered by believers ("We're praying for you") and unbelievers ("Best of luck—we'll keep our fingers crossed"). Today, if I had to answer the question "Where is God when it hurts?" in a single sentence, I would make that sentence another question: "Where is the church when it hurts?" We form the front line of God's response to the suffering world.

"This is how we know what love is: Jesus Christ laid down his life for us. And we ought to lay down our lives for our brothers. If anyone has material possessions and sees his brother in need but has no pity on him, how can the love of God be in him? Dear children, let us not love with words or tongue but with actions and in truth" (1 John 3:16–18).

20

A Whole New World Outside

Grief melts away
   Like snow in May,
As if there were no such cold thing.
               George Herbert
               The Flower

For the person who suffers, Christianity offers one last contribution, the most important contribution of all. As we have seen, the entire Bible, representing 3000 years of history and culture and human drama, focuses like a magnifying glass on the execution at Calvary. It is the crux of history, the cornerstone. But death is decidedly not the end of the story.

After three days in a dark tomb, Jesus was reported alive again. Alive! Could it be? The news was too good to be true. Not even the disciples dared believe the rumors until he came to them and let them touch his new body with their own fingers. More, he promised that one day each of them would receive a resurrection body as well.

The resurrection and its victory over death

brought a decisive new word to the vocabulary of pain and suffering: temporary. Jesus Christ holds out the startling promise of an afterlife without pain. Whatever anguish we feel now will not last.

The Christian's final hope, then, is hope in a painless future, with God. Yet today, astonishingly, people are almost embarrassed to talk about belief in an afterlife. The notion seems quaint, cowardly, an escape from this world's problems.

Black Muslims have a funeral custom that symbolically expresses the modern view. When the body is laid out, close friends and family encircle the casket and stand quietly, looking at the dead person. There are no tears, no flowers, no singing. Muslim sisters pass around small trays from which everyone takes a thin, round peppermint candy. At a given signal the onlookers pop the candies into their mouths, and as the candies slowly melt the funeral-goers reflect on the sweetness of the life they are commemorating. When the candy is gone, that too has meaning, for it symbolizes the end of life. When it simply dissolves, there is no more.

Actually, most moderns cope with death by avoiding it altogether. We hide its blunt reminders—mortuaries, intensive care rooms, cemeteries—behind high walls. But when death cannot be avoided, the modern response differs little from that of the Black Muslims. A creeping paganism invites us to view death as the last phase of the cycle of life on earth, not as a violent transition into an ongoing life. Elisabeth Kübler-Ross defined five stages in preparing for death, with the clear implication that the final stage of "acceptance" is the most appropriate. Ever since, health workers have been helping patients strive toward that ideal.

I remember one evening in my Make Today Count group when a woman named Donna, who was in the final stages of leukemia, mentioned how much she was anticipating heaven. The comment provoked an awkward response from the group: a long silence, a cleared throat, a few rolled eyes. The social worker then steered the discussion toward how Donna could overcome her fears and progress toward the acceptance stage.

I left that meeting with a heavy heart. Our materialistic, undogmatic culture was asking its members to defy their deepest feelings. Donna had, by sheer primal instinct, struck upon a foundation stone of Christian theology. Death is an enemy, a grievous enemy, the last enemy to be destroyed. How could members of a group who each month saw bodies deteriorate before their eyes wish for a spirit of bland acceptance? I could think of only one appropriate response to Donna's impending death: "Damn you, death!"

Not long after that I came across a quote from Blaise Pascal, who lived during an era when thinkers first began scorning "primitive" beliefs in a soul and the afterlife. Pascal said of such people, "Do they profess to have delighted us by telling us that they hold our soul to be only a little wind and smoke, especially by telling us this in a haughty and self-satisfied tone of voice? Is this a thing to say gaily? Is it not, on the contrary, a thing to say sadly, as the saddest thing in the world?"[1]

What inversion of values has led us to commend a belief in annihilation as brave and dismiss a hope for blissful eternity as cowardly? How can it be noble to agree with the Black Muslims, materialists, and Marxists that this world, malignant with evil and suffering, is the designed end for man? Such a notion only appeared after 7000 years of recorded history. Every known primitive society and every ancient culture included elaborate beliefs in an afterlife. (Apart from such beliefs, archaeologists would have a very difficult task, for the ancients buried their cultural clues, conveniently, in sealed tombs.)

In great contrast, the Bible refers to the afterlife with a spirit of joy and anticipation, not embarrassment. This is a groaning planet, and Christians expectantly await a world where every tear will be wiped away.

Easter Faith

We have only shadow notions of that future state, longings that the untroubled joy eluding us now will one day fill us. We are locked in a dark room, like the setting of Sartre's play *No Exit*. But chinks of light are seeping through—virtue, glory, beauty, compassion, hints of truth and justice—suggesting that beyond those walls there exists another world, a world worth all enduring.

Christian faith does not offer us a peaceful way to come to terms with death. No, it offers instead a way to overcome death. Christ stands for Life, and his resurrection should give convincing proof that

God is not satisfied with any "cycle of life" that ends in death. He will go to any extent—he *did* go to any extent—to break that cycle.

In October of 1988 one of my closest friends died in a scuba diving accident in Lake Michigan. The very afternoon Bob was making his last dive I was sitting, oblivious, in a university coffee shop reading *My Quest for Beauty,* a book by the famous therapist and author Rollo May. The book tells of Rollo May's lifelong search for beauty, and among the experiences he recounts is a visit to Mt. Athos, a peninsula of Greece inhabited exclusively by monks.

Rollo May was beginning to recover from a nervous breakdown when he visited Mt. Athos. He happened to arrive just as the monks were celebrating Greek Orthodox Easter, a ceremony thick with symbolism, thick with beauty. Icons were everywhere. Incense hung in the air. And at the height of that service the priest gave everyone present three Easter eggs, wonderfully decorated and wrapped in a veil. "Christos Anesti!" he said—"Christ is Risen!" Each person there, including Rollo May, responded according to custom, "He is risen indeed!"

Rollo May was not a believer. But he writes in his book, "I was seized then by a moment of spiritual reality: what would it mean for our world if He had truly risen?"[2] I returned home shortly after reading that chapter, and was met at the door by my wife who conveyed the news of Bob's death. Rollo May's question came back to me many times in the next few days. What does it mean for the world if Christ has truly risen?

I spoke at my friend's funeral, and there I asked Rollo May's question in a different way, in the context of the grief that pressed in on us from all sides. What would it mean for us if Bob rose again? We sat in a chapel, numbed by three days of sadness. I imagined aloud what it would be like to walk outside to the parking lot and there, to our utter amazement, find Bob. Bob! With his bounding walk, his big grin, and clear gray eyes.

That conjured image gave me a hint of what Jesus' disciples felt on Easter Sunday. They too had grieved for three days. But on Sunday they caught a glimpse of something else, a glimpse of the future.

Apart from Easter, apart from a life that continues beyond this one, apart from a new start, a re-created earth—apart from all that, we could indeed judge God less-than-powerful or less-than-loving or even cruel. The Bible stakes God's reputation on his ability to restore creation to its original state of perfection.

I confess that I too used to be embarrassed by talk about heaven and an afterlife. It seemed a cop-out, a crutch. We ought to make our way in the world as if that is all there is, I thought. But I've changed over the years, mainly as I've watched people die. What kind of God would be satisfied forever with a world like this one, laden with suffering and death? If I had to stand by and watch lives like Bob's get cut off— suddenly vanish, vaporize—with no hope of future, I doubt I'd believe in God.

A passage in the New Testament, 1 Corinthians

15, expresses much the same thought. Paul first reviews his life, a difficult life that included jailings, beatings, shipwrecks, and gladiator-style contests with wild beasts. Then he says, in so many words, I'd be crazy to go through all this if it ended at my death. "If only for this life we have hope in Christ, we are to be pitied more than all men." Along with Paul, I stake my hope on resurrection, a time when Christ "will transform our lowly bodies so that they will be like his glorious body" (Philippians 3:21).

Home Beyond

Scottish author and theologian George MacDonald once wrote a letter of consolation to his stepmother after the death of her good friend. "God would not let it [death] be the law of His Universe if it were what it looks to us," he said.[3] It's up to us believers to tell the world what death looks like from the perspective of One who faced it—with fear and dread—but then came back to life.

The tangible help this belief can give to a dying person is starkly portrayed in the documentary film *Dying* shown on the Public Broadcasting System. Producer-Director Michael Roemer obtained permission to follow around several terminally ill cancer patients during their last months. "People die in the way they have lived. Death becomes the expression of everything you are, and you can bring to it only what you have brought to your life," said Roemer after the filming. Two Boston families, especially, show the extremes of despair and hope.

Harriet and Bill, thirty-three, are seen struggling

with a failure of nerve. In one scene Harriet, anxious about her own future as a widow with two sons, lashes out at her dying husband. "The longer this is dragged out, the worse this is going to be for all of us," she tells him.

"What happened to the sweet girl I married?" Bill asks in reply. Harriet turns to the interviewer, "The sweet girl is being tortured by his cancer. Who's gonna want a widow and eight- and ten-year-old sons? I don't wish him dead, but if he's gotta go why doesn't he go now?"

In the last weeks of their life together, this family tears apart, unable to cope with their fears. They whine and shout, attacking each other, shattering all remaining love and trust. The specter of death looms too large.

The response of Rev. Bryant, fifty-six, the dying pastor of a black Baptist church, provides an amazing contrast. "Right now I'm living some of my greatest moments," he says. "I don't think Rockefeller could be happy as I am."

The camera crew records Rev. Bryant as he preaches on death to his congregation, reads the Bible to his grandchildren, and takes a trip South to visit his birthplace. He displays calm serenity and a confidence that he is merely heading home, to a place without pain.

At his funeral, the Baptist choir sings "He's Asleep." And as mourners file past the bier, some reach down to grasp his hand or pat his chest. They are losing a beloved friend, but only for a while. They believe that Rev. Bryant faces a beginning, not an end.

The film clips from Rev. Bryant's church seem authentic to me because of my wife's experience among senior citizens in Chicago. About half are white and half are black. All of them, in their seventies and eighties, live in constant awareness of death. Yet Janet has noted a striking difference in the way the whites in general and the blacks in general face death.

Many of her white clients become increasingly more fearful and uptight. They complain about their lives, their families, and their failing health. The blacks, in contrast, maintain a good humor and triumphant spirit even though most of them have more apparent reason for bitterness and despair. (Most lived in the South just one generation after slavery, and suffered a lifetime of economic oppression and injustice. Many were senior citizens before the first Civil Rights bills were passed.)

What causes the difference in outlooks? Janet has concluded the answer is hope, a hope that traces directly to the blacks' bedrock belief in heaven. "This world is not my home, I'm just a passin' through," they say. These words and others like them ("Swing low, sweet chariot, comin' for to carry me home") came out of a tragic period of history, when everything in this world looked bleak. But somehow black churches managed to instill a vivid belief in a home beyond this one.

If you want to hear up-to-date images of heaven, attend a few black funerals. The preachers paint word pictures of a life so serene and sensuous that everyone in the congregation starts fidgeting to go there. The mourners feel grief, naturally, but in its proper place: as an interruption, a temporary setback in a battle whose end has already been determined.

It is, of course, wrong to use heaven as an excuse to avoid relieving poverty and misery here on earth. But is it not equally wrong to deny an authentic hope in heaven for someone whose life is ending?

One Foot in the Air

Belief in a future home beyond this one should affect more than how we die. It should also affect how we live.

J. Robertson McQuilkin, former president of Columbia Bible College, was once approached by an elderly lady facing the trials of old age. Her body was in decline, her beauty being replaced by thinning hair, wrinkles, and skin discoloration. She could no longer do the things she once could, and she felt herself to be a burden on others. "Robertson, why does God let us get old and weak? Why must I hurt so?" she asked.

After a few moments' thought McQuilkin replied, "I think God has planned the strength and beauty of youth to be physical. But the strength and beauty of age is spiritual. We gradually lose the strength and beauty that is temporary so we'll be sure to concentrate on the strength and beauty which is forever. It makes us more eager to leave behind the temporary, deteriorating part of us and be truly homesick for our eternal home. If we stayed young and strong and beautiful, we might never want to leave!"

If there is a secret to handling suffering, the one most often cited by those I interviewed was along this line. To survive, the spirit must be fed so that it can break free beyond the constraints of the body. Christian faith does not always offer resources to the body. Neither Brian Sternberg nor Joni Eareckson Tada has been healed, despite thousands of prayers. Yet God does promise to nourish the spirit that will one day rejoin a perfected body. Brian will leap again—like a calf released from the stall, says Malachi; Joni will be on her feet dancing.

"Do not be afraid of those who can only kill your body; they cannot kill your soul," Jesus said as he sent out his followers. Because physical death is not the end, we need not fear it inordinately. But because it is the enemy of Life, we need not welcome it either.

In short, because of our belief in a home beyond, Christians can be realistic about death without becoming hopeless. Death is an enemy, but a defeated enemy. As Martin Luther told his followers, "Even in the best of health we should have death always before our eyes [so that] we will not expect to remain on this earth forever, but will have one foot in the air, so to speak."

Having that one foot in the air gives one a new perspective on the problems of pain and suffering. Any discussion of suffering is incomplete without this view from the vantage point of eternity.

A skilled polemicist could defend pain as a good thing, better than any of the alternatives God might have allowed. Perhaps. But actually pain and suffering are far less than half the picture.

How to imagine eternity? It's so much longer than our brief life here that it's hard even to visualize. You can go to a ten-foot blackboard and draw a line from one side to another. Then, make a one-inch dot in that line. That dot, to a microscopic germ cell undulating in its midst, would seem enormous. The cell could spend its lifetime exploring the dot. But if you, a human, step back to view the entire blackboard, you'll be struck by the hugeness of that ten-foot line compared to the tiny dot the germ cell calls home.

Eternity compares to this life in the same way. Seventy years is a long time, long enough for us to concoct many theories about God and why he sometimes appears indifferent to human suffering. But is it fair to judge God and his plan for the universe by the swatch of time we spend on earth? No more fair than for that germ cell to judge a whole blackboard by the tiny smudge of chalk on which it spends its life.

Are we missing the perspective of the universe and of timelessness? Would we complain about life on earth if God permitted a mere hour of suffering in an entire seventy-year lifetime of comfort? Now, our lifetime does include suffering, but that lifetime represents a mere hour of eternity. As St. Teresa of Avila audaciously expressed it, from heaven the most miserable earthly life will look like one bad night in an inconvenient hotel.[4]

In the Christian scheme of things, this world and

the time spent here are not all there is. Earth is a proving ground, a dot in eternity—albeit an important dot, for Jesus said our destiny depends on our obedience here. Next time you want to cry out to God in anguished despair, blaming him for a miserable world, remember: less than one-millionth of reality has been presented, and that millionth is being lived out under a rebel flag.

To view the role of pain and suffering properly, one must await the whole story. Promises of it abound in the Bible: "And the God of all grace, who called you to his eternal glory in Christ, after you have suffered a little while, will himself restore you and make you strong, firm and steadfast" (1 Peter 5:10). "These troubles and sufferings of ours are, after all, quite small and won't last very long. Yet this short time of distress will result in God's richest blessing upon us forever and ever! So we do not look at what we can see right now, the troubles all around us, but we look forward to the joys in heaven which we have not yet seen. The troubles will soon be over, but the joys to come will last forever" (2 Corinthians 4:17–18 LB).

I have always been curious about one detail often overlooked at the end of Job, that great story of human suffering. The author takes pains to point out that in the end Job received double all he had lost in his time of trials: 14,000 sheep to replace the 7000; 6000 camels to replace 3000; a thousand oxen and donkeys to replace 500. There is one exception: previously Job had seven sons and three daughters, and in the restoration he got back seven sons and three daughters—the same number, not double. Could the author have been silently hinting at the eternal perspective? From that view Job did indeed receive double, ten new children here to go with the ten he would one day rejoin.

Death and Birth

An irony: death, the one event that causes the greatest emotional pain, in reality opens a doorway into the great joy of eternity. Speaking of his own death, Jesus used the analogy of a woman in the labor of childbirth: she travails until the moment of delivery, when suddenly ecstasy replaces anguish (John 16:21).

Death like birth—the analogy goes deep. Imagine birth from the perspective of the fetus.

Your world is dark, safe, secure. You are bathed in a warm, cushioning liquid. You do nothing for yourself. You are fed automatically, and a murmuring heartbeat assures you that someone larger than you is meeting all your needs. Life consists of simple waiting—you're not sure what to wait for, but any change seems faraway and scary. You encounter no sharp objects, no pain, no dangers. A fine, serene existence.

One day you feel a tug. The walls seem to press in. Those soft padded walls are now pulsing wildly, crushing you downward. Your body is bent double, your limbs twisted and wrenched. You're falling, upside down. For the first time in your life, you feel pain. You're in a sea of roiling matter. There is more pressure, almost too intense to bear. Your head is squeezed flat, and you are pushed harder, harder into a dark tunnel. Oh, the pain. Noise. More pressure.

You hurt all over. You hear a groaning sound and an awful, sudden fear rushes in on you. It is happening—your world is collapsing. You're sure it's the end. You see a piercing, blinding light. Cold, rough hands grasp at you, pull you from the tunnel and hold you upside down. A painful slap. Waaaahhhhh!

Congratulations, you have just been born.

Death is like that. On this end of the birth canal, it seems a scary, dark tunnel we are being sucked toward by an irresistible force. None of us looks forward to it. We're afraid. It's full of pressure, pain, darkness . . . the unknown.

But beyond the darkness and the pain lies a whole new world outside. When we awaken after death in that bright new world, our tears and hurts will be mere memories.[5]

Do you sometimes think God does not hear? That your cries of pain fade off into nothing? God is not deaf. He is as grieved by the world's trauma as you are. After all, his only Son died here.

Let history finish. Let the symphony scratch out its last mournful note of discord before it bursts into song. As Paul said, "In my opinion whatever we may have to go through now is less than nothing compared with the magnificent future God has planned for us. The whole creation is on tiptoe to see the wonderful sight of the sons of God coming into their own. . . .

"It is plain to anyone with eyes to see that at the

present time all created life groans in a sort of universal travail. And it is plain, too, that we who have a foretaste of the Spirit are in a state of painful tension, while we wait for that redemption of our bodies which will mean that at last we have realized our full sonship in him" (Romans 8:18–19, 22–23 PHILLIPS).

As we look back on the speck of eternity that was the history of this planet, we will be impressed not by its importance, but by its smallness. From the viewpoint of the Andromeda galaxy, the holocaustic destruction of our entire solar system would be barely visible, a match flaring faintly in the distance, then imploding in permanent darkness. Yet for this burnt-out match, God sacrificed himself.

Pain can be seen, as Berkouwer puts it, as the great "not yet" of eternity. It reminds us of what we are now, and fans in us a thirst for what we will someday become. I can believe with confidence that one day every bruise and every leukemia cell, every embarrassment and every hurt will be set right, and all those grim moments of hoping against hope will find their reward at last.

At the height of his suffering, Job spoke:

How I wish someone would record what I am
  saying
Or with a chisel carve my words in stone,
  and write them so they would last
  forever.
But I know there is someone in heaven
  who will come at last to my defense.

I will see him with my own eyes,
and he will not be a stranger.
(Job 19:23ff. *JOB FOR MODERN MAN*)

Where Is God When It Hurts?

For a good portion of my life, I shared the perspective of those who rail against God for allowing pain. Suffering pressed in too close. I could find no way to rationalize a world as toxic as this one.

As I visited people whose pain far exceeded my own, though, I was surprised by its effects. Suffering seemed as likely to reinforce faith as to sow agnosticism. And as I visited those with leprosy, particularly, I became aware of pain's underlying value.

The problem of pain will have no ultimate solution until God recreates the earth. I am sustained by faith in that great hope. If I did not truly believe that God is a Physician and not a Sadist, and that he, in George MacDonald's phrase, "feels in Himself the tortured presence of every nerve that lacks its repose," I would abandon all attempts to plumb the mysteries of suffering.

My anger about pain has melted mostly for one reason: I have come to know God. He has given me joy and love and happiness and goodness. They have come in unexpected flashes, in the midst of my confused, imperfect world, but they have been enough to convince me that my God is worthy of trust. Knowing him is worth all enduring.

Where does that leave me when I stand by a hospital bed the next time a close friend gets

Hodgkin's disease? After all, this search started at a bedside. It leaves me with faith in a Person, a faith so solid that no amount of suffering can erode it.

Where is God when it hurts?

He has been there from the beginning, designing a pain system that, even in the midst of a fallen world, still bears the stamp of his genius and equips us for life on this planet.

He transforms pain, using it to teach and strengthen us, if we allow it to turn us toward him.

With great restraint, he watches this rebellious planet live on, in mercy allowing the human project to continue in its self-guided way.

He lets us cry out, like Job, in loud fits of anger against him, blaming him for a world we spoiled.

He allies himself with the poor and suffering, founding a kingdom tilted in their favor. He stoops to conquer.

He promises supernatural help to nourish the spirit, even if our physical suffering goes unrelieved.

He has joined us. He has hurt and bled and cried and suffered. He has dignified for all time those who suffer, by sharing their pain.

He is with us now, ministering to us through his Spirit and through members of his body who are commissioned to bear us up and relieve our suffering for the sake of the head.

He is waiting, gathering the armies of good. One day he will unleash them, and the world will see one last terrifying moment of suffering before the full victory is ushered in. Then, God will create for us a new, incredible world. And pain shall be no more.

Listen, I tell you a mystery: We shall not all sleep, but we will all be changed—in a flash, in the twinkling of an eye, at the last trumpet. For the trumpet will sound, the dead will be raised imperishable, and we will be changed. For the perishable must clothe itself with the imperishable, and the mortal with immortality. When the perishable has been clothed with the imperishable, and the mortal with immortality, then the saying that is written will come true: "Death has been swallowed up in victory."

"Where, O death, is your victory?
Where, O death, is your sting?"
(1 Corinthians 15:51–55)

Sources

Chapter 1: A Problem That Won't Go Away
1. C. E. M. Joad, *God and Evil* (New York: Harper & Brothers, 1943), 28.

Chapter 2: The Gift Nobody Wants
1. R. J. Christman, *Sensory Experience* (Scranton, Pa.: Intext Educational Publishers, 1971), 359.
2. Ibid., 361.
3. Maurice Burton, *The Sixth Sense of Animals* (New York: Taplinger Publishing Company, 1972), 9.
4. Thomas Lewis, *Pain* (New York: The Macmillan Company, 1942).

Chapter 3: Painless Hell
1. Ronald Melzack, *The Puzzle of Pain* (New York: Basic Books, Inc., 1973), chapter 1.

Chapter 4: Agony and Ecstasy
1. Augustine of Hippo, *The Confessions of St. Augustine*, translated by John K. Ryan (Garden City, N.Y.: Image Books, 1960), 186.

Chapter 5: The Groaning Planet
1. G. K. Chesterton, *Orthodoxy* (Garden City, N.Y.: Doubleday and Company, 1959), 144.
2. Ibid., 78.
3. C. S. Lewis, *The Problem of Pain* (New York: The Macmillan Company, 1962), 93.
4. Blaise Pascal, *Pensées* (New York: E. P. Dutton & Co., 1958), 55–56.
5. Chesterton, 80.

6. John Donne, *Devotions* (Ann Arbor, Mich.: University of Michigan Press, 1959), 108.
7. Ibid., 141.

Chapter 6: What Is God Trying to Tell Us?

1. "A Luckless City Buries Its Dead," *Time* (June 7, 1976).
2. Klaus Kloch, "Is There a Doctrine of Retribution in the Old Testament?" in *Theodicy in the Old Testament*, James L. Crenshaw, ed. (Philadelphia: Fortress Press, 1983), passim.

Chapter 7: Why Are We Here?

1. C. G. Jung, *Answer to Job* (Princeton, N.J.: Princeton Publishing/ Bollingen Series, 1973), 15ff.
2. C. S. Lewis, 39–42.
3. John Hick, *Philosophy of Religion* (Englewood Cliffs, N.J.: Prentice-Hall, 1963), chapter 3.
4. Bernard Seeman, *Man Against Pain* (New York: Chilton Books, 1962), 96.
5. Albert Camus, *The Plague* (New York: Vintage Books, 1972), 203.
6. Daniel Defoe, *Journal of the Plague Year* (New York: Penguin Books, 1966), 33.
7. "In Tornados, Some Trust God," *Psychology Today* (August 1974, 36).
8. Anita and Peter Deyneka, Jr., "A Salvation of Suffering: The Church in the Soviet Union," *Christianity Today* (July 16, 1982): 20.
9. David Watson, *Fear No Evil* (Wheaton, Ill.: Harold Shaw Publishers, 1984), 7.

Chapter 8: Arms Too Short to Box With God

1. Harold Kushner, *When Bad Things Happen to Good*

People (New York: Schocken Books, 1981), 43–44.

2. Frederick Buechner, *Wishful Thinking* (San Francisco: Harper & Row, 1973), 46.

3. Quoted in William James, *The Varieties of Religious Experience* (New York: The Modern Library, 1936), 281.

Chapter 9: After the Fall

1. Brian Sternberg with John Poppy, "My Search for Faith," *Look* (March 10, 1964): 79–80.

2. Ibid.

Chapter 11: Other Witnesses

1. Paul Tournier, *Creative Suffering* (San Francisco: Harper & Row, 1982), 2.

2. Ibid., 29, 37.

3. Quoted in David J. Garrow, *Bearing the Cross* (New York: William Morrow and Co., 1986), 532.

4. C. S. Lewis, 108.

5. Monica Hellwig, "Good News to the Poor: Do They Understand It Better?" in *Tracing the Spirit*, James E. Hug, ed. (Mahwah, N.J.: Paulist Press), 145.

Chapter 12: Extreme Cases

1. Terrence Des Pres, *The Survivor* (New York: Oxford University Press, 1976), 162–63.

2. Bruno Bettelheim, *Surviving and Other Essays* (New York: Alfred A. Knopf, 1979), 313–14.

3. George Mangakis, "Letter in a Bottle," *Atlantic Monthly* (October 1971): 253.

4. Viktor Frankl, *Man's Search for Meaning* (New York: Washington Square Press, 1959), 103–5.

5. Reeve Robert Brenner, *The Faith and Doubt of Holocaust Survivors* (New York: The Free Press, 1980), 94–95, 103–4.

6. Elie Wiesel, *Night* (New York: Avon Books, 1969), 44.
7. Ibid., 8–9.
8. Ibid., 79.
9. Ibid., 75–76.

Chapter 13: Frontiers of Recovery

1. Quoted in Douglas Colligan, "That Helpless Feeling: The Dangers of Stress," *New York* (July 14, 1975): 32.
2. Jean Vanier, "Hearts Awakened by the Poor," *Sojourners* (January, 1982): 17.

Chapter 14: Fear

1. Donne, 36.
2. Steven Brena, *Pain and Religion* (Springfield, Ill.: Charles C. Thomas, 1972), 78–81.
3. Melzack, 29–30.
4. Betsy Burnham, *When Your Friend Is Dying* (Grand Rapids: Chosen Books/Zondervan, 1982), 71–72.

Chapter 15: Helplessness

1. Colligan, 28.
2. James D. Hardy and Harold G. Wolff and Helen Goodell, *Pain Sensations and Reactions* (New York: Haffner Publishing Co., 1967), 117.
3. Eric J. Cassell, M.D., *The Healer's Art: A New Approach to the Doctor-Patient Relationship* (New York: Harper & Row, 1976), 44.
4. Jürgen Moltmann, *The Power of the Powerless* (San Francisco: Harper & Row), 142.
5. Norman Cousins, *Anatomy of an Illness* (New York: W. W. Norton, 1979), 153–54.
6. Benjamin M. and Carol Weir, with Dennis Benson, *Hostage Bound, Hostage Free* (Westminster/John Knox Press, 1987) as excerpted in *Leadership* (Winter 1989): 54.

7. Barbara Wolf, *Living with Pain* (New York: Seabury Press, 1977), 107.

Chapter 16: Meaning

1. Quoted in Mark Krum, "The Face of Pain," *Sports Illustrated* (March 8, 1976): 62.
2. Donne, 109.
3. Sharon Fischer, "What to Do When You Don't Know What to Do," *Worldwide Challenge* (June 1983): 20.
4. Henri Nouwen, *The Wounded Healer* (Garden City, N.Y.: Doubleday & Company/Image Books, 1979), 66.
5. Jürgen Trogisch, "Congenital Subnormality," in *God and the Handicapped Child* (London: Christian Medical Fellowship Publications, 1982), 41–45.

Chapter 17: Hope

1. Armand Mayo Nicholi II, "Why Can't I Deal with Depression?" *Christianity Today* (November 11, 1983): 41.
2. Colligan, 30.
3. Quoted in Nicholi, 40.
4. Bruce Larson, *There's a Lot More to Health Than Not Being Sick* (Waco, Tex.: Word Books, 1981), 90.
5. Quoted in Joseph Frank, *Dostoyevsky: The Years of Ordeal* (Princeton, N.J.: Princeton University Press, 1983), 157.
6. Moltmann, *Experiences of God* (Philadelphia: Fortress Press, 1980), 7.
7. Bettelheim, 296.

Chapter 18: Seeing for Himself

1. Robert Coles, *Children of Crisis, Vol. 2: Migrants, Mountaineers, and Sharecroppers* (Boston: Atlantic Monthly Press, 1967–71), 612–13.

2. Dorothy L. Sayers, *Christian Letters to a Post-Christian World* (Grand Rapids, Mich.: William B. Eerdmans Publishing Company, 1969), 14.

3. Cornelius Plantinga, Jr., "A Love So Fierce," *The Reformed Journal* (November 1986): 6.

4. Harry R. Boer, "And a Sword. . . ." *The Reformed Journal* (December 1984), 3.

5. T. S. Eliot, *Collected Poems 1904–1962* (New York: Harcourt, Brace & World), 187.

Chapter 19: The Rest of the Body

1. Quoted in Brennan Manning, *Lion and Lamb: The Relentless Tenderness of Jesus* (Old Tappan, N.J.: Fleming H. Revell/Chosen Books, 1986), 77.

2. Dorothy Clarke Wilson, *Ten Fingers for God* (Grand Rapids, Mich.: Zondervan, 1989), 145ff.

3. Donne, 107–9.

4. Alan Paton, et al., *Creative Suffering, The Ripple of Hope* (Kansas City, Mo.: National Catholic Reporter Publishing Company, 1970), 17.

Chapter 20: A Whole New World Outside

1. Pascal, 57.

2. Rollo May, *My Quest for Beauty* (Dallas: Saybrook Publishing Company, 1985), 60.

3. William Raeper, *George MacDonald* (London: Lion Publishing, 1987), 133.

4. Peter Kreeft, *Making Sense Out of Suffering* (Ann Arbor, Mich.: Servant Books, 1986), 139.

5. Joseph Bayly was the essential source for this analogy.

Among the titles available are:

On the Anvil
Max Lucado

The Jesus I Never Knew
Philip Yancey

Lord, Teach Me to Pray
Kay Arthur

The Knowledge of the Holy
A. W. Tozer

Encourage Me
Charles Swindoll

The Pursuit of Holiness
Jerry Bridges

Six Hours One Friday
Max Lucado

Heaven: Your Real Home
Joni Eareckson Tada

What Happens to Good People When Bad Things Happen
Robert A. Schuller

I Am with You Always
G. Scott Sparrow

Strength to Love
Martin Luther King Jr.

And the Angels Were Silent
Max Lucado

Apples of Gold
Jo Petty

The Best of Catherine Marshall
Edited by Leonard LeSourd

Book of Hours
Elizabeth Yates

Brush of an Angel's Wing
Charlie W. Shedd

Finding God
Larry Crabb

A Gathering of Hope
Helen Hayes

Getting Through the Night
Eugenia Price

To Help You Through the Hurting
Marjorie Holmes

To Mother with Love
Helen Steiner Rice

A Treasury of Christmas Classics

The Wonderful Spirit-Filled Life
Charles Stanley